The World Is Never Enough

Sarah Donohue

Book design – Andy Screen @ Golden Rivet
Cover photography – Mike Cohen
Other photography – Lowell Mason, Men & Motors PR, Chris Davies, powerboatracing.be, Gary Tapp. Billy Bingham, Raffaello Bastiano, David Williams of 'Bond Pix', Graham Rye at 007 Magazine, Kos Photo's whom I worked with on the Bond Film, Keith Slater and Gordon Smith.
Author – Sarah Donohue Publisher – Deringer Publishing
www.deringerpublishing.co.uk
ISBN 978-1-9999837-0-3

Dedicated to my best friend Charles Burnett III.
I'll miss you always

Contents

Dedication

Charles Burnett III – Speed King

31 May 1956 – 17 January 2018

A life-long friendship brought to an end too soon.

Charles was my oldest friend inside and outside powerboat racing.
He gave me the chance to have so many experiences across the world, gave me fond memories and a friendship many never get to experience.
All his family and close friends are devastated.
He was a great man that gave the world and everyone around him so much in everything he did. I'm numb.
Charles made my world a better place.
I loved him and will continue to love him.
He is a huge part of this autobiography and this book was being finalized at the time of his death. I haven't changed any details as he continues to live on in my thoughts and my heart.
CBIII the man that gave me and others so much life and love.
I wish I could spend just one more day with you Charles.
I have so much I want to say to you. We are all heartbroken and miss you every moment.
Rest in peace my dearest friend. I will love you always.

Sarah

Foreword

I first met Sarah back in 1999, as the first journalist to interview her after she'd recovered from a near fatal powerboat accident in Venice in which she 'died' for four minutes.

Thankfully, not only did Sarah recover, but this feisty, charming, intelligent and crusading woman prove herself to be a vital force on so many fronts.

Working hard and taking risks are clearly embedded in her DNA, and the long standing list of her achievements speak for themselves.

There's no doubt her book will, itself, offer a thrill seeking ride for the reader.

Sarah's life has clearly been a roller coaster – from the highs of career success to the lows of cyber bullying. But this charming Yorkshire lass always comes out fighting.

I wish her every success.

Angela Epstein: freelance journalist and broadcaster

Preface

I have wanted to write my autobiography for many years but time and tide have held me back. Time has also beneficially added elements which will surely entertain and amuse yet there are scatterings of devastation along the way. It has been a rollercoaster of emotions and some situations I would sooner have not have been in, but all have taught me valuable lessons about life, myself and others.

Admittedly most of writing this has had me laughing out loud, almost embarrassed I'm laughing at my own hand. But with the ebb and flow of my colourful life and the friends that have surrounded me, my lifestyle and its memories are something I will always cherish and remember with great fondness. I still feel like life has only just begun.

It was reflecting on Chris Eubanks words back in 2009, when he invited me to his motivational talk in London that made me take this leap to write some eight years later. He told me, 'You've experienced many things that most won't ever get the chance to do, you should consider writing an autobiography, and motivational speaking can help others achieve great things. Think about this.'

It was with these words coming from such a great man that I knew it was time. I have had the highest of highs, but I have also had the misfortune to have had the lowest of lows. Betrayed beyond belief leading to soul destroying cyber abuse, and even a short spell on a life-support machine. I've cried whilst writing this book but I've also loved every minute of recalling most of the events because every day is a school day, and if we take something positive out of everything that comes our way, good, bad or ugly, then ultimately we become a better individual.

So many people have been an integral part of my life and writing this book. And here is where I say thank you. The people named below are those who have brightened up my ever-colourful life.

Giuseppe Bevilaqua for dragging my lifeless body from the water, resuscitation and ultimately giving me a second chance at life.

Bergamo Sub Rescue in Italy for their immediate assistance at the crash scene.

The Italian racing federation (FIM) for their full support.

The Venice Hospital and the surgeons and doctors in 'reanimation', and Nadia my personal nurse.

Giovanni Carpitella, Kristian Rivolta, Matteo and Luca Nicolini, Italian powerboat champions, for their friendship.

Martin Lai, Enrico Bucciero, Deborah Cottrell, Karen Benson, Ian Cutler and Ricky Hill, my team mates from across the world. I love you guys.

All my racing friends worldwide for being awesome.

Andy Screen, career Lothario, bon vivant and former Royal Marine. One the world's top pinup artists for gifting me my book cover.

Mike Cohen my friend and cover photographer.

Martha Dolak my friend and make up artist.

Lee Barrett my Royal Marine protector and gorgeous husband.

Mark Time former Royal Marine and author of *Going Commando* for allowing me to lean on him.

Craig Downing, Royal Marine and expensive whisky tasting and drinking buddy.

The military men and women I have had the pleasure to have met along the way.

Charles Burnett III for giving me the opportunity to have this lifestyle.

My parents for simply being the best.

Miles Jennings powerboat champion, for always supporting me.

IP Barrister Guy Tritton at Hogarth Chambers for protecting me against myself.

Richard Clegg at GMS Law for continued support during my cyber abuse.

Advanced Wear Safety race overalls keeping me fire proof since 1997.

OSBE helmets for protecting me.

La Diva Design for the beautiful jewel-encrusted bikini.

My friends Lowell Mason show photographer and Averil Henry his better half (and my maid of honour) for their continued support.

If I had the chance to live my life again. I wouldn't change a single thing.

I also dedicate this book to all powerboat racers past and present and to those who ultimately lost their life doing the sport they loved.

And to the President of the United States of America. Albeit he should try building bridges instead of building walls.

Prologue

It's time to go. The explosion at MI6 means it won't be long until the chase is on. With my heart jumping from my chest, my left knuckles whiten on the wheel and my right hand pushes the throttle forward. I'm launched ahead as the propellers dig into the murky water of the Thames. I look beyond the G36K heavy machine gun mounted on the stern of my Sunseeker Superhawk and see below the sand and malachite ziggurat of the MI6 building, white water trails of a tiny black speedboat, waspish and lithe, as it zips behind in pursuit. I swerve into a slow winding 'S' to create a wake big enough to destabilise my pursuer, it works – the craft nearly capsizes yet rights itself and persists in its chase. As it's far more manoeuvrable than my 34-foot craft, it's a fly I can't swat away and bounces over my wake zipping into my port quarter. To my left I see heads peer from the Houses of Parliament windows, even the MPs are alarmed at the events before them. The pursuing craft nearly bounces into my stern under the shadow of Big Ben but cuts away before it kills us both. We both shoot through the shallow arches of Westminster Bridge and as I try to keep a visual on his zipping from starboard to port quarter my long dyed-dark hair disguise virtually blinds me. I'm at top speed yet the speedboat now speeds past on my port bow. I turn sharply into him, causing him to swerve away from certain death. I turn hard to starboard and drench my pursuer in white water yet I can't avoid a riverbank pontoon. The boat's hull vibrates as wooden panels are torn under my bow, glass explodes as I tear through the pontoon's café, yet any terror it's customers may voice is drowned under the gnawing of the engines accelerating from my destruction. The pursuer is now in front. I cut a hard right into the narrow passage of Java Wharf sending another 20-foot wall of white water into the glum London air.

I'm now speeding through Royal Victoria Dock. The speed limit here is 5 mph but when you're being chased by MI6, rules rarely apply. I take a hard left onto a wider canal of millionaires' apartment blocks where I set up an ambush to await the speedboat shooting from the junction. I swivel the G36K on its monopod and spit 5.56 mm rounds down the canal towards the black target hurtling through the water. Sparks fly from the hull and canopy of my pursuer as rounds ricochet anywhere but the driver, still debonair in his dark suit. He closes in, forging through the horizontal rain of bullets that still miss him. He's so close I see the whites of his eyes. He's heading straight towards me. He's not stopping. I dive for cover in the foot well of my boat. Shards of fibreglass and metal detonate around me as the maniac powers his craft over my stern, barrel-rolling in the air destroying my G36K before landing miraculously in the water.

I power off again this time alongside him. Grenade rounds splash the river covering his boat in water yet he stays parallel to me, a median strip of water traffic separating us from collision. I pass an old wooden barge that explodes into a million pieces and shatters my eardrums, shrapnel flies through the air behind me but I must I keep my eye on the craft, spry and fleet, that hounds me so.

I approach Glengall Bridge as its two halves descend together. It's suicidal to approach a drawbridge at such speed yet I have to pass through before it fully closes. I speed up, unsure whether I am going to make it. The red and white hazarders swing perilously low as I approach. I duck just in time – decapitation would make a terrible mess of this tight burgundy leather number I'm squeaking in.

It seems impossible, but he's still in pursuit. There's only one escape route – a low concrete bridge with its entrance blocked by a harbour patrol vessel carrying two fluorescent-jacketed officials. There's no way around it so I use an old Marines' trick – stacks of smoke and straight up the middle. I slice through the wooden vessel as if it's butter missing the two men on the bow by three feet. Another explosion tears through my wake and my pursuer gives up the chase, even he's not stupid enough to drive through an inferno of burning oil and wood.

I'm cruising to my destination – a rainbow coloured hot air balloon anchored at the base of the Millennium Dome shimmering in the laziness of a late afternoon sun and to my front I see it – the black speedboat, a nemesis that will never give up. Shooting ahead of it directly towards me are two streaks of white water bubbling just under the surface. Torpedoes. I turn virtually 90 degrees to my right and speed towards the dirty beach where I slide up the sand, smashing into the wall and through a metal fence that I jump over into soft mud just as the torpedoes hit the stern sending my boat into a fiery cloud of fragmenting fibreglass and molten metal. As I lay on the ground the pursuer, looking quite magnificent in his bespoke suit, jumps from his jet black speedboat. He's dashingly handsome and is a face I recognise. His name's Bond... James Bond.

Chapter 1

007, The world's most famous number

'I couldn't have been more Northern if I'd crammed an Eccles cake into my gob.'

Shooting machine guns off the back of a Sunseeker on the River Thames being chased by James Bond may have been a fantasy I'd only ever had in bed up until that day but life often turns out in the oddest way if we put our necks out and strive for success.

I'd never set out to work as a stunt double, I always had eyes on getting my Equity card in the hope of becoming a TV presenter, so when opportunities come knocking you could be excused to think that I'd jump at the chance and not nearly ruin it by being a tit on the phone… well you'd be wrong.

It was just another mid-racing-season day, one of maintenance, planning, drinking tea and lurid jokes, when my cell phone rang.

"Is that Sarah Donohue?"

I never confirm; I ascertain the caller's identity before I decide on affirming or denial.

"It's Eon Productions, the makers of the Bond movies, and we wondered if you have a few minutes to chat?"

A big grin appeared on my face. "Yeah course it is; is that one of Scott's mates? Tell him he's a tosser." Scott was my partner in crime and drinking buddy on the racing circuit.

"No, I'm one of the casting directors from Bond," said the voice.

"Of course you are, tell Scott to stop being a twat…" I cut her off and carried on with my daily routine. Two minutes later my phone rang again. "Wanker," I laughed down the phone before cutting off the caller.

She was persistent, I'll give her that, it rang a third time. "Scott can you stop fucking about I've got shitloads on," I laughed awaiting for a guffaw down the phone. The guffaw didn't happen.

"Sarah don't put the phone down, it's Annabel, I'm calling from Eon at

Pinewood Studios and I just need a few minutes of your time. Please don't put the phone down."

By this time, I was still dubious but the voice did sound official. If it was indeed Scott taking it this far he could expect Deep Heat in his undies for a month. I decided to play along. "Sorry about that, I race with a fleet of guys and we are always joking around so I just presumed it was another one of those days, my apologies. What can I help you with?"

"We'd like you to come to Pinewood for a meeting with the stunt department. We've a boat chase sequence in Bond 19 and we need a female driver."

"Err yeah OK." My heart raced, my lips went dry – *fucking James Bond!* "Can I pass your details over to my manager Suzanne Martin and let her deal with it?"

"Of course, we can deal direct with Suzanne if that suits you better. We're looking at a meeting in a week or two if that suits you whilst we put everything in place?"

"Whenever is fine it's no problem for me and thanks for getting in touch. Look, I'm really sorry I kept putting the phone down on you."

She laughed, and passed her details over, I also passed Suzanne's details on to her before I put the phone down. I just sat there, with a frown, half expecting Scott or one of the lads to call and give me shit for falling for their prank. It didn't happen. I've had a lot of strange calls in my time but that was the strangest. I checked my watch; it was almost lunchtime. *Fuck it, I'll run down to Suzanne's office.* It was on Greek Street only a few hundred metres away from my Soho flat. I'd need to speak to her before one of her legendary all afternoon PR lunches, which was a dignified disguise of a piss-up on Old Compton Street.

By the time I arrived, Suzanne had received Annabel's call and was already on arranging mode, sorting out my needs for the interview.

"Sarah, you know I love you dahling, but you just can't meet the producers of a Bond film with an accent like yours."

"Behave Suzanne, I'm Northern, get over it."

"Seriously dahling, this is too good an opportunity to overlook. Anyway I've already booked you the best dialect coach in London. I'll also organise a designer to dress you."

"I'm off to work with the stunt department, who cares how I look or sound?"

"Saying 'I'm off to work' should give you a clue. Anyway it's done. You look great, you've done loads of TV so this is the icing on the cake to make sure you get the role."

As my manager, Suzanne always knew best, so I humoured her.

I arrived at a leafy street in one of London's more salubrious suburbs. Wealth oozed from the brickwork as I looked for the house number. The elocution coach Suzanne had sent me had worked with Tom Cruise, Nicole Kidman, Brad Pitt and whole host of other 'A' listers to improve their English accents. I'm already English so how hard could this be?

I rang the doorbell, a charming looking old lady answered the door. "Sarah?"

"Yeah, Suzanne sent me, y'allreyt? Nice to meet yer."

I was confronted with a palm in my face, "No dear, the correct salutation would be 'Hello, it's awfully nice to make your acquaintance, I'm Sarah.'"

Oh for fuck's sake, it was going to be one of those days.

I was taken to the first floor and shown into her quaint sitting room. It seemed very prim and twee more like a country cottage than a London pad; everything was lightly flowered as if Laura Ashley had vomited all over the room. Although an older lady, her wrinkles were smoothed by her brown hair pulled tightly into a bun that sat atop a kind face. She was the poshest person I'd ever met and it made me giggle, I never thought people spoke in such a manner any more. I was truly Eliza Doolittle in Professor Higgins' study and I may as well have been starring in *Pygmalion* when we did actually recite lines such as 'How now brown cow' and 'The lazy dog....'.

With a mouth now full of marbles I went to see a dress designer. I would much preferred to have rocked up at Pinewood Studios in jeans and a T-shirt but instead I was fitted with designer shoes that made me wobble and a dress that made my boobs look twice the size. Maybe Suzanne had briefed them and wanted my chest to get me the job.

My first interview was with Michael Apted, the director; Barbara Broccoli the producer; the dashingly handsome Simon Crane, second unit stunts, and a couple of others who I didn't notice due to staring a Simon. The meeting went well, my background and posh accent seemed to impress them sufficiently to invite me into Simon's office to outline the sequence they wanted me involved in.

The storyboard for the entire boat sequence hung on Simon's office wall. It was brilliantly sketched out like a comic book and looked awesome as he described the scene in detail.

"What do you think?" Simon asked.

"Easy," I said, retaining my Queen's English reserve; "No problems."

"Good, that's what I like to hear," he said with a smile that made my knees go weak. "First, what we need to do is audition you to make sure you can do the job."

Confused, I blurted out, "Come again? You're auditionin' me? What fo'? All a do is boat shite." I couldn't have been more Northern if I'd crammed an Eccles cake into my gob.

Simon's grin widened as did mine when I realised what I'd just said to the number one stunt guy on a Bond film. "Because we haven't worked with you before, we need to take a look. I've seen you in action so I don't see there being any issues."

"Na no issues there, easy, it's what a do. I'm looking for'ard to it." My cover was blown. It didn't matter, I was Sarah Donohue, Northern lass now Bond stunt girl. I thought life couldn't get any better. How wrong could I be?

***

I had always wanted to do TV presenting or work in movies and had been at Oldham Theatre Workshop for many years prancing around on a stage. OTW is where most of the cast of *Coronation Street* originated from, but sometimes life changes direction albeit the end result can often remain the same. However my need for adrenaline started at a young age and never did subside.

We lived off the beaten track down a private lane on the edge of the Saddleworth Moor. It was a place that had untold beauty with hills and waterfalls, a child's dream where our parents took us to the waterfalls with a picnic during the summer as we played with the other children jumping into the cool clean water. Rickety-Rackety bridge was also a place of beauty, no more than 200 metres from our front door and under the Rickety bridge was a smaller sloping waterfall we could slide down, plunging into the cool water at the bottom. We caught fish in our nets and enjoyed the water with our parents watching over us, preparing the sandwiches. The bridge looked about 1000 years old, broken wood with planks missing, but we loved it there. I am fortunate to have lived the dream as a child and to have had parents that filled us with love and gifts of outdoor activities as a healthy family, something missing from this era as the world evolved, and children all now stare at tablet screens and social media as their childhood seeps away, never to return.

Where we lived, in our cottage, we had loads of scope for being daft with the safety of not being near a road, eliminating getting hit by a car or being abducted. I was supposed to be the sensible one as the only girl amongst six boys, yet often I'd be the one losing skin, much to Mum's annoyance. I was brought up with three brothers and three boys in the adjacent cottage. I was usually the one that encouraged stupidity and my mum has never got over the hydraulic pogo stick fiasco. I bought one for my brothers and with scientific mumbo jumbo tried to explain the height that could be reached if you jumped off the garden wall on it. Of course with any theory it has to be demonstrated. The stick was jacked up so high that on jumping off and hitting the ground, with me on it of course, it fired me off so high that the pogo stick and I parted company somewhere in the clouds and I crash-landed in a field and the pogo stick narrowly missed Dad's car, much to my brothers' hilarity and Mum's hard stare. It was a common theme with us siblings. I always bought them stupid presents from which I could get entertainment/trip to the hospital, and Mum's most used phrase was "I've got my eye on you!" It's something that has never left me, with my most recent encounter with the X-ray coming shortly after I said to my mum, "Mum I'm 46, I know what I'm doing," which then followed a Christmas day-trip to A & E with a broken collar bone.

I came back from London with two mini motos in my car, not an easy task with a smart car, but I squeezed them safely in there. I dived in my parents' house excitedly looking for my two younger brothers, with mum wondering what was going on. I found them in the garage outside, it was a big garage and more of a small house that Dad had built, it was never really meant for a car – it was a den we could all congregate and hide things from mum and dad in. It was a 'man cave' and had loads of tools and gadgets in it, as well as a loft area for storage or for when one of my brothers got locked out of the main house overnight by accident. With my brothers sat on the comfy couch chilling out, I burst in, smashing the door open telling them to come and see what I had. By now Mum just knew instinctively I was up to something and had followed me to the garage and was stood behind me, all 5'1" of her, hands on hips asking what we were up to. A guilty wide-eyed look was cast over her by all three of us yet my brothers didn't have a clue what I was about to reveal but knew mum wasn't going to like it and they wallowed sinking in guilt with me. "I've got my eye on you," she said as she disappeared back across the garden and into the house.

Like Roadrunner whipping up dust, the three of us couldn't get out of the man cave quick enough as I reversed my car up to secretly pile the bikes out of the back into the cave for a check over. To say my brothers loved them was an understatement. I was going to buy just the one but ended up with two because I couldn't help myself. The only reason I didn't buy three was because they wouldn't fit in my car.

"Have they got fuel in?" Robin piped up. Sam disappeared to grab fuel and some 2-stroke; we stood the mini-motos next to Sam's Hayabusa, the fastest production sportsbike in the world, they do up to 200 mph and are huge. Sam did offer me a go on it a few times, me having the Honda CBR600 as they had sponsored me for a short time, but I always refused. Sam is 6'4", Robin 6'3" and me 5'7". I didn't fancy dropping Sam's pride and joy and getting a broken leg in the process. The paintwork was beautiful – bronze, silver and black. The Hayabusa was a beast like no other and it could get you in trouble as quickly as it could get you out of trouble so I stuck to my smaller toys.

The mini motos were knee-high, red and white. They were exact replicas of 'grown up' bikes with racing numbers and that look of speed. Thick black tyres ready to rip along the ground and I could feel a day of fun ahead. Sam mixed the fuel and I could see Mum watching us from the house trying to see past the tree. She wasn't a nosey mum as such, her and dad are simply the best and most caring and thoughtful parents in the world, and to be fair me and my younger brothers would probably all be dead if it wasn't for them stopping us from being so stupid. Simon the eldest had way more sense. The fact that mum cared may have irritated us at the time but looking back, it's why I'm not badly scarred or six foot under. Ok they were fuelled, did we take them outside and start them up so Mum would know exactly what we were doing, or start them in the garage, choke ourselves with fumes – but at least we would be covered from Mum's death stare? Yep, we went for choking, it was safer than the wrath of mum. The lads gave both of them a quick pull with the cord and their little engines sang the sweet song of fine-tuning as we grinned and coughed, falling out of the garage, followed by bellowing exhaust fumes so we could breathe. It was playtime and although my brothers are always thoughtful and offered me everything first, I grinned and told them just not to fall off at full speed as Mum would kill me, and these little devils were 50 mph bikes. That's quick when you are only an inch off the ground, and with the lads being well over six foot this was going to be hilarious. Yup, their big sister had yet again done well and I could feel a bollocking from Mum coming on already, as Sam with his knees now situated by his ears, shot off over-revving over the bushes and up the private lane, wobbling all over the place due to him being so tall. He simply needed practice.

We could hear the moto ticking over at the top of the lane but Sam was out of view, suddenly an almighty noise, mimicking a huge swarm of bees, came down the dusty lane as a tiny red blur, and Sam shot past us still at full tilt and across the lane to the cottages at the end of the path. To much amusement he said it was way easier to balance at speed. Robin was next; Mum had now exited the house and was on the patio arms folded and frowning, I'm sure she was speaking to us but I just got Sam to keep the revs up so I could avoid acknowledging her. Robin slightly misjudging the fork in the lane went down into the field at a pretty high velocity – he backed off before actually jumping off and the bike came to a halt skidding on its side in the grass as we howled laughing. Mum didn't laugh, she glared at Dad and told him to do something. Dad just laughed and said, "Don't worry Pat, they'll break an arm or a leg soon and then they'll stop."

In my youth we even built a zip wire on a large drop bank from one tree to another. It wasn't a safe one by any means, it was a simple taut rope and we used a pair of handlebars to slide down on. The landing end also wasn't properly thought out. That tree was over a large drop bank as well and you either let go of the handlebars, dropping into the field below, or hit the tree square on and land all bloody in the harsh gorse bushes surrounding it. I was the first to test it, scaling the huge oak tree now 50 feet off the ground with the handlebars shoved firmly down my pants at the back. Over the rope they went, and down I went at some speed, letting go just before I face planted into the tree or the gorse, dropping down 20 feet onto the turf below, and being aware that the handlebars could in fact twat me in the face as they followed me. Next was one of the lads we lived next door to – they were like my brothers. He fell off midway and broke his arm; needless to say neither set of parents were happy and we later found our new toy cut up into much smaller pieces, not even capable to be used as dog leads.

Every summer we used to pack up home in the Saddleworth hills and disappear to France for four weeks, camping at 'Les Sables Blancs' (the white sands) situated right on the beach in Brittany, just 20 yards from the water's edge. It was an adventure like no other, we wanted for nothing and even caught our own shellfish right from the water's edge, which Dad promptly cooked for us whilst Mum made garlic bread for dipping. For us as youngsters it was a month learning a different language.

The campsite had few buildings, just an expanse of canvas and the odd set of caravans stretching for a couple of miles around the water's edge in what I remember as a big semicircle. There was also a centre section for those not wanting to wake up every morning to the lapping ocean, separated from the beach lovers by a lightly dusty road used by Frenchmen on bicycles, tiny old corrugated bread vans selling freshly baked wares to the campers; their croissants you could smell all over the site, a luscious ice cream van and other delicacies which filled the air with Frenchness. There were always two different types of beach sellers, one shouting *"Ouest France"* as he kicked his way through the sandy beach, clutching a sack of newspapers, and the 'glace' man selling ice creams on the beach. The site shop sold the fun stuff inflatables and sunscreen, as well as incredibly colourful fruit and veg bursting with life in comparison to the grey mush we get in the UK.

I did once get in a dinghy and got caught by a rip tide. Mum, a good French speaker, very quickly grabbed a local to speed out to me in his little boat and bring me back. I didn't get a bollocking that time, the tide simply went over to Carnac just across the water and it was never rough, she just shook her head. I did make my parents panic when the tide was completely out and I was looking for razor clams. All they heard was a high-pitched scream as I stood static in a shallow puddle on the beach with something wrapped around my leg almost thigh high. I can't have been more than nine years old. I had stood on a stingray that had been left behind when the tide ran out, so it had flicked sandy water over itself in the puddle and was hiding patiently to be picked up again by the incoming tide few hours later. As I stood there with this huge monster wrapped around my leg, a Frenchman beat my mum and dad in a race towards me. He told Mum and Dad, *"Arrêtez"* as he approached me. He pulled gloves out of his back pocket – he was a local fisherman and he slowly unwrapped the stingray as Dad quickly picked me up. We watched the old bearded fisherman pull the ray by its tail all the way into the sea, having to let go every few seconds because it was trying to sting him. Needless to say even to this day I avoid all puddles no matter where they are.

Holidays like this are what make a family really bond, being at one with the outdoors. No computers, only board games played at night via gas lanterns and no fast food outlets. I wish all children had an upbringing like mine. I was lucky to have parents that took a real interest in what we did and the way we lived our life. Mum and Dad even sent me and my older brother Simon to the small onsite shops or to the bread van that came around every morning encouraging us to speak French, so every day was a learning day. We had ten francs pocket money every day but we didn't need it.

As I approached age eleven, my mum registered me with Oldham Theatre Workshop under the rule of the formidable David Johnson, and it was from here my love of the bright lights began, and where I had true discipline drilled into me, a discipline which wasn't far off those from the military received and one which would stay with me to this day. David was famous for his ability to work with a hundred children in one room and have complete control, even to when they breathed. It was remarkable, and only those having been directed under David could truly understand. It was through his ability to teach and control that a large percentage of those attending you will see on screen every day in many UK TV dramas and films.

If you dared enter his workshop late he simply would not accept you, but not before he screamed at you. If you entered during registration he would scream at you. If you dared to utter a word or even cough you would be met with the same. He walked a little knock-kneed and twine-toed and rarely if ever smiled. To get a smile off him was the best feeling in the world because it was rare. He spent a lot of his time with one arm folded across his chest and the other elbow resting on it, with a finger to his lip looking at the floor in concentration as he listened to children and teenagers read their lines, listening for the timing of each sentence and interjection. You couldn't afford to even be a nanosecond out and god forbid if you forgot your lines or your dance moves. As we sang, David used to stay in that same stance and walk up to each and every one of us, looking at the ground concentrating and put his ear next to our mouth to listen to the tone of our voice; it was terrifying. If we were too quiet or if he didn't like the tone he used to tap the individuals on the shoulder, stop the entire rehearsal and get those he had tapped to step forward in front of the entire group and sing solo one by one. Really harrowing if you weren't a singer or were fairly introvert, new or nervous. It happened to me once. Even me a total extrovert almost crumbled terrified of now having to sing in front of a hundred other kids and belt it out like no tomorrow, without piano backing. I could feel the embarrassment crawl all over me, my hair stand on end and I felt sick. It's when I look back, I realise that David wasn't there to embarrass us, he wanted the best from each and every one of us. He wanted us to overcome our nerves to shine on stage and be a star and to make his musicals the best musicals in the business, and even though we were just children and from all walks of life we did just that. And for that I salute him and miss him greatly.

The kids of the Oldham Theatre Workshop were famous all over the country and although parents paid huge amounts to send their kids to theatre schools such as the Sylvia Young Theatre School, our parents at OTW paid less than £1 per attendance, as this school wasn't for profit. This was a donation so the workshop could continue to run and even underprivileged kids could attend, showing that you don't need to spend loads of money to make your child a star. Even the adult staff were all volunteers, and my mum often volunteered helping David at his workshops and backstage at the theatres. You simply need to find the best directors who love what they do and give all their energy to you in their spare time for free because they are passionate and love you, the children, and the theatre.

I remember David shouting that if we didn't have discipline how could we ever expect to take direction and work in a theatrical environment where timing was key? He wouldn't tolerate anything; yes he made everyone nervous, but we all returned week after week, year after year and when we performed on stage, he wanted perfection, nothing more nothing less. I learned everything from David and his discipline helped me in later life and with my future heading towards TV, stage and putting on my own shows later down the road. I couldn't have done any of it to the standard I did it without him. He was my mentor and clearly one of the best theatrical directors in the country, if not the best. He was a breed apart from any other director who came through the door after David sadly went into retirement. So those that read this book that have been under my direction in theatre or heard the stories. Now you understand why I am like I am and why your stage and my production was the best in the business for what we do. Average was not an option, entertainment, timing and precision are key.

During my time at OTW and my later years at school, I didn't stay on to the sixth form. I wanted 'A' levels but time was best served getting them at college so I enrolled at Oldham Tech to do 'Fashion and Textiles'; my mum and my grandma were ace dressmakers and I had got pretty good at it, and as I loved the theatre so much I knew I never actually wanted a 'normal' job and was prolonging my decision into what to do whilst still doing something

I enjoyed. I told my mum at a young age that I would never work nine to five and I never have. Oldham Tech was great. Their art department that also encompassed fashion and textiles was known as one of the best in the country for design. Phil Chisnall was in charge, he was the one that interviewed me and became my tutor for two years. He spent a lot of time stroking his beard as if in deep thought and always came out with something profound, was always softly spoken and incredibly nice and helpful.

I remember my initial meeting with him. It was in the art department, a massive room the size of six tennis courts back to back very open plan with partitions for the different skills in art. The offices were small and in between the partitions, and as I sat down retrieving my artwork from my bag, so he could see my skill rather than talk about it, he told me that the head of fifth form from Saddleworth School, Mr Atack had sent him a letter prior to my arrival to ensure I wasn't taken on the course. This fashion course was one of the most popular courses in the North West when it came to entry and getting in was tough enough, without some asshole of a teacher attempting to use the old boy network to not only scupper my chance of a place on the course but what could be my future. He told me of the letter and its contents saying he was advised not to offer me a place. Phil asked for my thoughts.

I had in all fairness expected to be greeted with this because Mr Atack had told me, "Donohue. I will make sure that when you leave this school no one anywhere ever takes you on. Nothing will ever become of you." Funnily enough I now appear in the 'Hall of Fame' at that school. For years he had to endure walking past a huge picture of me in the corridor feeling like the twat he was.

I told Phil I was expecting it. So the overly rotund head teacher had kept to his word. Mr Atack looked like Dennis Healey after eating an entire Kiplings' factory. He was a little over six foot or he appeared that way because I was so small, and he was just as wide. He always wore a dark grey suit, his massive gut straining the buttons and pulling the threads. A murky white shirt with faint pinstripes rolling down his ugly carcass, and often a burgundy tie which matched his nose. His face was red through broken blood vessels, with spider hairs sticking out of his nostrils and ears like a troll, greasy dark grey hair stuck to his head in no particular style, his eyebrows were so wild they ruffled in the wind wisping up like wings, and he had one of those faces that crumpled together with skin folds like a mastiff, but not as cute. He was so overweight that he could barely fit through a door and he waddled side to side when he walked always with intent, usually to bollock me for something regardless of if I had or hadn't done it. Why anybody would want this man as a role model for their children is beyond me.

I was the only girl he called by surname, relegated to being spoken to and treated as a boy for the entire year. I spent my entire fucking last year at school in detention and I absolutely hated him. At this point even my parents were sick to death of him because I didn't lie to Mum and Dad and if I said I had done nothing wrong they knew I hadn't and living in a remote area, detentions became a pain in the ass for my parents especially in winter – it was dangerous for me getting home. I was simply lively and gregarious as children of that age should be, never ever swore at a teacher, never answered back and I never played truant and he hated that. As time at school drew to a close, he took me in his office and asked me what I wanted to do when I left. As soon as he had extracted the information he wanted, the ogre told me he would be contacting the college ahead and making sure I didn't get on the course. He then told me I had detention that night. I walked out and didn't do another detention after that as I simply refused to stay. My parents were happy with that. In short, a man such as him should not have held a position in the education system and whilst it was fair to say you shouldn't speak ill of the dead, he is certainly one man I will never regret not meeting again.

As 'O' Levels closed in I contracted glandular fever, not just a small dose of it. I was wiped out to the point that I was so tired that if I went to go to the toilet I would fall asleep halfway up the stairs. I had this for around four months and it was decided by the education board I took my exams at home under the same rules imposed at schools with an assessor as I lay on the couch under a blanket. What a great way to take my exams and get the results I needed.

As I sat with Phil Chisnall, it soon became apparent to him that I didn't like Mr Atack and it was reciprocated. It also became clear to him that I had a talent he wasn't used to in someone who had never studied clothing design, and as I pulled out of a huge bag outfit after outfit I had made without utilizing a shop-bought pattern he was surprised on how I had actually made garments without it. Much of the clothing I made for myself I learned from my mum, and it was made by a process called moulage. I simply used cheap cloth on myself or a mannequin and cut and pinned it around the body in the design and shape I wanted it. I drew and wrote directions and cut around it on the body before removing it onto the floor and using that as the pattern transferring it to the real fabric. I also made an amazing humpty dumpty that that made him smile because it was so perfect and cute. It was around 12 inches tall and had yellow checked trousers – the remnants of a suit Mum had made Dad. Dad was of a loud gregarious nature just like me. It had little black boots on with yellow laces, a purple velvet upper body with little hand-stitched hands, big eyes and a smile, with a few strands of wool for hair. He asked if I had pattern for it. I just said no and that I had cut directly into the fabric and hoped it worked. He loved it as he held it up in the air on the palm of his hand with a big smile.

Phil told me, "We always discuss every applicant before making decisions on who to interview and who to then take on the course because we get hundreds for just twenty places. Your school report is in fact the worst I have ever seen, but what you are capable of is the best. I have to report to someone above me who has also read this report and I was in fact asked not to see you because we don't interview everyone. I will be putting forward that I want you on my course, so leave it with me and as long as you promise me that I won't regret it then I hope to see you in September." We shook hands and I left knowing my future for the next couple of years.

My new classmates were awesome and I remember our first week, five of us stayed in the studio for lunch and locked ourselves in the pattern paper storage room so we could do the Ouija board. We all pulled a chair in and tried not to giggle, drawing attention to ourselves, because students weren't allowed in the design area over lunchtime. We sat there silently giggling until we heard the final person leave. Wayne, the only guy on the course led the séance and it didn't take long for Janet, our extrovert with blonde and pink spiky hair, to scream and jump out of her skin as the glass flew across the board and hit the wall, which in turn made all of us scream. We all instantly blamed each other whilst nervously laughing, but all of the shushings in the world didn't help the fact we had blown our cover as Phil ripped open the storeroom door and went mad at us.

The group always had fun and worked as a well-oiled team and life at Tech was awesome. I stuck to my word and in his words "became one of his best students", always working hard to get grade A's and distinctions. All the time I was at Tech, I was also at Oldham Theatre Workshop walking from Tech just a quarter mile to rehearsals, getting home by 21:00 each night to do my homework often not getting to bed until the early hours. From an early age juggling study with theatre and loving it.

I later went to further my education and during this time started modelling, which took me on many travels and many exciting shoots. I found a home in modelling for many years, and am still doing it to this day in some capacity, My then agency was Manchester based Boss Models/Nidges. It was during my time with them I became close friends with five young men, better known now as Take That. One of them becoming my long-term boyfriend, and all of them becoming very close friends as I met them up and down the country in hotels as they toured. There were six people who knew the band were going to split months before it was announced in 1995. The sixth being me. When the news eventually broke it seemed the whole of the UK was devastated. I was almost relieved that I would see more of my friends, however the last time I saw Robbie was grabbing his arse on Oxford Street as he signed an autograph whilst trying to hide under a large-brimmed cap. We grabbed coffee out of the way of prying eyes and soon he shot to superstardom and his feet haven't touched the ground since.

Chapter 2

Silk stockings and Soho nights

'Hair flicking, high kicking, back bending.'

I'd participated in the Oldham Theatre Workshop since the age of around eleven years old and this is where I had met Mark Owen from Take That prior to him joining the band. I had appeared in too many musicals to remember, but stage, theatre and TV were where I wanted to be. There was only one place to make it happen – London.

I moved to London aged twenty-two with aspirations of becoming a TV presenter and back in the day such a position required an equity card. One of the best ways to get it was to dance. I'd danced tap, modern and jazz with the Oldham Theatre Workshop since the age of eleven and had appeared on stage countless times in innumerable musicals. As long as you could dance with showgirl talent, had a great body and the right look then there was always a possibility you may get hired at Paul Raymond's 'Raymond Revuebar' – the most prominent entertainment venue in London. Of course, there were many dodgy clubs out there who I knew would take me at the drop of a bikini, but I've never been one to take the easier option – I wanted to dance for the best show.

I didn't have a clue about flat-hunting, I'd lived with my parents up until now apart from a few weeks here and there living with friends and of course my years at Uni, so finding accommodation was all a bit hit and miss. Michael, who I had started dating, lived in London and offered me a bed at his place, but I didn't fancy that as I didn't want to be 'living with someone' at such a young age so I bought a newspaper called *Loot* and looked for a flat share and room rentals anywhere in London. It was literally pin the tail on the donkey as I didn't really understand locations, prices, nor transport links, so I looked at rooms that weren't too expensive around the East End. I saw a couple of real shitholes where as soon as the occupants opened the door

I didn't even enter and I also saw a couple I didn't even bother ringing the doorbell of as they looked perfect places for serial killers.

I finally settled on a room in East Ham. It was a flat share with three Australians. The house was hardly the Ritz but to be fair I didn't care as I spent all day out at castings or buzzing around the West End, and in the evening I hoped I would be working. The main thing was that it was clean and warm. Neither the kitchen nor bathroom looked like they had been decorated since the 60s but both were clean. Nothing in the house seemed to fit and I wondered whether it was subsiding. The carpet throughout was bloody awful. Badly fitted, within its frayed edges big orange and brown swirls looked like a dog had shit chocolate oranges everywhere – it was right out of the 70s, but as I'd be keeping my shoes on I didn't care, and in the room that I would take I'd put a big rug down anyway. I don't mind rolling around in my own filth but not anyone else's

The room where I would sleep was in a peculiar place, just off the living room next to the massive bow window that fronted the street, meaning to get to my room door I would have to walk in front of the TV, meaning there would be no escape from my housemates, but for that price nowhere was going to be perfect. The girl opened the door and showed me the room. It was badly lit but I didn't mind. The wallpaper was disgusting and I swear it had been decorated by either a blind man or someone just taking the piss. It contained a single bed, a small table and an old veneer cupboard, straight from the war. She hurried me in and out but I saw enough to see that it was clean, my main priority, and that the people seemed nice enough. If you are too fussy, house-hunting in London can be epic as you battle your way through hundreds of trivial discrepancies and unless you have a sheikh's wallet there will always be something you're not happy about. I gave them the deposit right there and then, darted back home in the North, collected some stuff and returned to the flat all before they could make tea.

It wasn't until my first couple of nights in there I realised the room was freezing. I don't just mean a bit nippy, I mean really, really cold as if it was actually outside – indeed, I would have been warmer sleeping in the bush that I could always hear swirling in the wind.

Mum came down to visit the following week to make sure everything was OK. She walked in and within seconds said,

"This is the bloody conservatory. The cheeky buggers have wallpapered over all the windows. I'm not surprised it's so cold! They can't expect you to pay rent for sleeping in the conservatory. It's got no heating and it's not even part of the house."

I never spent much time in my room as I was out all the time and been so busy I hadn't even noticed; it was merely somewhere to rest my head. I only stayed two weeks. I took back my deposit and left. My next port of call was Michael's. I moved in as his flatmate and stayed in the second bedroom. I had way too much going on in life to be tied down.

Thursday was always the day I eagerly awaited, as it was when *The Stage* newspaper was released. It was always full of jobs and castings, adverts for singers, dancers and actors trying to find work, stories about theatres and other thespian paraphernalia. I used to try and get it the night before at 5 pm as there were a couple of stalls on Tottenham Court Road that got it the day prior. Jobs in *The Stage* went so quickly it was imperative I get ahead of the game, so I would wait around the stalls with baited breath as the bundle was dropped off ahead of schedule.

I applied for an audition at Paul Raymond's Revuebar and got my date and time at the club located on Walker's Court Soho, where I knew I'd be under the critical glare of either the famous flouncing Frenchman Gerrard Simi – Paul Raymond's right-hand man – Carl Snitcher and sometimes even Paul himself. My parents were fully aware what I was doing and supported me, as they always did in my decisions although Dad warned me jovially about 'them blokes in frocks'.

Soho at that time was known as a seedy haven for rain-coated perverts and lost souls. During the early morning one could trip over tinfoil takeaway trays swimming in piss and fag butts, walk into a sex shop for a breakfast thrill before getting your choice of addiction sorted in the adjacent tobacconist/off licence. On a grey day the place looked as run down as the cleaners who wiped clean the leatherette chairs in the £1 peep show booths. But as the sun fell from the sky Soho would come alive. Like a Christmas tree brightening up a lounge, once the neon was turned on Soho was vibrant, exciting, full of London's characters and creatives and a million miles away from the commercial sedatives of Bond and Oxford Streets shopping meccas that bored me to death.

I arrived for my Revuebar audition and spent an age changing into my most stunning dancewear and heels before meeting Gerrard. He was around my height with a surly face framed by a wispy beard and an 80s football mullet that wafted down to his neckline. His side-kick and assistant choreographer

Bob was also as camp as a row of tents. As a former ballet dancer Bob had the longest legs and a Leo Sayer barnet. Gerrard was the usual strict abrupt choreographer, he had no time for a smile nor niceties, he was there to do a job and that was it.

His introduction was, "Show me your body." His accent was so French it spat mustard and his wildly erratic hands impressed upon me that he wasn't in the mood for waiting.

It seemed the time I'd spent trying to impress him with my dancewear had been time wasted as he made me take the whole lot off until I stood there butt naked in front of him. As unusual as that may sound, if you haven't got the confidence to stand naked in front of a professional choreographer then you haven't got the minerals to dance on the Revuebar stage.

He looked me up and down without any hint of emotion, told me to put on my G-string, bra and heels before taking me through part of a routine that I would have to instantly memorise. I would need a frigging photographic memory to perfect it in the time he allowed, and his continual screaming at any slight mistake made me even more determined to show him I could do it. He then called in other dancers from their dressing rooms to see if I suited the line up. As they walked on stage they all grinned at me as they'd all been through this same inquisition.

Gerrard clapped and screamed at us to get into position. With a tap of his foot and a "five, six, seven, eight," I was straight into the routine. I fucked up. Gerrard squealed in anger and screamed for the music to stop. The girls on stage grinned at me wondering how I was coping being screamed at. Coming from a theatrical background it was situation normal for me.

We set again and restarted on cue. I nailed it on the second attempt, thank fuck. He then shooed the girls back to their dressing rooms with a flick of his hands. "Sarah you start rehearsals in one week by which time you will be fluent. You'll be on stage for the opening and closing within four days of rehearsals. You'll also have a double routine that you'll learn within that same week and the week after you'll learn your solo. We work on it as many hours as it takes for you to get it right! Understand?"

I nodded, taken aback by the swiftness of it all.

"In one hour from now, Joan the dressmaker will arrive and measure you for all your costumes. A shoemaker will arrive at the same time to make your shoes. You are on full pay as from today."

He directed me to Paul's office to sign the contract. As I exited the stage door I popped my head into the top dressing room to tell them I'd got the gig.

"Have you met Carl Snitcher yet?" asked one of the girls.

"I'm on my way over to meet him now."

They all started giggling before Kay said, "Good luck."

I got it… titillation sprung to mind. Kay walked over and zipped my top up to the very top and suggested I keep it that way.

This was the first time I had met Carl Snitcher. He was well fed but not fat – as if he was a cheap November turkey. His face matched his surname – with pokey squinty eyes that sat close together, his whole face sagged downwards with a deep thin philtrum that looked more like a scar. His face looked like it had never cracked a joke nor a smile in his entire life, and left me with a feeling his head had actually been transferred from a dusty corpse.

His office was resplendent in female nudity with magazine pictures covering every inch of wall and his body odour made the room smell of sage and onion stuffing. I was fully dressed but felt naked as he overtly undressed me with his beady eyes. I felt remarkably uncomfortable as he asked me when my first rehearsal would be. "I'll come across to watch," he added with a smile slimier than what was left of his balding hair. He added the excuse that it would be when he would bring the contract over.

I wasn't that naïve. We'd rehearse with very little on, after all it's a show where the female body is key and the lighting is done to emphasise the body and to highlight or hide certain areas at key points. All Gerrard's girls had perfect bodies. Any straight, red-blooded man would kill to watch rehearsals.

Joan the costumier arrived in the dressing room. She was a lovely old lady who I kept in touch with until just a few years ago when she became ill. It was through Joan I met Ellie, another costumier who did my wedding dress and makes many of my clothes for me. The girls sat and watched in the dressing room while Joan went over what I would be wearing and took all my measurements. The girls assisted, offering comments while they sat around in various states of undress. I couldn't believe how helpful they were to me, the new girl. I'd never experienced anything like it. They were just amazing.

I loved the outfits, they were larger than life and so colourful. If they used blue it was the bluest blue you could ever see, if they used crystals they were bigger and brighter crystals than you could ever find. Everything at the Revuebar was louder and more colourful and absolutely everything was covered in glitter, even your food you brought in to snack on ended up powdered in glitter. After about a fortnight I'd ingested so much I actually had sparkly faeces. And from experience I can confirm that the proverb is true.

The shoemaker arrived soon after. I explained my right foot was about a size bigger than my left, much to the amusement of the other dancers. He made me three sets of 5-inch heels especially for dancing, plus a pair of boots. I still have my black patent leather silver studded dance shoes now. When I left I took them with me, I just had to. It's virtually impossible to make heels feel like slippers but these fitted like a glove. They are divine.

Gerrard always insisted on made-to-measure footwear no matter the cost because it was imperative to him that all girls could be on their feet all night safely. Fuck, I loved my new job. The money was fantastic. Two shows a night, six days a week. It was all cash back then and working a maximum of thirty hours most of which were back stage drinking and having a laugh. I earned double what some of my friends earned in a week and they were doing the usual forty hours of mundane life-sapping work. I didn't even count it as a job; it was pure fun. It was fun from start to finish with never a dull moment. I loved going to work, I loved my girls and I loved the theatre staff and I loved being on stage. The Revuebar was just a dream to work.

My best friend soon became Kay. Kay was also a model and had an amazingly dry sense of humour. She was 5'10" and because of this, her made-to-measure shoes were only 2 inch heels because all the dancers had to be the same height. Kay had the best boobs I had ever seen, with inverted nipples that only popped out to the feel of silk. Because they were perfectly round and natural she looked like she had a couple of Dunkin's stuck to her chest so it wasn't long before I nicknamed her 'Donuts'.

The changing room was like a professional sports team's, with allocated seating for the dancers. Kay sat one side of the door with me on the other. In the corner sat Mousel, then Charlotte, Christine and finally Rachelle, a Scouse brunette with a great smile. Mousel was stunning with her English rose porcelain skin fronting her long black hair that cascaded down a blemish free body that I would die for. Charlotte was hilarious, very extrovert and totally beautiful with red hair and bright green eyes.

Despite us all looking so different, once on stage everything had to be the same. It was epic once we had our makeup on, we all looked cloned. The girls taught me how to apply a new type of stage make up and Kay took me to a stage make up boutique called 'Charles Fox' in Covent Garden to get the correct glitter and pancake so I could truly trowel it on under the heavy lights.

The make up was very 'drag queen'. Our lips were always the reddest of red and the lip glitter had to be a specific red for it to be used at the Revuebar. The eyes were always heavy with black eyeliner, blue-shaded in the socket with white highlighter, and we wore huge eyelashes so long they could sweep the floor. We had pancake base on our face and heavy blusher giving great definition, giving us all the look of a doll. Gerrard would come round and check us all, including our perfectly manicured bright red nails, like a primary school teacher checking pupils' hands for lunch, before we got on stage. Heaven help anyone who he didn't find perfect. It was so important that every girl looked the same that if we wore wigs on stage, you couldn't tell who was who. My parents came to watch the show and both failed to identify me until I was introduced to do my solo routine. There were so many feathers and crystals, neither did they realise we were topless.

Under amazing lighting, the show was so dramatic. The opening was eleven girls on stage, all with a chair that was part of the routine. We all dressed in black, silver and red, wearing studded heels with ankle straps, black fishnet stockings and suspenders, a heavy leather studded body harness which had a neck collar with studs running down from the collar between the breasts and around the waist, fastened a huge belt to pull the waist right in. From the collar were also attached studded epaulettes over the shoulders and studs running down the arm to just above the elbow, and a fastening around which was met at the elbow by long black gloves and a small black G-string. The headdress was a leather cap with a chain at the front and sequins on the peak. On top it had attached layers and layers of torn red and black net to give it height and width and the wildness of dancing flames. The chair routine was amazing. The opening was my favourite, we used to have so much fun. I still remember the entire routine to this date.

The secret game during the opening, but god forbid if Gerrard found out, was to try and flick open the collar of the person in front of you but without the audience seeing you. If you could flip open the collar, the entire harness fell forward off the shoulders and it would totally fuck you up on stage. Many a night someone would get caught out and it was always about being aware who was behind you or next to you. The idea was to hold and refasten it quickly before it fell or before someone noticed. The best time for attack was on the final bow just before the curtain closed after the opening, if you could open it at the bow it just tumbled and there was no stopping it. We devised many pranks for minor amusement if we knew the choreographer wasn't watching. Another one was to tear someone's stocking just as we were lining up for show opening. It was so incredibly unprofessional and childish but hilarious, as a stocking can be changed, it's just incredibly inconvenient, so each night at the five-minute call we would be lined up looking like a load of schoolgirls dancing around like cats on hot bricks trying to avoid our stockings being torn prior to the curtain being raised.

My solo was 'The Final Countdown' the song released in 1986 by the Swedish rock group Europe. I wore a red white and blue American football outfit and my prop was a huge football helmet. I had heavily sequinned red ankle boots with gold stars and long white socks with a blue stripe around the top. The routine consisted of lots of hair flicking, high kicking, back bending and salaciously caressing the oversized helmet. It was so over the top but brilliant. I supported huge cage shoulder pads under a top that I eventually ripped off before revealing a sequinned body harness and not much else… It was all about dancing with curves and making the most of what you had, and I loved it, although I can't stand that song any more I've heard it so many times. The other dancers would sometimes hide behind the curtain whilst I was on stage doing their level best to put me off because if Gerrard was watching and I made a single mistake he would absolutely kill me.

Our audience was a mix of rich locals, inquisitive tourists and the occasional dickhead. Every Friday without fail a friendly vicar used to come up to visit the girls on what could be considered his preaching of the Lord's word. Now call me old fashioned but I thought a church may be the best place to spread the love, but this vicar thought it far more ecumenical to offer us a private audience in the dressing room, clasping his Bible without any sermon, while we were conveniently half naked or getting in and out of the shower. On the first occasion I witnessed him, I looked at the girls and asked why the fuck a man of cloth in a collar (and not a leather studded one) would wander around while my tits were out. The girls just grinned. It was normal for all the girls to be polite and entertain him for five minutes. I just found it weird but apparently he had visited for as long as the oldest transgender could remember.

We had two transgender dancers. You would have no idea, and Christine and Amanda were beautiful, much better than most women I have ever seen, bearing in mind that thousands of girls audition for the Revue but only the best of the best get picked, with only fourteen of us who would make the grade. It became quite normal to work with transgenders, there are more in this game than you can imagine and the chances are you wouldn't have a clue. Christine, for instance, I didn't know was a transgender until several years later when I was out with my best friend in the world, Talisa, a TG herself and one of my gorgeous bridesmaids on marrying Lee in 2015, again so beautiful you would never know. We saw Christine at the Café Royal club in Leicester Square and said hello. I hadn't seen her for years and was shocked that Talisa knew her. The last I had heard Christine had gone from the Revue to Australia. As I hugged Christine and she floated off to the bar I asked Talisa, "How do you know her?"

"She's a tranny darling, we all know each other."

"Fuck off, there's no way Christine is a tranny. I worked for years with her naked in the same dressing room, not a fucking chance!"

"Isn't she fabulous?"

I was in shock, I would never have guessed. The tits, even the voice and hands, nothing would have led me to believe it. Neither would I have guessed Amanda was a TG, the only weird thing about her was that she was way too beautiful and perfect for a female. Before my time someone from *Vogue* had come in to see the show and wanted Amanda to test for the front cover. He was that impressed he really begged the Revuebar to arrange it. Amanda refused. She said simply that she had escaped from being born male and being on the cover of *Vogue* would surely bring people out of the woodwork who knew her as a man when she just wanted a nice quiet life living below the radar as a woman. I still keep a picture of the girls I worked with in my bedroom. We loved each other as sisters.

The Revuebar dancers were a different breed of showgirl, we were beautiful, disciplined, talented and very content in everything we did and helped each other on and offstage. We were a family.

After a few months a Danish girl called Sara joined us. She was very plain without makeup but as soon as it was applied, she transformed into one of the most beautiful girls I had seen in my life. As she was vegan she wouldn't use any products tested on animals, which in those days severely limited availability and lived on a diet of beans and lentils and thought it natural to fart in public. Due to her lack of product use, it wouldn't be long before she stunk of body odour, which is not cool especially in a dressing room where all we do is sit around naked in close quarters with each other. While we couldn't stand it, we didn't want to make her feel overly uncomfortable, we wanted all the girls to feel part of the family and in such delicate situations it would be easy to upset the group dynamic. Fortunately Gerrard, with less tact, walked in just as Sara let one rip. As she had also been rehearsing she was pretty heavy on the BO. Kay and I escaped to the corner burying our heads into Mousel's breasts trying not to inhale the smell.

"What in god's fucking name iz zat 'orrible stench?" he screamed.

Sara owned up to it and offered her reasons for not showering here because of animal testing on products. She barely finished her sentence when Gerrard pushed her in the shower and turned it on.

"Kay, give me your fucking shower gel." He threw it at Sara. "Never, ever secrete any stench ever again in my fucking theatre," he squealed before storming out. From then on she smelled of roses (and rabbit death).

I couldn't believe the amount of money I was now raking in. I had so much money it was like a dripping tap and never-ending, as on top of my Revuebar wage I also worked my free day times as a model going from casting to casting in London. I was on the books with Boss Models in Manchester and in London I had signed with Marco Rasala, and then later to the agency owned by the gorgeous Page 3 pin up from the 80s, Linda Lusardi. My day would begin with calling into the agency first thing in the morning and again last thing in the afternoon to see what castings/auditions had come in. The 'booker' – mine was the lovely Jo – would read names and addresses of where I had to be and who to see, and if I had a time slot or whether I just had to go there and wait. The details of the job would also include what is was, e.g. swimwear, lingerie, fashion, nude, semi-nude or clothed; and what it paid. Nude was always tasteful yet many girls didn't do it so it was highly profitable for those that did. There were many horror stories of girls being manipulated or exploited but with the decent agencies all work goes via them so everyone was totally protected. The client paid the agent within six weeks and the agent paid the model, skimming their 20% commission.

I'd finish at the Revue Bar around 11.30 pm and I'd either go to the Boardwalk bar on Greek Street for a drink, or if I had a job or casting on the next day I would go home. I started at the Revue around 6 pm so whatever modelling job I had I needed to be clear so as not to be late. Sometimes my day would start at 7 am and I'd be in bed for 12.30 am. We all knew that to work hard we needed to play hard or we'd go mad. This lust for life would eventually be our undoing at the Revue. While working there was a dream, we were all young and adventurous and when even the best jobs become mundane a few of us decided to look for work at other venues.

Coincidentally, I received a phone call out of the blue from Bob, our old assistant choreographer who was now living in Amsterdam with his boyfriend, inviting both me and Kay to fly out to visit him. We thought it was a good chance to check our options

When Kay and I landed in Amsterdam it was great to go to Bob's house. It was very flamboyant, filled with framed pictures of old movie stars and film posters as you walked down the long hallway into the living area. It was very black and white with touches of red. It was classic and stunning with black leather sofas and chrome ornaments, which on closer inspection, were very erotic. His spacious kitchen was tiled in black and was filled with chrome. It was incredible. He played Sinatra in the background and he always wore neat black jeans, black polished shoes and either a black shirt or a flamboyant silky shirt with his Leo Sayer hair and moustache.

Bob told us to leave the Revue and work in Amsterdam. We were at a loss what work we could do there. We weren't hookers and we didn't do the sort of shows that Amsterdam is infamous for. Bob suggested a club that was similar to the Revue, so we thought we would take a look. However, it appeared that since Bob's last visit several years ago it had changed somewhat and even though we were guests of the club, so didn't pay for entry or drinks, we soon spat our drinks over each other as we stared and watched. I don't need to go into detail about what we saw but it was one of those shows where you tilt your head and wonder how they put that thing where they did. On a flexibility scale they were very impressive, and what they could do with certain implements was rather imaginative – so too the activities of some of the audience. It clearly wasn't the direction we saw our careers heading. On the way out Kay asked the whether Amsterdam needed erotic dancers who didn't get naked or indulge in live sex? We were politely escorted out and thanked for our visit. We spent the rest of the day at a selection of canal-side bars drinking and wondering how many women they could actually fit on a sex swing.

Putting a big black mark through Amsterdam we sought pastures new. Kay and Christine went to the Crazy Horse in Adelaide. Known as the city of churches, Adelaide has a rather demure reputation with its ageing population and serene nightlife, yet is home to Miss Nude Australia, probably the craziest pageant on the planet. Mousel went to Vegas. I went to that little place in Paris called the Moulin Rouge...

Chapter 3

Moulin Rouge to the dog house

'I almost expected a fairy to sail down a zipwire.'

I arrived in La Pigalle area of Paris at an apartment shared with another dancer. Many of us back in the day adopted pseudonyms for safety and privacy, even at the Revue I used a different name and had a bank account in a different name. It was an age when opening a bank account without ID checks was common. Pigalle was an area not too dissimilar from Soho with the brightly coloured lights and interesting characters. The Moulin Rouge is crowned with a huge and glorious bright red windmill towering over everything, making it a spectacular landmark and the surrounding buildings made it look like something out of Disney, I almost expected a fairy to sail down a zipwire at any moment, sprinkling her fairy dust. The windmill of course doesn't function and the only grinding going on in that building is kept purely to the stage, but it is truly monumental and beautiful.

Pigalle was the red light district, no different than Soho drawing in punters, voyeurs, perverts and the simply intrigued from all over the world. The rich and famous to the down and outs hung out in Pigalle and that's what made it such a trendy place. There were peep shows and sex shops and dodgy cinemas on every corner with the Rouge standing proud and always busy. All sorts of things went on down the back streets, men in long dirty macs through to women in Gucci sharing the midnight air, as the ladies of the night walked the streets looking for their next client. It's a magical place in many ways and a place that everyone should visit at least once and everyone should most certainly book early and reserve seats at the Moulin Rouge.

I remember meeting my friend after the show one early morning, he was picking me up under what I called 'Rapunzel's tower' which was just to the left of the Rouge as you faced the entrance. I often imagined a long ponytail cascading down whilst the fairy flew overhead. He had come in to see the show with his sister, he had in fact seen it many times and yet he could never spot me on stage; that time was slightly different, a girl had slipped on stage and that girl was me. I hadn't gone arse over tit, but catch a rogue feather on the floor at the wrong time and trust me, that theatre had more feathers than a peacock farm and it becomes lethal. All dancers are pretty much taught to slip and fall and continue with grace as are runway models. My smile didn't move an inch and fortunately I was upstage so at the back but my arms threw a windmill larger than the one sitting on top of the building as I battled to stay upright. And not tear any muscle in my groin. I came offstage my heart still pounding with the two girls on stage either side of me giggling at my misfortune. This is not a stage for fuck-ups and accidents don't happen at the Rouge. I prayed no one had spotted my gyrating routine as I continued the evening and changed into my bright red can-can number praying no more feathers were floating around.

Backstage was like a rabbit warren with so many dressing rooms it was the Revue just bigger. There were huge feathers everywhere. It was sweetly ironic that I was here at the home of the can-can, as when I was a small child, my babysitter Mariah was a dancer with the Bluebell Girls and awesome at the can-can. It was only when talking to her as a teenager I became interested in being a Showgirl.

The Rouge was colourful and vibrant, beautifully classy. I sank into the dressing rooms on the luxurious red wine coloured carpet that had the deepest pile I'd ever seen. The dressing rooms had cream coloured walls and insanely high ceilings to give unrestricted access for the huge feathers cascading from the headwear. A head high shelf ran all the way around on top of where beautiful headdresses were kept out of harm's way. Underneath the shelf hung dresses or other costumes. Where the hangers stopped there would be a row of desks for each performer to have their space with their own drawer for makeup and a personal mirror space.

The stage was a lot bigger than the Revue, there were lots more performers for a start and it was way more demanding. There were also men in the show, which didn't exist in the Revue, although when I left they did bring in two men.

The Moulin Rouge emphasised more on dance ability so before I auditioned I had gone 'back to school' 121 training for a top up and plenty of classes. I spent a lifetime in demanding rehearsals, a studio part mirrored and part scattered with gym equipment was to be my home. I also had many costume fittings before I hit the stage with the can-can one of the first things I learned to perfect. The can-can is more than merely leg kicking. The best girls could kick off a man's hat without hitting him in the face – not something I would recommend attempting half-drunk in a pub. The skirt has to be held at all times whether lifting it to the front, side, the back, with the many petticoats and garter always on show. The head was always held high, there was always a smile on our faces, and our backs were always rod straight. It was fast and furiously paced and required a high level of fitness, something that non-dancers take for granted. We'd jump into the splits and get up just as quickly and carry on. It took so much out of us and we had to be so precisely in tune with each other on stage or we'd never catch up because of the tempo. There was no room for error.

The girls were from all over the world, the Rouge auditioned in many different countries and the choreographers pushed hard to get the best out of you at both the auditions and in rehearsals. They knew so much about dance styles and the way everything was put together was mind-blowing. The Revuebar was my love and passion but the Rouge went to an all new level of professionalism. The main choreographer didn't flounce like Gerrard and he wasn't as hot tempered, but he did get what he wanted

I loved the Rouge, after all it was the most famous Showgirl venue in the world.

The whole setting was above and beyond. It was romantic and warm and classically done and with such expertise. I know that Gerrard at the Revue always wanted his show to be of the standard of the Paris show and in many ways it was, but there were so many more dancers in Paris, the theatre held so many more in the audience and there were so many more staff. People from all over the globe worked there, it was incredible. It was a well-oiled machine and if you fucked up then you were out of the door. It may seem boring but performers just didn't fuck up there and never turned up late. The Rouge wasn't just a job, it was a career, a lifestyle and only the best of the best work there and once you got the job, you embraced it even though the rhinestone G-strings hurt like hell.

There are many people who think of the Moulin Rouge as just a movie. I have to be honest and say I haven't seen it as I don't want any memories tarnished, and more annoyingly all I'd do is sit there shouting "What a load of rubbish, that wouldn't happen there," no different than when a war film comes on and my husband, a former Royal Marine of twenty years, sits there swearing.

I enjoyed my short time there, but Paris and the spectacular show which was Formidable wasn't for me. London seemed much warmer and more like a village. When I lived in Soho in London everyone knew each other in all the bars and shops and peepshows, it was safe it was home and it felt cosy. Paris wasn't like that possibly due to cultural and language differences, so I never really felt safe or at home and my feet had become itchy again to move on.

I eventually returned to London and bought *The Stage* newspaper again and went on the hunt for what else was available in Europe. I saw an ad looking for professional dancers at the Beverly Hills club in Vienna. Pre-internet we didn't have information and research at our fingertips so we took most things on face value. I called the number and spoke to a girl called Cassie who asked about my dance background. I told her I worked the Revue and the Rouge so with that information I was hired. I had several important questions for her about the venue. I asked if the venue had an elevated stage away from the audience and that I wasn't expecting podiums and nor would I dance on a podium. She answered positively. I also checked that there was no consummation as I was a professional showgirl. She said there was absolutely no consummation. This is the lengthy name for having to talk to clients to earn money. She assured me that it was the same as the other venues I had worked in, that I would be fitted for costumes and footwear and I would be going through rehearsals and then onto perform.

With my concerns allayed I put down the phone and awaited Cassie to send me my travel itinerary and tickets. I got on a plane with barely any money as it was all stashed away in savings. I'm not usually that stupid and I always carry cash (I'm not encouraging anyone to rob me on the street, however). I had my itinerary, they had sorted my accommodation, would pay for my meals and I would be paid at the end of every working week. With everything in my working life being great, what could possibly go wrong?

***

A Beverly Hills club representative met me at Vienna Airport and all seemed fine. I had asked if I could see the venue before I was taken to the apartment so I could take a look and get my bearings and possibly meet the girls before I started. Even at night I was awestruck by Vienna's beauty. Snow falling lightly added to its charm, and lining the roads subtly lit buildings exuded class. We stopped at the famous Beverly Hills club and with what I'd seen in the car was tremendously excited. We entered through the front doors of the venue which was both unusual and a first as I am used to rear stage doors. The stage was tiny, a lot smaller than expected but had great lighting, and I was introduced to the staff. I said hello to the girls backstage and went Front of House again. The room was mainly lined with curved high-backed velvet-covered bench seats with lots of chrome and glass top tables. It was clean and professional looking but one thing confused me – why were there half-naked girls lap dancing for men and girls sat at tables canoodling with punters? I presumed Cassie had forgotten to tell me there were different things going on at the venue. I wasn't overjoyed with what I saw but I could ask questions the next day.

A chauffeur took me to the venue the following night to presumably run through routines and rehearsals, albeit I thought it late. The whole thing was odd as I was just shown the beautifully fitted out dressing room and given a space. I asked about rehearsals. The girls looked at me like I was mad. The girls at the Rouge and the Revue had all been trained in some form of dance to a high standard so the way they walked and spoke was just elegant. There was a discipline and respect amongst the performers that didn't exist at the Beverly Hills club. I spoke to the manager who simply said that I started at 10 pm. The job was a spot on stage every hour and the rest was consummation.

It then dawned on me. I was working in a high-end strip joint. These girls were strippers and hookers only interested in money. There is nothing wrong with that, I've known plenty in my time and everyone in everyday life prostitutes their services in someway. But it's simply not for me. It wouldn't take much for me to break the wrist of any man that dared touch me or even look at me in the wrong manner.

"Cassie said there would be no consummation," I said.

The manager simply replied, "Cassie has nothing to do with it. You're contracted for three months. Be ready at ten."

I'm sure it has happened to other girls and they have just sucked it up. I thought '*fuck this shit.*' I was now on automatic '*Where's the exit and how do I get my ass out of here?*'

The problem of coming away with little cash now dawned on me. I knew that for one night I had no choice but to play the game so I gave my excuse of not going on stage the first night because I had my period. It was too intimate for me but moreover it was a waste of my time as there was no money to be made onstage and as I had been lied to, they could fuck off.

I was absolutely fuming, had Cassie been there I would have punched her into the following week whilst standing on her feet hoping she would spring back like a jack-in-a-box so I could punch her again. We should always be given the chance to say no but to say no we have to have the full story so what didn't she understand about 'no' consummation? How a woman could do this to another woman I have no idea. My aim was to visit her and make sure she didn't do it to anyone else but I couldn't track her down. I think my voicemail messages to her weren't encouraging enough for her to call me back and invite me for high tea at the Ritz.

I wanted to leave the club immediately and the thought of having to talk to some pea-brained overweight dickhead staring down my cleavage all night for cash made my skin crawl. I had to get them to ask me to dance so I could earn per dance. I worked as professional dancer and showgirl not this shit. I know many girls earn from doing this. Good for them, my temperament isn't suited to this type of work because I just had visions of head-butting some pervy bastard. I already knew approximately how much flights were so I gauged how many dances I needed to do. It wasn't that many but if I could do them all with one person there was less chance of me either pouring a drink over them, insulting them or worse still them touching me and then I punch them right in the face.

Before I had chance to even walk the floor to see what the entire club was like the manager came over. "That gentleman over there would like you to join him."

I would have liked to join him to a live electric cable but I smiled and sat down with him nonetheless. The seats were dark velvet and could well have been new or refurbished as they hadn't yet been spoiled by sweat, jizz or beer. I just wanted to throat-punch him but smiled nicely whilst visualising sticking my thumbs into his eye-sockets for staring down my chest. He took a drink of whisky before breathing halitosis over me. I was hoping he would choke on it and collapse on the table but he didn't. He offered me a drink, I said yes just so I needn't go anywhere else. I only had Coke and we chatted. I pretended to be mildly interested in his bullshit spewing forth from his noxious mouth but acted sweetly and thought about my ticket home. I was so sick of him chatting to me and poisoning me with his breath I just asked him, "Do you want me to dance?"

He answered positively and over the forty-five minutes I sat with him I danced for the five songs I needed to pay for my flight.

It's a funny thing dancing for someone that isn't remotely attractive. I can honesty say that all I did was smile and think *'you pathetic perverted freak, parting with cash and giving it to a girl that doesn't give two fucks if you drop dead on the spot. Yep you mug give me your cash.'* When girls chat to guys in these clubs do they really believe for one minute she likes anything other than his wallet? When the money dries up and he just wants to chat she will exit and go to the next man. Of course many men play the game as well but there is only one loser. And it's never the girl.

I visualised wrapping his tie around his fat neck and draining the life out of him until he turned blue. On the fifth song I took his payment, thanked him said I would be back and needed the ladies room. He didn't really seem that happy with the deal; however, I thought he was lucky to still have the use of his eyes and legs.

I took my bag from the dressing room and escaped through the fire exit. I jumped in the first taxi, returned to the apartment and packed. It could have been around midnight. I stayed up all night and wedged myself behind the locked bedroom door. When I heard the other girls come in, I left as soon as they settled. It was 5 am and fucking freezing.

I reached the travel terminal and waited outside in the snow until it opened. I went shivering into bookings. My lips had almost turned blue and my toes seemed to have disappeared. An attractive young man behind the desk asked if I was OK. I said yes but it was obvious I wasn't. I hadn't slept, worrying that because I had ran out of the club someone might come to get me. On processing my booking it appeared I didn't have enough money for a flight. My parents were in Spain and I couldn't reach them. I suddenly became really distressed. The ticketing agent asked what had happened and why I was in Vienna. I just babbled helplessly about my thirty-six hours of hell. As soon as I mentioned the 'Beverly Hills' club he looked horrified and told me to wait a moment. He came back minutes later tapping away and printing. He handed me an airline ticket and a ticket for a bus to the airport. He told me to keep the money I had for food and phone calls and said,

"Take care of yourself. I'm sorry what happened to you." He then took me outside and put me on the bus. This guy, whoever he was, had just saved my ass. The company clearly had a slush fund for fuck-ups and a kind boss.

I slept like a log on the plane and took the tube to Soho and carted my case up the stairs to the flat I had kept. I lived above Charlie's Bar right above the chaos of drinkers. I put my key in the lock but I couldn't open my door, probably due to lack of sleep. I was irritated and kicked my suitcase down the stairs. A pretty girl dived out of the way and said, "Hi! You must be Sarah? I'm your new neighbour. Looks like you've had a shit day. Get your arse in the bar for a drink."

Talisa and I became inseparable. It wasn't long before we had moved bars and were shooting tequila's in a Tex Mex restaurant called 'Los Locos' in Soho Square whilst raggedly holding onto a mechanical bucking bronco. This was the basis of my lifelong friendship and soul mate with Talisa Garcia.

***

I was actively encouraging everyone in our new bar to drink more and ride the mechanical bull when Tim the manager spotted me and offered me a job on the spot. I initially declined as I was with a model agency and I'd served my years as a barmaid going through university.

"How does £300 cash for two nights work sound? You'll only work three hours each night."

Such a sum for only six hours work only 200 metres from my flat in a restaurant I frequented anyway was too good an offer to turn down. Los Locos (translated 'The Crazy Ones') had a new beer launching and Tim had seen me in action, and encouraging people to drink copious amounts of booze was a speciality of mine.

All I had to do was stand on a small platform dressed like Daisy Duke from *The Dukes of Hazzard* and sell bottled beer from an ice bath. Even if people didn't like beer, by the time I had smiled at them, taken the top off with my teeth and thrust it in their hands they had already handed over their money. Admittedly men seemed more interested in the product than women but as they were bigger drinkers Tim was more than happy, even if it did take the punters away from the bar.

Tim loved me, the staff thought I was hilarious and carefree and, in a way, I was. I didn't really need the money, this was just a heap of fun working in a bar where drinking while working was actively encouraged. I could shout and play about with customers so how could anything top this? It was none stop laughter as the DJ and I gesticulated to each other all night. Dion the hot Kiwi waiter always offered me shots and a smile. After Paris and Vienna, I was home.

I had only been there two weeks when a guy about 6'5" walked in wearing a blue Stetson and a ghastly coloured shirt. He stood out like a sore thumb so I beckoned him over. He scrambled his way through the drunken hordes and asked what I was doing.

"I'm selling you a beer, sir." I talked through the USP of the new beer and how it was laced with tequila, took the top off with my teeth, thrust it in his hand and asked for two pounds with a massive smile; my pearly white teeth and my ample cleavage popping out of my bikini top.

He smiled and in a Texan accent said, "I don't drink beer I only drink vodka."

"You do now" I retorted, "It's opened and got your name all over it. When you've finished be sure to come back and get another one."

Before you knew it, it was in his hand and he had given me £20. "Keep the change," he said and wandered off.

I saw him a few times throughout the night and even my best smile couldn't convince him to try another beer I was waving at him. Near closing time he finally bought another beer. As he put his hand in his pocket to pay I told him not to. After all, his initial tip was so big I told him I was buying that one for him. He smiled, raised his bottle to me and walked off. As I packed away the bar Dion came up to me.

"Do you know who that guy is in the blue Stetson?"

"No idea." I just did my job, drank loads and carried on drinking at the bar until 2 am.

"It's the owner, he's a Texan billionaire. Charles Burnett III."

"Good for him, nice guy," I muttered on the way to the end of the bar – my usual place for beverages. Behind the bar I always looked at the pictures above the bottles. They were of brightly coloured racing boats with Los Locos branding down the side.

The manager Tim approached me and amusingly said, "I hear you met Charles? He likes you, he wants you to work for him."

This is how my powerboat journey started – in a club, drunk, biting tops from beer bottles. Before I knew it, I was in a private helicopter heading off to Lake Windermere to assist Charles with some PR.

I had been pulled in for a quick meeting with Charles (CBIII he was often called) before our professional relationship started and he spoke about the race team and what he did and about me helping with PR. He always wore this blue Stetson with a brown and white feather centre front and a brightly coloured shirt. I can't say they were particularly classy, more like a child had been having paint throwing frenzy, but dress sense apart we got on like a house on fire. I remember being picked up by a car in London and taken to Selfridges to meet him before our trip to Speed Week at Lake Windermere where there was an awards dinner. CBIII's family, the Weston family own Selfridges but back then he just had an account with them. He took me up to the Personal Shopping Department where they were expecting me and asked the ladies to dress me for an important dinner. I told Charles not to worry I had plenty of nice outfits and I didn't need more clothes, basically he needed me out of the way for an hour as he had meetings so I wasn't really given a choice as he reiterated to the ladies to arrange me an outfit. They asked what I liked and arrived back with a large dress rack whilst I drank my coffee and ate my salmon and cream cheese sandwiches I had been brought. I stood there as they ran through the designers and the clothes and asked what I would like to try on.

"None, I don't like any and I really don't need anything,"

"It's so refreshing to hear a young lady say that, however we have to find you that outfit as Charles has asked us to. Would you like to come onto the shop floor with us and we will bring the rail and just point at what you like and we will bring it upstairs for you."

So there I was with two personal shoppers and an open expense account. Not one. Two. In Selfridges designer department. I was just a tomboy from the Yorkshire moors the only thing I was missing was the stereotypical whippet and flat cap. First stop was Gucci and then Versace and so it continued. I met the trolley full of goodies plus accessories, handbags and shoes upstairs. The Jacket was a chestnut brown cashmere and wool mix woven tightly with a cerise pattern trimmed with silver thread, short kimono style sleeves, a fitted bodice, wide collar and beautifully tapered back. I teamed it with deep cerise velvet trousers by Gucci, a beautiful silk floating bodice top, leopard skin heels and matching bag and a stunning chestnut coloured belt like a horse's bit. It worked beautifully together and to this day I still have everything as it was all worn only once with Charles. The lady popped it all in pretty boxes with ribbons for me and then into bags and asked me to sign for it. Well shit me I hadn't seen a bill that big before. Just as I signed CBIII thanked the ladies and grabbed me saying we were late and we needed to rush. Behind Selfridges a Rolls Royce sat there as he opened the door for me and we jumped in. We were on the way to the airport via my apartment for my bags.

Biggin Hill airport is a small airport for private planes in a nice quiet area outside of London. We clambered on board CBII's helicopter to take us to the Lakes. I'd never been in one before and I was like a kid in a candy store as I was passed a headset so we could all talk as it was so noisy after take off. We flew over the beautiful green pastures of the English countryside, CBIII gave me running commentary of what was below us and the different counties as we flew above them. I remember it being a stunning clear day and a most enjoyable flight.

We had checked into the Low Wood hotel, the most beautiful hotel in the Lakes, all painted white situated on green pastures overlooking the lake. It was an English summer's day as we headed down to the waters edge where 'Speed Week' was getting underway. As we walked into what's known as the 'pits' the first thing I saw was this huge fluorescent yellow boat. It didn't look like what I had always known a boat to be, but then again, I was from the Yorkshire moors. There really wasn't much call for a powerboat on Saddleworth Moor unless you were the unfortunate winners of Bullseye. The closest thing to a boat I had ever been on was a Brittany Ferry with my parents or a wooden rowing boat on Hollingworth Lake. It was huge and had two giant pointed hulls like two boats stuck together, each with a bright orange tip with a number two on each tip and cockpits on top of each hull again with orange lids. It had 'Los Locos' written down the side and a huge cartoon vulture painted across the deck. The boats name was *Cultured Vulture*. Los Locos was the name of his chain of London restaurants, and it supported two huge outboard engines hanging off the back with black pipes coming out running into the boat itself. My eyes were wide open. I had never seen anything so beautiful in my life and then the engineers started her up. The noise bellowed out. My eardrums trembled, as did the air. There was a hose attached to what I saw as the lower part of the engines, presumably mimicking the boat being in water and the engines just spat out fumes and water as the engines were flushed and checked. Then it all went silent as they were turned off.

A swarm of people were polishing this already highly shiny beast sitting in front of me. I was lost for words, I had never seen anything like this nor did I understand anything that was going on, but soon it would all change. CBIII introduced me to his team. They were all incredibly polite and shook my hand. I asked CBIII what he wanted me to do that day and he gave me team clothing to wear and just told me to look pretty and if people wanted pictures taken with the boat then to bring them over and get the team as much PR as possible. Fuck, and I was getting paid for this? So the restaurant paid my wage but instead of actually working I was in a private helicopter at a stunning hotel at a powerboat event. I don't consider looking pretty and talking to people work. Life was good.

Admittedly I still didn't know what was going on at the lake apart from 'Speed Week.' Some racers were there to try and break world or national records and some were there to get the most out of their boat for race preparation as it was all officially timed and the flat water made it perfect for testing different set ups and propellers. CBIII impressively took a world speed record which still stands to this day and is in the *Guinness Book of Records*.

The precise time is taken over a set one kilometre. There is a run up so at the start of the one kilometre mark you should be at full speed, holding that until you complete the one kilometre, with a run off at the end to slow down. Safety boats are up and down the course, naturally anything at speed can be highly dangerous, indeed Donald Campbell lost his life in the Lake District whilst attempting a record in *Bluebird* on Coniston on 1967. Speed Week is hardcore and safety is key. For those with a fully canopied boat, the crew must pass a dunk test before being allowed to drive in this type of boat to ensure they can escape should there be an accident. The cockpits are protected by canopies designed like F16 fighter plane canopies. They are made so if the boat splinters apart, the crew should remain intact. In theory it's great, in practice it's not always so great. Remember there is always drowning to contend with. There were so many boats at Windermere it was a carnival of colour like a parade of peacocks strutting their stuff as they made their way onto the water one by one to go all out for the coveted prize of getting in the K7 speed club.

Everyone in all the different teams was super friendly and after a few days we flew home with CBIII asking me on the flight,

"What do you think about the boats then?"

I loved them and he knew it and it wasn't long before he invited me down to Southampton to visit their workshop and learn more about racing. As I arrived in Southampton CBIII picked me up from the train station in his big yellow Hummer and took me to their workshop under the Itchen Bridge. The team were buzzing around as he took me to the outside area and told me he had bought me something. As we passed under the dusty metal shutters I was stopped in my track by a small yet immaculate yellow boat on a trailer. I didn't think anything of it as I stared at her beauty all shiny yet missing the decals which all race boats need.

"Here ya go, she's all yours," he said in his Texan twang. I stared at him and then the boat and then him and then the boat. All I could muster was the word, "What?"

"Well you said you liked the racing and the boats were lovely so I bought you one. It needs some work doing, we need to adjust the driving seat to your position and of course you need to give her a name and then I'll get Mary Montague to do the artwork, and we'll get your license sorted out and then all we need is a female navigator and you will be the only all female team in the world." What the fuck had just happened? I stood there silent. I had no idea what was going on. Just then the engineer came over and told me to hop in. I did as I was told still speechless and bemused. CBIII had a big grin and joked, "Are you going to say anything?"

I replied, "What the fuck, I don't understand,"

He answered, "we now have a two boat team, we just need to get you out on the water and get as many hours as possible under your belt before the season starts and of course you need to do all the navigation exams and safety at sea tests, rules of the road, medicals, but we will sort all that out."

"What are you going to call her?" he asked.

"*Vulgar Vulture*," I replied. CBIII's 28ft Skater I had fallen in love with was *Cultured Vulture* and had a cartoon eagle across it. I knew then I wanted a female vulture wearing lipstick, a pink polka dot bikini and holding a compact. Yep a *Vulgar Vulture*. This was the start of my racing career. They hired in Pete Little, four times world champion, to come down and work with me. The only thing I didn't have was a navigator, but it didn't take long for CBIII's private pilot, Stef Kondac, to offer the services of his wife to the team.

This pairing wasn't long lasting for sure, after the first few events of us getting lost several times during the races, the team got rid of my teammate and put a new one in called Deborah Cottrell. UK races back in the day were not like many other countries and certainly not the same as today's events. Our navigation was tough and some legs could have been twelve miles in distance. There was no room for error and we didn't use GPS systems. Deborah was amazing, she was one of our racing rescue divers – hard as nails, a buxom blonde, and knew the waters well.

The evening the initial navigator was sacked, I didn't even know about it until she attacked me in the bar on Bournemouth pier where the offshore party was. She ran towards me like a screaming banshee, dived on top wrenching my hair and swinging like a mad woman, kicking and punching. The guys grabbed her and pulled her off. I didn't retaliate I just let her hit me and covered as best I could holding onto my own hair as if it were a wig and not wanting it to come off. She was summoned by the race committee at 0800 the following morning and had a race ban for the next half of the season. I came away with a fat bloody lip and a bit of a swollen eye, not great for my modelling career so maybe it was a good thing that this sport was male-dominated and the only girls were me and Deborah. The rest of the evening was great, me and my fat lip were always treated like a princess, I got on with all the teams really well and mucked in where I could. It was my new teaming with Deborah that changed everything, we were great together.

Many people think that a race boat is just a boat, that it simply has stop and go and steering wheel, but its far more complex, and the bigger and faster the boat the more complex it becomes. Offshore race boats have a water tank at the front called a ballast tank, or bow tank for short. These tanks hold a huge amount of water and if the sea condition is rough or there is a huge head sea with waves coming towards you, you have the option to fill the tank adding weight until the boat runs level. If you turn into a following sea then by the time you have turned the tank must be empty otherwise the nose becomes too heavy and it will stuff into the water. Timing is key. Some boats have two hulls so therefore a tank in each hull, maybe more than two tanks and the water can also be pumped from tank to tank until the balance is perfect.

On top of this we have inboard engines and outboard, so let's talk outboard. These engines have lifters, meaning the engines can be lifted higher in the water or dropped lower, they also have a trim tucking the engine in or bringing her out all having different effects on the boat. The trim, lift and tanks are operated to give optimum balance and speed throughout a race and all work in conjunction to each other. There is also the propeller or propellers. These are not standard. These are 'worked' propellers and can cost literally tens of thousands and many things can be done to them to stabilise or increase speed, and you would have both flat water props and rough water props, because all props work differently on different boats in different types of water – and so the list goes on. The better you are at balancing the boat in all conditions the more you will run at optimum speed, and the more level the boat the less stress on both your body and the equipment, so the less breakages. I talk to Deborah during the entire race. She tells me where to go (literally sometimes) and I tell her if I need more water in the tank and I tell her when to start releasing water. If she feels we need an alteration in balance she also has the option to tell me she is making changes so I understand why the boat may be handling differently.

The sea is the most unpredictable racing surface in the world. It changes underneath you every second, holes open up and swallow you without warning and seas change direction without notice. Wind against tide is often the most unforgiving and uncomfortable but you don't have time to think about discomfort. It's about survival especially in British waters. We have been out in swells so big that I was actually driving up a wave at a forty-five degree angle with the nose of the boat pointing at the sky. I couldn't back off because we would plummet backwards and swamp the boat, the engine was fighting so hard and it seemed an eternity that we gazed at the sky trying to mount the crest. This particular race lasted almost three painful tiring hours and when a wave crashes into the boat or you nosedive into the water (stuff it), then it's a bilge system that has to pump out the water, and if the electrical one fails you also carry a hand pump and sometimes both are required because it's so severe. Races now last a maximum of one hour. This is because officials noted that most accidents occurred in the later stages of the race especially in demanding conditions.

My life was never the same after I had met Charles Burnett III, for he took me all over the world and introduced me to experiences very few get to experience. Every day was an adventure with CBIII by land, by air, by sea, by jet. Salt flats to mountain tops, forests to deserts. I knew my life would never be the same with Charles in it…

Chapter 4

Country girl to racer girl

'It's like standing in a cold shower and ripping up £50 notes.'

'Call me Ishmael.' Any sailor will tell you that the sea is a cruel mistress with more faces than Mount Rushmore; the weather can change in an instant so, when it comes to powerboat racing, pre-race weather briefings are more important than popping a toilet roll in the fridge after a particularly potent King Prawn Vindaloo. If the weather looks changeable it's not unusual to get called back for an update but even the most up-to-date report cannot control the unpredictable creature that is the sea. It could be as flat as an ironing board one minute and then suddenly a massive hole will open up and, like Odysseus on his ill-fated voyage back to Ithaca, pull you in between the arms of Scylla and Charybdis. Unlike some competitors, I hate racing in flat water, it's slippy and I don't like slippy – if I can't feel it I don't like it. Like couples with joint Facebook accounts, there's no trust.

Then there's the other end of the spectrum – the wild sea; the briny equivalent to going ten rounds with Chris Eubank with your hands tied behind your back. My preference are big seas. I like the pain it brings – it keeps me focused. The boat sometimes doesn't reach from one wave to the next and this can prove to be awkward – stuffing it through an oncoming wave is sometimes the only way and, in an open canopy you have to duck, lest your head be summarily removed from your shoulders. If you can get on top (and stay on top) then it's always better if the distance between waves is the same and if you can get over the top it's great, but invariably the landing sends shockwaves up the spine and you are constantly bracing yourself for impact. The reality is, racing in big seas is like standing in an ice-cold shower, ripping up £50 notes.

Like any motorsport, the start of the race is always the most dangerous. Like the pied piper, the start boat leads the racers up to the milling area where all boats congregate and travel in an anticlockwise direction until further notice. Helicopters hovering overhead indicate that the flare is about to go up so, if we don't hear the helicopters we know we have a few more minutes of lulling. Boats are least controllable at this very low speed and with lots of them in a small area it's more like the opening of a Walmart on Black Friday than the start of a race. Some of the big boats drift out a fair bit to give more space but the primary concern is always your position on the race line and being able to see the flare. You know where you want to be on a race line as you know where the first mark is, but many people want that same position, so depending where you are when you are milling in that large circle often depends on where you will end up in the start line.

Powerboats work a rolling start typical of all offshore race events. Once the orange flare has gone off, you need to batten down the hatches and make sure you are race ready, eagerly watching for the start boat. The start boat carries a yellow flag held up in the air – two minutes later the start boat will take a straight line across the racecourse in front of your bow usually from landside to the centre of the race course. At this point you must get yourself in a position pointing forward – not as easy as one thinks depending on where you are when this happens, especially if there are thirty boats all jostling for the best position.

As the start boat slowly makes that 'line' across your bow, and she gets to the inside line at the end of all the race boats, she will turn and face down the racecourse with you, slightly in front and off to the side. All boats must stay behind her and away from her. She will be ahead on your port side, preparing to lead you towards the first turn mark. Once she sees that all of the boats are in a line (or as near as damn it) she will start to accelerate away down the course increasing speed still holding the yellow flag up high. At no point can you overtake her or run with her or you will be penalised.

The start boat is always a fast boat. She won't drop the yellow flag and raise the green 'GO' flag until she makes sure all boats are as level as they can be and if any boats are too close pulling away she will signal that boat to drop back. When they are happy they will take you up to speed until the boats are almost at race speed and, at this point, they will drop the yellow flag and raise the green. And they're off! All boats will accelerate past her at an astonishing speed leaving her stood still as she pulls off to her port side into the safety of the centre of the racecourse where she will sit and monitor on the start/finish line.

This is the most exhilarating part of the race. No one wants to be in the centre of the race line where the water is choppy and aerated, but most will invariably end up there. Aerated water makes it difficult for the propellers to get a firm bite in the water and the stern of the boat fishtails, often forcing the bow into a direction you don't want. For the driver it is often easiest to tell the throttleman (who controls the speed and trim of the boat) you are heading for an area of clear water as yet undisturbed by the racers. Even if it is slightly off course it is quicker and safer to run into the clean water to gain both control and speed and then cut across back into the line when you really need to. The start chute is a race in itself; a tactical game of 'find the clean water' – the Moby Dick to the racer's Ahab, so, if you can get ahead on the start chute and leave everyone else in your wake then you have an expanse of clean water ahead – this is ideal although not always possible. It's so fucking exciting the hairs on the back of my neck stand up just writing this. In the smaller boats and when I first started racing, the driver was also in control of the power, but as the boats get bigger the driver and throttleman positions are split so you must think as one.

Racing in big seas are always the most memorable. One particularly memorable race took place in Cowes where I was racing with Deborah. Only five of us managed to finish the race – all the other boats turned around and headed back as they weren't prepared go around the island. The sea was mountainous. It was so big I thought I was going to drown in my crash helmet, not only due to the deluge of water but also the seemingly endless waves of vomit leaving my stomach and sloshing around my helmet like in a washing machine. I can assure you having a helmet full of regurgitated carrots is really unpleasant and confusing, especially as I'd not even eaten any carrots.

We went through every wave and the bilge pump was working overtime, and Deborah was using the hand bilge as well, right up to the point where it launched itself out of the boat. It was freezing cold. It was so hard – we weren't able to get the boat on the racing plane as we couldn't gain enough momentum to get on top of the waves. We struggled to see the turn marks because they just disappeared behind a sea of angry waves. I remember trying to drive the boat up a wave (yes, not across it) and completely fucking it up, providing me with an impromptu, albeit brief, view of the sky. We even tried to drive in the opposite direction of the race to gain some momentum; driving with the following sea to enable us to get on top of the water so we would loop around but all attempts were futile. There were no other boats in the vicinity for it to be dangerous. Most had returned to harbour or had broken down and we had no sea safety other than the helicopter on the far side of island due to it being too dangerous. The sea was merciless but we eventually finished in second place. Deborah was covered in blood – her hands ripped to shreds from operating the hand bilge like an overeager Amish butter churner and I couldn't walk for two weeks – the constant battering through the waves had compressed my spine so badly that every step I took felt like someone was punching me in the kidneys. Deborah hadn't told me that during the race her seat had been ripped out of the runners. She had to hold herself into the seat, and the seat into the boat by holding onto the runners which added insult to injury to her already shredded hands. It was either that or drowning. We loved it! It has to be said that Deborah at one point let out a caterwaul of continuous painful yelps. I was concerned and naturally asked if she was OK and did she need me to turn back. Despite her predicament (and in between the shrieks of pain) she told me to, *"Shut the fuck up and keep your foot down."*

It was this infamous race where I had won 'first lady driver', a beautiful perpetual trophy with names on such as 'Lady Aitken, The Countess of Arran' and Gina Campbell, daughter of legendary Donald Campbell. When I was told I would be awarded this, much to Lord Normanton's surprise I told him that they were welcome to engrave my name on it and proud to have my name alongside those so great, but I wouldn't be getting up on stage and accepting it because I was the only female driver and I hadn't earned it, and racing is racing – male or female. It was like being congratulated just because I had a pair of tits. This trophy is a prestigious trophy and women since me have gladly accepted it and boasted of it even when they are the only ones in that event, but why? I was 'one of the lads' and expected to be treated as such. They removed it from the awards table and I alongside Deb took the trophies we had earned through hard work, not through birth.

***

Some time later I was presenting the Royal Yachting Association's awards with none other than the moustachioed F1 world champion Nigel Mansell, where I had the honour of being the first ever female on the panel of judges. Over a dinner conversation with Nigel he said he'd only been taken out in a powerboat once and after that, would never race in one as he found the whole experience a bit on the hair-raising side. I had to admit that I felt the same – I had been out in an F1 at Silverstone and found that very frightening so we mutually agreed that our respective motorsports, were where we both intended to stay. I've done many a track day where friends like CBIII have hired out circuits like Silverstone or Brands Hatch but that doesn't mean I particularly like it. What I do love is the adrenaline rush. There's always plea-sure in pain. Pain makes us feel alive, and death comes to us all… eventually.

The first time I went to CBIII's UK home I travelled by train from London to a small village train station where he picked me up in a Rolls Royce, doing his best Parker impression whilst wearing a chauffeur's cap and gloves. I went to jump in the front seat and reverently doffing his cap, he told me to get in the back. What then followed can only be described as a white-knuckle ride back to Newtown Park – a beautiful listed stately home in the New Forest. He floored it around every blind bend and country lane on the way and seemed to be oblivious to the fact that the car actually had brakes. His driving used to drive me mad as I'm the first to admit that I'm not the best of passengers – regularly pressing the imaginary brake pedal and clawing ner-vously at the upholstery like the dutiful backseat driver. It was always quiet with no traffic and he was a heavily skilled driver in every sense, so I never had any real worries, but he secretly knew I hated it so made a point of doing it on purpose every time I got in a car with him.

Newtown Park is just the most gorgeous Georgian building with six imposing columns at the entrance to enhance its grandeur. I would often stay at Newtown Park while CBIII was in the UK; my room was known as the 'purple' room. I had so much fun with him because, like me, he hadn't grown up and was like a little kid with toys and boy did he have a lot of toys. We even converted one of his lounge rooms into a huge Scalextric circuit by moving out all the furniture to set up this mammoth track. We must have played on it for twelve hours straight into the early hours of the morning whilst drinking a gallon of vodka before hitting the cinema room to watch powerboat racing.

A very tight clique ran CBIII's UK race team. Whether I liked most of our team was up for discussion. Fortunately those particular guys I no longer have anything to do with but one thing was for sure, they made my first year of racing hell. They didn't take too kindly to having a girl on the race team and weren't happy with CBIII's decision to bring me on board and buy me a boat. This may have put other people off the whole idea but their resistance only made me even more resilient. They were all smiles and polite at the start, probably because they didn't think I would last but I did. It was out of nothing more than pure pigheadedness that I became good at what I did. I spent hours, days and weeks testing with Pete Little before we travelled to Italy for my first European Championships.

CBIII didn't understand why I wanted to travel to Italy with another UK team. I couldn't tell him that our team were a bunch of chauvinistic assholes, I didn't have the heart. He was so good to everyone and it would make me sound like I was trying to be a bitch and cause division in the team. So I set off in a campervan with Pete, Pat and Stef towing their boat.

We had made a little route plan and set off a few days early as we knew full well that our journey would inevitably get held up with several drinking sessions along the way. Pat and I had become very good friends through our mutual love of Chablis so the route was carefully planned using vineyards as waypoints. Once the ferry docked we made our way to 'Chabliville' where our sole intention was to drink the most expensive bottles of wine we could get our hands and lips on; and we did. When the bill came Pat had conveniently forgotten his wallet, frantically patting empty pockets and trying to look apologetic. We were all in hysterics – much to the chagrin of the waiter who was becoming more and more nervous as he clutched to a particularly massive bill in his sweaty hands. Pat found everything funny; life to him was just a whole barrel of laughs. I suggested he start washing up and we would pick him up after the race on the way back home. He tasked one of the lads to take a taxi back to the hotel to pick up his wallet – in the meantime, we carried on drinking.

As we travelled through the Alps, our next stop was the picturesque town of Chamonix at the foot of Mont Blanc. We stopped at one of the cheaper hotels on the outskirts where there was plenty of manoeuvring room for the boat and large camper. Pat checked us all into the hotel and, once in, we looked across in awe at the foot of the snow capped mountain where Chamonix or 'Shaminwax' (as we had now named it in a comedy French accent) stood.

We wandered into town and moved from bar to bar, all of them stunning little wooden chalets decorated with beautiful pictures. It was obvious that skiers and snowboarders alike were running them; the bartenders and waitresses mostly had golden tans with panda eyes and many had peeling noses. Chamonix was a place of beauty with the most incredible views, and we sat outside so many different bars each time edging for a better viewing portal up the mountain as we sipped exceedingly expensive beer.

Pat was (thankfully) picking up all the bills, which was rather nice, as 'Shaminwax' was a touch on the expensive side, but who cared – the views there, unlike the overpriced beer, were priceless. It wasn't long before the afternoon crept into night and it was safe to say that by ten o'clock Pete was so sick of Pat and I getting more and more pissed that he left, swiftly followed by Stef leaving the two of us embedded in a rather expensive bar across from a glorious hotel at the foot of the mountain:

"I bet that's pricey," Pat said as he ordered another round.

Most of the evening was a blur after that.

Things were decidedly hazy in the morning. Pat woke up and turned around and looked at me lying next to him – both of us fully clothed I hasten to add. In the immortal words of PG Wodehouse, "I sat up in bed with that rather unpleasant feeling you get sometimes that you're going to die in about five minutes."

"What the fuck are you doing in my room?" He laughed, looking rough as a badger's arse. He looked in the wardrobes as he wandered to the toilet.

"Where are my bags? Where's all my stuff gone?" The penny then dropped. "This isn't my room."

"It's not mine either," I croaked.

We both looked confused as the last piece of the post-alcohol jigsaw was placed in its hole.

"We aren't even in our hotel. Remember that hotel you said, 'Fuck me I bet that's pricey?'"

Pat stared at me blankly.

"Well, we are in it!"

We managed to crawl back to our original hotel just in time to meet a decidedly unimpressed Pete and Stef hooking up the boat ready to go. Pat and I sat in the back of the camper nursing two particularly vigorous hangovers. Through the intermittent groans and prayers for death, Pat loosely calculated that our pit stop in Chamonix for a quick beer and snack had cost [him] in excess of four figures.

We finally arrived at the pit area of the Lido di Jesolo race venue. I looked around and saw my boat and workshop but no team. It didn't surprise me; my team had made it abundantly clear that they didn't even want me there.

I called the team to say I had arrived but no one answered so I called

CBIII's PA, as he was scheduled to fly in from the US later. I was told to meet at the hotel foyer the following evening for a team meal after a day working on the boat. The following day the team still hadn't visited the pits and our workshop was shut so any help with the boat came from the other UK team I had travelled down with. We would be testing the following day and racing the day after but we had yet to receive any help from our own team.

The team meal was held at a nice restaurant in San Marco Piazza and we sat outside people-watching and taking in the beauty that is Venice. The entire Los Locos team consisted of about seven men plus Deborah my co-pilot and myself.

As our starters arrived so did a side order of snide comments from the guys about my boat knowledge and ability. Bearing in mind the world's best had taught me and I had put so much work into learning every aspect of my craft, I kept an unusually dignified silence. One of the guys asked me how to balance a boat. It was a highly patronising question requiring a basic answer and the arrogant prick didn't even allow me to reply, preferring to answer it for me by saying it was obvious I didn't know because, being 'a female' I was useless and had a lot to learn. The last point at least was true; everyone in any line of work learns something new every day. The moment you think you can't learn any more then prepare to fail or make mistakes.

The whole table just burst out laughing, apart from Deborah who was also sick of the constant barrage of chauvinistic digs. It was affecting her driver and she had heard enough. I stood up and walked across San Marco Piazza visibly upset. Deborah followed, put her arm around me and took me back to the pits where we joined Pat and the other UK team for a beer. I stayed with them in the pits and didn't return to the hotel. By the time my team had got their lazy fucking asses to the pits the following day, half the day had gone and the other UK team had already fuelled, checked and launched our boat. We were ready to test. Our team were pretty pissed off because without them and the keys to the workshop we would have been unable to test, which is undoubtedly what they wanted. I was keen to prove I didn't need them. The saddest thing about the whole debacle was that this was costing CBIII a fortune and yet he had no idea his team were trying to sabotage the whole thing – never mind that a competing team were picking up the slack. CBIII was paying all their wages and all of their expenses to look after the all-girl team, but they did the sum total of fuck all for the entire week apart from try and look busy when CBIII appeared.

We had a great testing session and we thanked Pat's team. At this point my team finally pulled their thumbs out of their asses by craning our boat from the water but only because the boss had come down to the pits.

As the morning of the race approached, Deborah and I were in the driver's briefing but our team manager wasn't. Not a single member of our team was at the boat for prepping even as the other boats were being launched. As it was the European Championships, Pete and Pat had their boat to deal with, but it didn't stop them helping us. They had started prepping their boat two hours earlier than planned, launching at 6 am, and by the time Deborah and I had got to it they had done our team's job and launched, prepped and chosen the correct propeller.

Pat smiled and said one thing. "You're good, but not good enough. We're going to win and you'll take second or third."

Returning a huge smile and gratitude both UK teams were ready to rock and roll and we went for coffee. I passed my own team on the way as they drove into the pits. I stopped their vehicle and told them, "You should have stayed in bed. The boat's already in the water. We don't need you."

In the European Championships there are two races over four days with points awarded for both heats. In this race we were competing against twenty-five other teams. We came fourth in the first race and invited onto the podium, although we did wonder whether they invited us up because the Italians had never seen girls race powerboats before, so maybe they really did want to congratulate us.

Pat and Pete won and I was truly glad for them, irrespective of the fact they'd helped us they were worthy winners. CBIII was over the moon with our placing – our team were secretly seething but were (unsurprisingly) more than happy to receive the boss' congratulations.

On the second race, as all teams do, we calculated where we needed to finish for us to place. Pat and Pete won again so they deservedly took the big title. We came third giving us an overall third place in our first European Championships. CBIII was ecstatic as were the Italian racing fraternity. My own team were gutted. I had proven that my driving ability didn't live up to their low expectations. Funnily enough, they never showed CBIII their disappointment.

I had finished my first season by placing third at the European Championships. I had gone from loving my new job to hating the people I was working with. If your environment is making you unhappy then you can't stay – no matter how much pleasure a part of it gives you. The team hated me because I was a female and because CBIII had gone out of his way to support me so much The attitude was more in line with a gaggle of schoolgirls than supposedly grown men – it was pathetic.

CBIII and I had done everything together and had become very close, something the team didn't like, so it was even harder to make the decision I was about to make.

I sat in the camper overlooking the pits with Pat. His engineer was still working away on the boats post-race and people across the pits were still celebrating. It was the sort of team cohesiveness I wished I was part of. I thought of the dinner in San Marco Piazza where the team had made me cry. It was disheartening yet I couldn't tell CBIII, he wouldn't believe me, and his team had been with him a lot longer than me. Pat could see I was troubled and asked what I was going to do.

I simply said, "Leave the team. It's the best time I have ever had in my life but I'm not putting up with that bullshit for anyone, those men are mean and I don't deserve it. It'll only get worse."

I saw CBIII that evening. I took a deep breath and walked up to him, gave him a hug and thanked him for all the opportunities he had given me, for all the fun we had together and that I adored him. "But I need to leave the team."

He was shocked. He laughed, thinking I was joking.

I couldn't tell him everything so just said, "Charles, the team is awful to me and I don't deserve it." At this point I left.

As I walked off Charles said, "But you love racing and without me you won't be able to race."

Charles wasn't being egotistical. He was stating that offshore powerboat racing is expensive and racers basically need a blank chequebook to continue. It was his way of asking me not to leave. I looked at him and he just looked upset and bewildered, but I knew if I stayed with him for too long I wouldn't be able to leave him so I walked away. I truly loved Charles, he was my best friend.

I returned to the camper. Pat and the lads looked at me as I sat there really upset. In the last year I had fallen in love with a new sport and met some of the best people one could hope to meet and yet, because of some sexist pigs, it was all about to disappear. I was heartbroken.

On my return to the UK, Pat invited me down to his home in Oxford.

Little did I know the lads on the UK circuit had been busy little bees behind my back. Over my first season I had made quite an impact on many of the UK lads. I had adapted well, mucked in like everyone else, I was low maintenance and loved racing. We had so many hilarious nights together, having a girl on the scene was a breath of fresh air.

Pat took me to see Taff. Taff was an older gentleman and one of racing's head officials. We all stood on the driveway talking, then without introduction, Pat pulled back a tarpaulin to reveal the boat he had won the European Championships in – the boat I raced against in Italy.

He said, "Here you go girl, here's your new boat."

I was stunned and speechless.

"We couldn't have you not racing."

Taff stood there and announced he would become my team manager. My navigator was Alan Layton, a hugely accomplished racing driver himself but was willing to take a back seat for the season. Another racer and one of Pat's best friends John Miller with whom I had spent many an incredibly drunk evening had stumped up the money for my license, entry fees, fuel, hotels and other expenses and Tohatsu had sponsored me with an engine and engineer.

What the fuck had just happened? OM fucking G I was back racing through the love of my fellow racers – the racers who I would be competing against that coming season. I was so gobsmacked I found myself in tears. I had my own boat, my own team and a team of guys who would have my back.

I went out testing the boat with Pete Little, Pat's former teammate, with whom he'd driven the boat to European victory. He taught me as much as he could about it and soon enough it was the first round of the British Championships.

The opening race to a season is always the toughest as drivers get into the swing of things. The sea was rough, cold and it would be a battle I would never forget. CBIII's team were there in *Cultured Vulture* and *Vulgar Vulture*; it was a new all-girl team but it was to be short lived.

All the teams took up the start position. The rolling start began, the green flag went up as the yellow flag dropped and we were off. It was a tough battle with us all jostling for position for well over an hour and I had Alan in the back screaming at me. By the time we had finished I was knackered and Alan slapped me hard on the helmet as we got the chequered flag and pulled into the centre of the course. "We fucking won girl, we fucking won the opening race!"

I couldn't believe it. I had beaten Pat who had given me the boat. He was finding it highly amusing that he had given me the winning boat, and I had beaten the current British Champion Ian Cutler (alongside whom I would later win the 2004 APBA One Design National Championships in the USA). The new all-girl team had broken down in a delicious slice of irony pie.

As stupid as it may have sounded, I had to ask Ian Cutler if he had let me win. Ian looked at me then laughed.

"Racers don't let other racers win, not when there is a championship at stake girl."

We went to the podium and it was the biggest welcome and cheer I could have ever wished for. All of the guys were so loud when our names were called out for first place in the opening race. Champagne went everywhere as Pat and Ian took second and third respectively. It was a weekend that will last with me forever. It wasn't money that I needed to race. It was friendship, loyalty and trust.

With my newfound love of the sport came many weekends of raucous fun. I had been brought up with six boys so race weekends with a hundred of them was a walk in the park and made me feel right at home. One of the guys, Tony Hamilton, had bought a pub close to one of the venues, so the Saturday night event was held at his place and we all piled in there for an evening's entertainment. It was going to be messy. The rounds came in thick and fast from all directions and Tony, nicknamed 'Mad Dog', who had become a very close friend of mine sat down with us and spoke about a new chilli sauce he had bought from the States and it was dangerously hot. He then brought this sauce over to the table and put a minuscule amount on the prong of a fork and told me to try it. Not being one for refusing a challenge, I opened my mouth as he wiped it on my tongue much to the amusement of the other guys. At first I felt nothing, then it heated up, then it felt like my eyeballs were going to fall out as my nose ran, my eyes turned pink, I could barely breathe, and I really felt my like my skin was peeling off as I reached for my pint which was swiftly moved out of reach as were everyone's drinks. I reached for anything I could find but the lads were making me suffer for my stupidity of accepting a challenge from Tony who was well known for pulling stunts on people. I swiftly ended up behind the bar with my head under a tap, the cool water running over my tongue. I stayed there for over five minutes. I couldn't come up for air as the air burned my tongue, everything was on fire. I helped myself to a pint pot of ice cubes and made my way back over to the table nursing my stupidity with a cube firmly held on my tongue, planted myself back down at the table calling Tony a wanker much to the amusement of the other guys. But I had my own plan for revenge.

"I'll give you a hundred quid if you put some of that on the end of your dick Tony."

Like myself, Tony was also not one to refuse a bet of any kind and certainly not one with the promise of a cash reward. He dropped his pants at the table and took control of the chilli bottle. By now I had noticed that it had a skull and crossbones on the bottle as well as other major warnings of potential burn implications all over it. He shook it gently as a drop came out of the end and landed right on the tip of his dick. Putting the bottle back on the table and dick in hand, he made eye contact with me. Under normal circumstances, it would be your lover looking deep into your eyes whilst holding his manhood and it would be in private however, we were in a busy bar surrounded by all the guys and there was Tony holding his dick in my direction staring at me. A sea of silence and most of the pub had realised what was going on as he slipped his chilli covered cock back in his pants and sat down still looking at me as I started to grin. A pin dropping a mile away could have been heard as the entire pub had stopped and everyone seemed to hold their breath. I could see guys grabbing their own crotch waiting to see a grown man writhe in pain. We all waited.

I had never seen a pub so still or silent with all eyes on the landlord. He tried to ignore the pain that had evidently started to wash all over his body. His eyes went pink and started to water. Every movement he made was clearly uncomfortable as the searing heat of the chilli began to burn his little man. The smile drifted from his face replaced by a pained grimace painted on what can only be described as a sweaty beetroot.

"Fuck me!" he shouted grabbing his cock, knocking the stool over he was sat on and he legged it through a door into the back. We all looked at each other wide eyed before bursting into fits of laughter realising the damage which could have occurred and the hilarity of it all. We didn't see Tony for almost an hour. When he finally reappeared, he limped sheepishly back into the bar hobbling over to the table.

"My fucking dick, my fucking dick is burned, I've just had it under the cold tap for twenty fucking minutes and it's fucking raw girl."

"Good job, see me down the pits tomorrow and collect your winnings," The guys fell about laughing as Tony sat there still visually very uncomfortable.

The following day arrived and I could hear Tony's boat start up from across the pits – it had the biggest engines and sounded incredible as the air vibrated. It had just been craned in so I jogged over to the crane and lay on the ground overlooking the craning in basin where Tony was stood on the deck of his boat releasing the strops.

"How's your dick Tony?" I shouted.

"Fucking sore."

I whipped out a hundred quid and waved it at him. He snatched it off me with the look of a man who knew it wasn't worth it.

"Have a safe race," I winked at him. I loved Tony. He had one of the biggest personalities on the circuit and he was a love or hate guy. Many people couldn't handle his gregarious nature. He didn't give a fuck about things and if he didn't like you he told you straight. I think the reason Tony and I got on so well was because we had similar personality traits. We were both loud and colourful and didn't really care about what people thought. We oozed confidence in our own personalities and enjoyed life and people – everything was about fun. Tony always had my back and I wanted for nothing when I was with him.

The comedy value was broken for a moment as I was accosted by Tony's wife under the crane as she homed in to deliver a bollocking.

Arms flailing and gesticulating wildly yet comically ranted, "I want a word with you. What did you do to my husband? You've ruined our sex life, he will be out of action for weeks his dick is that bad."

"Sorry, but he started it and it's cost me a hundred quid."

"You actually bet him to do it and now you've actually paid the idiot?"

"Yeh, I can't believe he even took it off me and revelled in it the cheeky fucker after he made me burn my tongue and my eyes nearly fell out."

"He had his dick under the tap most of the night. The two of you are as bad as each other," she answered trying not to laugh.

It was a great weekend, they all were and I used to live for race weekends. Racing became my life. It was more powerful than any drug could ever be. I was addicted to the lifestyle, the lads and the adrenaline. It was a passion that, to this day, still lives in me and, unlike Ahab, I did manage to take down Moby Dick... even if it was with the help of some chilli sauce.

Chapter 5

Lights, Camera, Action

'Get rolling. I have the first interview.'

Because of the hype surrounding me I had been nicknamed the 'Golden Girl' of racing and given so many interviews on radio, TV and in newspapers that publicity was drawing in so many opportunities. It was all a bit of a whirlwind and something I hadn't expected. All I wanted to do was race.

L!VE TV had been in touch with the United Kingdom Offshore Boating Association and asked if they could come and film one of the next UK races along the south coast and follow me for the weekend, promising not to get in the way of safety or any officials.

L!VE TV was run by the Mirror Group Newspapers headed by Kelvin McKenzie and Janet Street Porter and the only fully live channel in the country. They were given a race calendar of events and joined us at Eastbourne. Eastbourne is better known for its pensioners and graveyards and place where people go to die. I'd sooner swap it for racing in the Bahamas or Miami, but the exciting and colourful carnivals of highly tuned powerboats not only brightened the place but helped the council's coffers in attracting money and tourists. This was one of the things I liked about racing in the UK – we, albeit for a short while, helped the communities in which we raced.

L!VE TV's programme would be a mixture of pre-record and live which was unusual for them, but reporting live from a speeding race boat was impossible, so it was all carefully mapped out what would be happening and what they needed. The TV crew were incredibly polite and helpful and never got in the way taking into account racing came first and filming was secondary to me and the organisers.

The race was great, I placed on the podium, which wasn't unusual, and the TV crew were a lot of fun. I spent the whole weekend with them and tried my hardest to stay sober the night after the race as they were still filming. Me falling head first into my pint of cider may have made good TV but wouldn't have looked good for the sport. They asked me if I would be happy to interview some of the teams around the pits to add something different. I had no problem with that and grabbed the microphone and pin-balled across the pits chatting to the guys. Of course this wasn't particularly easy as the guys ripped the piss out of me and gave me stupid answers before being sensible but that was all a part of the fun. Without the guys, I wouldn't be racing so although the press focused on me I always spread around the PR because that was the right thing to do.

Within a matter of weeks Kelvin McKenzie rang me. He had watched me on the show and thought I was good in front of camera.

"We're pitching a new sports show. It's going live every night at 1800 for one hour, three hours on a Saturday and four hours on a Sunday. We're looking for presenters who would work a week on and week off with another female presenter, but would be paid full time. We'd like you to audition and we can work around your racing."

It sounded too good an opportunity to turn down so it was within the shake of a lamb's tail I was walking into the huge glass atrium of London's Canary Wharf Building, collecting my pass and heading up to the 24th floor where L!VE TV was based, it was so high I swear it rocked in the wind. I was let in via one of the girls on the desk and shown to a waiting area. The other receptionist, wearing a name badge 'Veronique' looked up at me from her desk and her first words were, "What are you looking at?" Yep I had met the rudest receptionist of all time, but I put it down to her having had a bad day. The irony of it was it amused me so much that during my time at L!VE Veronique became my best friend. Any girl with an attitude like that, I want on my side.

Kelvin came out of his office and introduced me to former Page 3 glamour model Gail McKenna who was very pretty with golden brown hair and quite petite with a strong scouse accent. Both of us were introduced to a producer that showed us to a small room where a camera was set up. He showed us how to use the camera and asked us to write a few scripts as if we were reading sport and talk to camera and just keep practising.

He gave us about an hour and then reviewed the tapes. We had of course been thrown in at the deep end but this was after all live TV and there wasn't the luxury of pre-recording and repeating something and cutting things out. It was just weird to begin with, neither of us had done anything like this and it was actually quite embarrassing talking to a camera at first. Neither of us were shy but we were well out of our comfort zone.

Pushing ourselves got us to the levels of success we had so far achieved so soon got into the swing of things and helped each other out, trying to appear natural to the camera, often with hilarious results. We worked hard in the given hour and our performance would be reviewed by the producer who gave us a copy on a VHS tape; I still have mine to this day. The producer must have thought we were both OK because we both were hired. We wouldn't work together but for the next two weeks he wanted us in five days a week to practice, to know our stuff, to get used to how studios worked and to watch and learn off people like Charlie Stayt, the now BBC breakfast presenter.

The first week of live TV went to Gail – I was very happy she went first. I was so nervous. The second week went to me and I was surprised that it was requested I wear a short skirt. I wasn't used to wearing skirts but L!VE TV was known for, amongst other things, trampolining dwarves reading the weather, so what else did I expect? We had a large glass table, the female presenters wore short skirts and low tops and that's just the way things were. We were asked to bring glamour as well as knowledge to the studio so we gave it our best shot, albeit I'm sure the viewers were more interested in our assets than our knowledge of sport.

I was present when they brought in dwarf weather readers. It was the oddest thing I'd seen and not exactly PC. A magnetic board with a cartoon picture of Great Britain was placed in the studio. Each of the three little men held magnetic stickers of the sun, rain and clouds. I watched bemused as one by one they took turns on a small round fitness trampoline jumping up and down sticking the stickers to the board whilst saying, "Raining in the north of England" or "Sunny in the south." They came unstuck for the Shetland Islands as none of them could actually jump that high and I have yet to hear any weather reader on any channel regularly mention the Shetland islands so my guess was that the scriptwriter was taking the piss and hoping they would stick on some more southerly random place. It was the only time the office actually stopped squirrelling and the staff watched. I never got used to it.

Weekend shows were the worry. We had to hold interest in a live show for three and four hours. Kelvin knew everyone in media so we had high calibre guests from all sporting disciplines.

I had always been a chatterbox and rarely at a loss for words so soon found my home in presenting. I really loved the thrill of being live on air. Quite often, because I was on talk back to the gallery, they used to try and throw me off over the weekend by saying something daft in my ear, so it was about learning to ignore the gallery whilst talking to camera or to the guest. What many viewers don't know is that back then and maybe even now, you can have your earpiece open or closed. Open means that you can hear everything going on in the gallery, and this is for those that can easily talk whilst blocking out someone talking in their ear. The other is closed and the only time you hear anything is when they want you to, such as counting you in and out of breaks, correcting you if you are wrong, passing you information, breaking a news story and at first the only thing you have to get your head around is listening to the gallery whilst listening to the person you are interviewing and making sure you only answer the person in front of you and not the gallery by mistake!

Always on a Sunday afternoon I had the gallery tell me a few choice jokes while on air. On one occasion I just giggled as I couldn't keep it in, only saved by co-presenter Rhodri Williams who had also heard the joke but was far more experienced.

L!VE had many amusing moments, apart from the dwarf weather reading – which they eventually became tired of, in favour of a gorgeous busty blonde weather reader. All seemed quite normal until she started to undress during a live broadcast. In fact, the further south they got the more she took off and they even did the weather in Spain which meant she totally stripped off keeping only her 'intellectual' reading glasses on, a G string and a very, very small bra with ample bust oozing out of it. I'm sure at some point she even went topless. So that is what weather reading had become. Titillation and no one cared what the weather was like, just as long as she made it as far down the coast as possible during her two minutes slot and across the channel into a warmer part of the world.

I was also sent out for outside broadcasts (OBs). Some were live for other shows or my own show and some were pre-recorded. I travelled near and far to football and rugby stadiums, either talking to the teams, coaches or fans. The outside broadcasts were fun as long as I didn't have to do something called vox pops. I really hated doing these and I'm sure many reporters do. They are always done informally in public places to get the general public's opinions via a couple of questions, but I hated them. Walking up to someone and shoving a microphone and camera in their face quite often made me feel awkward if they backed off or just ignored me.

However, it was great to work with a crew on the move and broadcast right from that very spot talking back to the studio, there was always that sense of excitement because broadcasting live from the street, always had an element of jeopardy.

My time at L!VE was so varied and I loved them all. I was sent to an England rugby league World Cup game and I was to interview their coach. The studio don't set things up, it's often just jump in with your press pass, hope for the best and see what you can achieve.

The evening prior to the interview I went to the studio to ask our resident expert some background of the team including the name of the England coach.

"Phil Larder, MBE," he said.

"Ha how strange I had a PE teacher at school with that name."

The resident expert showed me his picture. I nearly spat my coffee out. The England coach *was* my PE teacher at school. I had won shitloads under Phil, I was one of his best athletes throughout school.

I had a massive grin knowing I had a massive advantage in getting his attention even if he wouldn't really have time for anyone.

It didn't take long to find out what hotel they were staying in as and I phoned the hotel to speak with Phil; times change and nowadays data protection wouldn't allow it but back then it was a lot easier. I left a message at reception and it wasn't long before he called me back. Yes he was busy but he sounded really pleased to hear from me and asked how things were and what I had been up to. We chatted for about five minutes as he was due to give a team briefing and he said he would leave my name at the relevant place and myself and my crew could get in no problems with full access and if I was to just bear with him he would come and find me. Job done. I couldn't wait to see Phil, he was the best sports teacher, he ran me ragged on cross-country, but he was the only teacher I liked at school, I hated the rest, but Phil was ace.

My film crew and I pulled up at the stadium and climbed out of the OB truck leaving the tech guy inside sat in the back with all his gadgets, monitors and toys. We had already said we would get a pre-record with Phil and anything else of interest and some vox pops with the crowd, and do a live OB, adding the pre-records in. The camera and sound guys were ready and we didn't have a producer/director with us, because in these types of things you become accustom to knowing what is required and knowing what to do, so you work closely with the crew.

As they looked at me for direction I suggested a few vox pops with the fans to get the atmosphere and few cutaway of groups of people chanting and singing and then I led the crew into the stadium. We had security take us all the way through to the ground, which surprised the crew.

"How did you pull that one off?"

"Ahhh, all will be revealed."

We sat where I was told to sit and waited with the crew, hardly confident that we could get an interview.

Phil appeared from the stadium tunnel, with crowds still pouring in through the gates. It was great to see him. He gave me a massive hug and we did the small-talk shit for a minute or two before we got on with the job in hand. The interview was awesome, Phil had nothing to be cagey about because it was me, he was relaxed and was full of smiles and even added things in that I hadn't asked. Quite often, interviewees won't open up in case the interviewer digs too deep or asks awkward questions they would sooner not answer. I finished off my piece to camera actually mentioning that he was my old sports coach because on TV the interview would have come across differently than any of the others he would have done leaving people wondering why he was so relaxed before a big game, but it wasn't that. It was because he was with his star pupil.

The interview with Phil meant we could pack up and get back to the truck and studio asap as we already had a crew filming the game. Because I knew Phil it had saved us hours hanging around hoping to get a few words. Camera crews had already started arriving waiting for the same interview, BBC, Sky Sports, they were all there waiting. I could see them edging towards us microphones in hand ready to pounce on the England coach, and as we were rounding off they were ready to dive in for the next interview but Phil smiled as we said good luck for the game and left, shutting the door behind him not giving another interview before the game. This meant that we had the first interview to be broadcast. Something every channel wants. Nice. Kelvin McKenzie on seeing the interview on TV was suitably impressed. "How did you pull that off with Phil Larder?"

"He was the best sports coach I ever had at school," I said with a huge grin. "I've known him since I was twelve years old."

The following weekend I had to interview George Best in the studio. I was really looking forward to talking to such a legend. Yet by the time he was due to go live he still hadn't turned up. The gallery told me in my earpiece to fill time because he was currently in the pub enjoying a tipple. The first thing I would do on a weekend was get up very early and read the papers so I always had fillers keeping some articles on my coffee table to refer to. I was waffling for England to the ad break where I asked where the hell George was. It seemed that he had decided to do a Sunday pub-crawl and our chauffeur kept missing him. He had now left his second pub and moved on. It took a further ninety minutes to track him down and almost two hours to get him in the studio. As we were given the cue to introduce him after the break, I saw out of the corner of my eye a quite dishevelled George Best walk in the studio holding a pint of beer. He stood there swaying still supping his beer.

We cut to a break and Rhodri and I stood up to shake his hand and welcome him on set. His red face smiled and he stunk of alcohol. I gestured for him to sit down and quickly talked him through what we would be chatting to him about as a heads up which he most certainly needed and he slipped his pint of beer under the couch out of the way. George had actually taken the glass from the pub promising the landlord he'd return it. The ten second count to broadcast came through as George whipped out his glass and took another gulp. I told him to get rid of it and back we were on air with George Best for a great interview. He was amusing throughout, mildly intoxicated which was pretty much expected anyway, but jovial, polite and funny and we spent the next twenty minutes or so with him talking all things football past and present. As the show came to an end so did his pint, the car driver came to collect him and took him back to his local pub to duly refill his pint glass

The following week, L!VE decided to do a snooker programme – with a difference. The players were all female; however, none could really play but all of them looked great when bending over a snooker table. The programme was named *Short Skirt Snooker*. I don't think the programme was on longer than ten minutes a show, just time enough to have a few large breasted long legged girls rest their cleavage on the green felt table cloth and stretch for the furthest ball away from them making sure that at no time was their skirt covering their bum as they stroked their cue suggestively, whilst pouting and always missing every shot. Did someone actually sit in an office and get paid for thinking up all of these shows?

I had been given a heads up that I would be covering Euro 96. This was one of the biggest moments in English football history and Kelvin had given me the job of covering it. I was still quite new and in my eyes Euro 96 needed an expert. Kelvin told me I needed to take a crew down to the Haymarket, try and get an interview with Terry Venables from the Sports Bar Café where the major press conference was and get it back to edit and out asap. If I couldn't get Terry then I was to do a report.

Fuck, BBC Sports, ITV, CH4, Sky Sports, their experts would all be there wanting the same thing. The press conference room would be full of pundits and experts and be televised live across the globe. I wasn't looking forward to this at all. It was the most important time of Terry Venables' career, huge for English football and massive for the country and they had sent me – a newcomer who before L!VE didn't even follow football. I personally didn't think it was good for a novice to interview an expert in this type of situation as it could make the channel look bad because if he threw anything back at me then I wouldn't have clue. This wasn't good.

As the weekend of the Euro 96 interview closed in I voiced my concerns to a racing friend and said that I just didn't have the expertise for this interview and that was even if I would be able to reach him with the hundreds of press there all wanting the same thing.

"Terry Venables?" My friend repeated back to me. "He used to play football with Chris Augers dad."

Chris was one of the powerboat racers I had nearly drowned with whilst racing around the Isle of Wight, and his dad I had just found out was quite a decent footballer back in the day playing at the same club as Venables. Terry had sponsored Chris' early days of racing. Small fucking world. I just picked up the phone and called Chris without hesitation.

"Chris I need your help, I've got myself in shit. I've been asked to interview Terry Venables at the Euro 96 press call at the Sports Bar Café on the Haymarket in a couple of days and I know pretty much jack shit about football."

Chris laughed. "No worries mate, I'll sort it right now. Standby."

Ten minutes later the phone rang. It was Chris,

"Tel's got a club called Scribes in Kensington, it's a celebrity hang out. Can you get down there the day after tomorrow around noon? Terry will leave your name on the door and he'll be there to meet you for a drink and a chat."

He had just thrown me a massive life-raft and I was going to climb on that's fucker at all costs and ride the storm. Not only was I getting a personal interview it was a day before the world press would get to question him.

I made sure I was immaculately dressed, plied with studio information. I entered through an unassuming doorway with 'Scribes' written in italics above. A very smart lady sat at a small neat reception and took my name. I was shown downstairs to a beautifully decorated bar area, full of dark wood with a deep red and absolutely stunning bar running across it, manned by a handsome neatly dressed waiter who immediately came up to me and asked if I was Terry's guest. I sat in a lovely comfortable velvet chair and looked around the room, there were pictures of footballers up on the walls and a few well-dressed gentlemen in the other room laughing gently giving it a nice ambiance. I had about ten minutes of waiting to do as I had arrived early but I just wanted to get there and chill.

Terry was at that moment the most important person in sport. Daily, he was all over the news and omnipresent on TV. Many reporters had tried to rip him apart for many things, so a guy in his position will naturally always be on the back foot with reporters. I sat there with my frothy coffee, a long sugar stick protruding out of the clean white cup and steam pouring out of the top. I tried not to worry about looking like a novice twat, but I knew I was in good hands. Terry by now would know that I was a racer, racing against Chris so I awaited the man of the moment to enter.

I looked at my stunning Raymond Weil watch that one of the racers had bought me for winning my first race – it was noon and like clockwork a well-dressed Terry walked in the room in a smart grey suit, a white shirt and blue and yellow tie. He looked crisp. He said hello to his barman and then looked straight at me and grinned.

I held my hand out and shook his. "Thank you for seeing me, I've got myself in a right situation."

"I know," he replied with a grin. "Chris told me."

I wasn't going to hide behind professionalism, after all, he was a lifelong friend with a mate so in effect he was family by default. He started with getting me another drink and ordering himself one, then he turned to me with a grin and said, "So you race powerboats with Chris and you are the only female I hear? How on earth did you start racing? Its dangerous, I've watched Chris enough times to see that, you lot are crazy."

We started chatting about life and racing. It took a whole frothy coffee to actually get onto Euro 96 and it was Terry who brought it up. He asked me what my 'pickle' was exactly that Chris had said to him about the press conference.

I just blurted, "It's like this Terry, the bosses at L!VE have insisted I go to the press conference tomorrow to interview you even though the big boys from the other channels are there. I've only just started working in the football arena and I don't know anything about it. I asked them to send someone knowledgeable but they want me to do it. For me to speak to you about football is just embarrassing as you'll immediately spot I know fuck all and I'm actually really worried about it," I grinned and continued, "Just treat me gently because I'm shitting it to be fair. Euro 96 is the biggest thing ever right now as are you and I have no idea why they've asked me."

He sat there amused to say the least, chuckling while sipping frothy coffee as I spewed out my worries. He leaned back in his chair and said,

"Don't worry, I'll make sure I find you and we'll do an interview. It'll be very busy but try and stay somewhere where I'll be able to see you." He winked affectionately and continued, "You'll be OK I'll make sure of that. Do you want to ask me anything now for prep?"

I asked some questions in advance so I could get my head around his answers and understand them, I also asked him if there was anything he could think of that I should be asking him that would be expected of me. He gave me as much time as I needed and then as I left he gave me a pat on my arm and told me not to worry and I was priority.

Seriously, did that just happen? I phoned Chris and thanked him and told him the next race night was on me. The entire evening's drinking was on me. I was buzzing, I was no longer worried, I was happy and confident and I knew Tel would treat me gently. I worked all evening to make sure I knew as much shit as I could and prepared the best I could and then arranged to meet the OB crew down there well in advance of the press conference.

As dawn broke, it was a crystal clear day as I looked out across the streets of the capital. I put the coffee on the stove and sat with my paperwork knowing that today I was reporting on one of the biggest days in sporting history. If we didn't as a team come back with the goods our heads would roll.

As we got to the venue with the OB van round the corner, it was heaving with a sea of press. We gave our details on the door and crammed in. I, along with the crew, squeezed our way along a wooden floored corridor up a few stairs to an open area roped off with security refusing to let anyone up. The press conference had started. Sat at a long table were five people with Terry in the middle. It was laden with microphones with all the big players' logos on – BBC, BBC Sport, Sky Sports, Sky News, CNN, Granada. In front of the long table was a sea of 'important' press, the invited ones from the major channels and the big newspapers. All were waving notebooks in the vain hope of attracting Terry's attention. I was now on my tiptoes trying to see over the crowd in front of me and hoping Terry would look to his left.

Terry stood up to denote the end of the conference, waved that the questions were over and looked toward the stairs where I was stood. He saw me and nodded letting me know I had been spotted. He walked from behind the table and with two security escorts pushed through the scrum of journalists keen to get the first interview. We were being pushed further back, much to my producer's angst with people still shouting his name trying to ask questions and get his attention, Terry came down the stairs ignoring everyone then nodded at me and beckoned with a head nod to follow. He walked past surrounded by cameras as my producer started to panic saying, "C'mon you're missing him we need to get him he's leaving!"

I said with no sense of urgency or worry, "Don't worry we can catch him outside."

The producer's voice was getting stressed. We followed the crowds towards the door and the security let Terry out of the building but blocked the press from following, he put his hand up and looked at me and beckoned me and my crew to the door. Everyone turned around and looked at us as I pulled my crew through the pack and we went out onto the street to where Terry was stood with his other security.

A few press had already got out before us and were trying to speak with him but he didn't even acknowledge them.

"Get rolling. I have the first interview," I said to my camera guy.

The producer looked baffled as Terry smiled at me and waved me over. Other press flooded out of the door and chased us with cameras but security held them back and told them to wait as he had his first interview to do and then it was their turn. You could actually see the big press boys looking at me thinking, *'What the fuck?'*

Terry took my arm and we walked another few metres down the road so we couldn't hear all their shouting his name and questions. My camera guy was now rolling with my producer off to the side holding a couple of dummy boards with keyword prompts so I wouldn't miss anything important.

Terry clocked it and said, "Don't worry, if you forget, I'll fill in the blanks for you."

It was a long interview, highly unusual in these sorts of situations, usually crews would fight to get their questions in and they would take what they could get, but not us. We must have spoken for five or more minutes and left no stone unturned. We chatted as if it was just another day at the office and even had some banter.

"Terry, thanks for taking the time to speak to us here at L!VE TV on what is a very important day for you, it's been a great interview."

Terry replied, "Thank you Sarah for a great interview it's been a pleasure."

I shook Terry's hand leaned over to him and whispered, "Thanks for saving my ass, that was awesome."

He nodded, smiled and then signalled to his security to let loose the beasts. Hordes of journalists stampeded towards him to get a fraction of what we had achieved.

We hung out on the pavement as the OB techs did their stuff. The producer asked, "What the hell was that about? How did you do that?"

I just smiled and said, "It's not what you know, it's who you know."

L!VE immediately pumped out the interview and by the time we had arrived back at Canary Wharf the studio was buzzing.

Kelvin McKenzie came straight out of his office to greet us and asked the producer, "Do you know our interview went out before the BBC's? We had the first aired interview from the conference. How the hell did you pull that off?"

She just gestured to me, "Sarah knows him."

Kelvin looked at me and said, "That was amazing, I mean really amazing, that interview was just incredible."

"Terry used to sponsor one of the racers, I had a coffee with him yesterday in Scribes and asked him to go gently on me," I grinned.

Wide-eyed Kelvin looked in shock and as he turned to walk back to his office he looked right at me, pointed at me and said,

"You're one of the best presenters we've ever had. Is there anyone you don't know?"

Kelvin was great to work for; he always made me feel ten feet tall. Around 2013 I caught up with him again on Cleveland Street in central London. He owned a sports channel and I had been interviewed for *Talking Balls*, a football show and it was so great to see him in there. It had been some twenty years. His first words were, "You look great, you haven't changed a bit."

It's always nice to see an old friendly face when working in media and Kelvin was always an awesome bloke, albeit not everyone feels the same about him that's for sure.

It was safe to say my job at L!VE was secure, although I had no intention of joining their short skirt snooker team or their naked weather readers any time soon. L!VE TV sent me to many interviews, one I remember fondly was to interview Antonio Banderas and other celebs after the premiere of his film *Desperado* so I went to the after party and did the rounds. I took my cameraman, and my best friend Jane to keep me amused and so we could party afterwards. She was always good for a giggle as at our last event together she came running back to me howling with laughter saying she had been shimmying on the floor with a guy.

He said to her, "Wow you smell really nice."

Jane replied in her broad Yorkshire accent, "Thanks, I've just farted," and ran to me giggling like a schoolgirl all pleased with herself. I had to laugh until she pointed to whom she had said it to. It was only Bill Murray, the famous American actor.

We sat at the bar and waited for *Desperado* celebs to arrive in their droves. I returned from an interview, to find Jane had made the most of the free booze.

She slurred, "That bird there just tried to pinch your bloody bar stool. I wasn't having that, I told her "Oi get your fat ass off that chair."

I asked who was sat on it because everyone in the bar was famous. She pointed to a lady dressed in pink, "Her," she said.

Oh fuck, it was Vanessa Feltz the presenter. I couldn't help but laugh. I then briefly went to the toilet and when I returned Jane was sat in the middle of Jonathan Ross and Paul Young.

"Look who I've accosted for you to interview. Get your cameraman and get over her and I'll swap places."

All I could do was shake my head and laugh. To be fair it was a big pull so I sat slap bang in the middle of them and did a great interview. It wasn't long before Jonathan invited me onto his hit TV show *They Think It's All Over* and both me and my boat were in the studio playing 'feel the sportsperson' with the rest of the racers in the live audience watching.

As all things, my stint at L!VE came to an end. I went on to work with Granada for around six years working on three separate TV shows including my own extreme sport shows on the Men & Motors channel, filming all over the world trying my hand at every extreme sport we could muster from skydiving to snowboarding.

Prior to Granada I auditioned to be a presenter on Channel 4's *The Girlie Show* and it was between me and Sara Cox, we were both blonde and both northern. They went for Sara but I was one of the first people they interviewed about racing. I also auditioned for *Top Gear Waterworld*, and applicants were whittled down to the final two – me and Kate Humble. Kate pipped me to the post, albeit I knew Andy Wilman the producer would have gone with me if he had the choice because of my knowledge in that arena as a powerboat racer, but it was at a time when BBC didn't do accents so they went with Kate and told me my accent was too strong. Again I was one of the first people they interviewed for my racing.

I did however get to do a TV show with Tiff Needell in Dubai about powerboat racing and Tiff remains a good friend to this day. You win some you lose some, it's like everything in life, everything ebbs and flows I have to say that I loved my life in media, it was just a riot from start to finish no matter what I did and even if I fucked up or was pipped to the post for a job I didn't mind. I got back on the horse. Every day is a school day and we learn something new with everything we do.

Chapter 6

Life after death

'It's starting to look like a bloody morgue in here.'

I flew to Venice, Italy for the European Offshore Powerboat Championships where I met up with Giovanni Carpitella – a very well-known Italian powerboat racer and one of the world's best. At 6'2", he was tanned and strikingly handsome with long blond hair and electric blue eyes. He was also racing and although a competitor, we were inseparable like brother and sister. When together, he always made sure I had everything I needed and would take me to the best dining and drinking establishments.

After the race day's weather briefing it was time to get on the water. I had jumped in a boat hundreds of times but for some reason there was something dark and foreboding nagging away at me. I had no idea why and I can't explain it to this day, but it ate at me so badly that I phoned Fiona Pascoe, a British race coordinator and family friend, to tell her that if anything happened during the races in Italy, she would be the first point of contact, not my parents, because Mum would sooner have someone she knew speak to her if anything happened. Fiona was understandably a little confused about this, but not half as confused as Mary Arthur, Taff's wife. Taff was my team manager back in 1994. He was an old boy and a damn good scrutineer and official, albeit now retired. I walked up to Mary who was quietly sat on a bench in the pits.

"If anything happens in the race can you please contact Fiona Pascoe, she'll know what to do. I don't want anyone else contacting Mum and Dad, especially not an Italian because of the language barrier."

Mary looked really puzzled as I gave her Fiona's number.

"Just please contact Fiona. Sorry I have to go, the whistle's blown and I've got to get to the boat."

And as soon as I had arrived I was gone. Mary just frowned questioningly at me as I ran off to the jetty.

There wasn't anything out of the ordinary about the Venice race that day. I just couldn't shake this weird feeling. I was driving for an Italian team with Enrico Bucciero and the intensity of the race soon focussed my mind on the task at hand pushing these strange feelings from my mind.

We were racing Class III 2 ltr and our boat was a catamaran. Catamarans have two sponsons (hulls). Enrico's boat was delightfully quick. We had tested it the day before and she ran like a dream and now we were running amongst the front few.

We were over half way through the race battling a beam sea. I hated beam seas where the waves run perpendicular to the direction of travel so getting the boat perfectly balanced isn't that easy, nor is keeping a consistent speed and keeping on top of the waves. It is quite simply awkward to race in. It's hard enough to coordinate the basic functions of life let alone try to navigate, steer or control a highly powerful beast in fucked-up water. Think of being on a bucking bronco while being smashed with a high-pressure hose and you sort of get the idea.

We headed towards a turn mark at about 80 mph. Water is a moving and unpredictable racing surface so is double the sensation to land therefore the equivalent of driving 160 mph in a rally car, and in a crash hitting water at such speed is the same as hitting concrete with the added dangers of drowning and hypothermia. As the beam see hit the boat, the engine shifted. It offset the balance of the boat and I saw my sponson (hull) disappear into the water. It was so quick yet I watched it in slow motion. I just remember thinking, 'Oh fuck'. There is very little recovery on a multihull in such rough water especially with offset balance. We were fucked.

The right sponson dug into the water causing the boat to barrel roll forward, stopping dead and upside down.

Death without knowing death is surely the kindest death.

***

I opened my eyes. Beyond the blur all I could recognise was the sterile white of a fluorescent strip light. I tried to swallow but a pipe plugged my parched throat and nauseating pressure flattened my tongue. I tried to move but couldn't. I just lay there peacefully. I wasn't in pain, I wasn't tired, I wasn't emotional, I wasn't confused. I was simply a body that could see.

Studious white coats, like geeky wood nymphs, swirled around my vision.

With so much activity I thought I may hear a mechanical hum, clumsy rattle or careful word to bring me comfort, but no, nothing. Maybe I was already dead and playing out my last memories before infinite sleep. Pure darkness had already consumed me before drifting slowly towards inviting light. Whatever situation I was in, it wasn't ideal. I closed my eyes again to see only the aqueous silver of closed eyes under the sterile white of a fluorescent strip light.

I woke again. I felt a hand on mine. Mum gently stroked my head as if I was made from porcelain whilst looking down at me. "See, I told you I've always got my eye on you."

The white coats were still busying themselves with mysterious equipment. I tried to work out what was going but in the rubble of a bombed out brain it was like piecing together a jigsaw with too many missing pieces. Darkness seemed easier so I just let my eyes close and slowly fall back to sleep. Realisation then hit me. *'Oh bollocks, I crashed. If I'm not dead, Mum's going to kill me.'*

Mum was still holding my hand when I opened my eyes again. *When did mum get to Italy?* I just wanted to tell her, 'I'm sorry' but my words were stuck like stilettos in mud, only my eyes told the story. I tried to squeeze her hand but I couldn't. My body was catatonic. The white coats gathered again, rushing around reading displays that told me where I was and what had happened – I'd woken from a coma and on a life support system in intensive care. In Italy they are romantically called 'reanimation rooms'.

Every time I opened my eyes Mum was still there. Even in such trauma our predisposition is to know where we stand in the passage of time and Mum's alternating top was my only notification that a day had passed. While her red eyes were the battle scars of emotion, Mum would never openly cry in front of me whilst I was awake. Mums are the strong ones, they want you to think you are OK and if they cry that could only add doubt. Mums are ace at lying to give comfort. It's a rare talent.

I just lay there with wires and drips hanging off me. I did wonder why I never needed the toilet but of course my nurse Nadia had fitted me with a bag. My jaw had been broken in two places, yet it wouldn't stop me from trying to talk, I'm a Northern lass after all, however I barely had the energy to breathe. A noise finally passed my lips – it was more of a low sibilant whisper but enough to give me confidence. Within a few days I managed to say "pen" through a glued mouth but without the 'P' so it sounded more like "hen" – I must have looked like the Tin Man in *The Wizard of Oz*. Mum searched her bag and gave me a pen. I couldn't grip it, in fact I couldn't even move my hand so she carefully cradled it in my hand. She knew I wouldn't be able to write but that's what mums do, they do anything to offer comfort and help. My wrist was utterly destroyed; the bone had actually pierced my skin. My arm was also broken. My shoulder was broken, so too my collar bone. Indeed, my whole right side was a mosaic of smashed bones.

I was eventually moved from the reanimation room to a private ward. I don't remember when, I'd been pumped with so many drugs lucidity was rare. When the morphine started to wear off I would beg for that lovely big needle to be stabbed in my arse to take away all my pain, but it was on a strict schedule and it wasn't enough. Morphine was the love of my life in those moments and our meetings were always the highlights of my day.

Now I was finally out of a coma, the doctors had started to plaster me up and fix me. I desperately wanted to leave the hospital but the doctors all told me I was in the best place in my condition. I woke up one day to see my arm and wrist had been plastered, I don't remember them operating on my arm but I had continuous pain from where the bone had said hello to the world. I also don't remember them pushing it back in my arm, which I'm actually very pleased about.

I was hooked up to a drip, I was in serious pain, my jaw was incredibly sore, it would be, it now had two titanium plates screwed in to it hold it together. My broken ribs meant any rasping cough from a dry throat was like being kicked by a mule and even moving was an exercise in teeth-gritting to fight the agony albeit I had knocked out most of them. My migraines felt as if my head was about to explode and made me so photophobic I felt like a vampire, not that I could really see anything through my blurred vision. Nor could I voice my frustration, I still couldn't talk.

After a period of time I could attempt wire-jawed murmurs and grunts, incoherent to anyone but Mum, who was always beside me whenever I opened my eyes, often accompanied by Giovanni who looked after her every move to and from the hospital. I asked for a mirror, but Mum wouldn't allow it, she wanted to protect me. Although I looked at myself as just 'me' my looks had earned me a decent wage and I could see Mum was worried how my new look could affect me mentally, after all a girl likes to look good, right? However, there was no getting away from the fact that the accident had left me with a head like a smashed crab so I needed to see for myself just to know what obstacles I had to overcome. She finally relented to my continual requests for a mirror, probably fed up cleaning up my dribble as I slurred with a toothless droopy mouth hunched up in bed like Charles Laughton's Quasimodo.

I raised it to my face slightly nervous of what I was to see. My hair was a mess and still covered in blood from the accident. I had a fractured skull and blood crusted my body and hair and could see it still under my acrylic nails all of which were intact, my body may not have withstood the impact but my manicure was still perfect. I would have smiled if I could. I had lost most of my teeth, my jaw sloped like I had Bell's Palsy as the nerves in the right side of my face had been severed, I had black eyes from my broken nose.

"Do I still have model looks hu hu hu?" I mumbled as my parched throat made me laugh like Frank Bruno, which made me laugh even more hurting my broken ribs.

Mum laughed with me immediately apologising by saying, "I shouldn't laugh," before continuing our giggles. It was great to see Mum's face finally light up.

I managed to tell her that I needed to wash my hair. My hair is naturally curly so I was paranoid it would matt together. Forget the fact I had actually died and been on life support, my main concern was that my hair needed washing and that is all I wanted. She told me not to worry and to rest.

But I couldn't rest with dirty hair, all I wanted to do was wash it. Drugged up and in pain, I tried to move to wash it myself but couldn't, I would have cried through frustration, but didn't have the energy. My mum helped me sit up. She knew that until my hair was washed I would be really stressed. My mum although tiny helped me out of bed, managing to untangle me from the web of wires, tubes and wheeled drips that accompanied me to the bathroom along with my urine bag, that followed me everywhere like a faithful dog. She held me up whilst I shuffled, hunched over like I was about to die. Nadia, my nurse, flew alarmed through the door. Mum rolled her eyes to Nadia to let her know that I 'had to' wash my hair. They both carried me to the sink. Mum told me to put my head over the sink while she splashed my hair with water.

"There you go, love, all done. You're all beautiful again," she said before slowly escorting me back to bed. The reality was she'd put an eggcup full of water on my hair, how would I know any different? I was sky high on drugs and was about to pass out yet again.

After about ten days in the hospital I just wanted to come home. Mum and Nadia had already had to contend with reporters and photographers in the hospital wanting access and she allowed he who offered the highest price the picture and interview and awaited a contract from the paper before she allowed access. Mum had it all in hand, she has always assisted me and knew how I worked and as I mumbled her, "Bills still have to be paid. Charge them."

***

The men, other than Dad and my brothers, I really wanted to see were Giovanni and the other racers. Once allowed, they would come to see me every day and I could see how difficult it was for them to tell me what had happened but they knew better than to argue when I insisted on them taking me through the events that led to me laying here with a piss bag strapped to my leg.

After we had crashed, the next two race boats on the circuit immediately stopped to give assistance. This is mandatory in powerboats. In car racing, crashes are simply flagged; in powerboating, because of all the extra dangers, the first people on the scene of an accident will always be another racer. Enrico had been thrown clear and was in the water. He shouted to Giuseppe Bevilaqua and another team that he couldn't find me. My body should have been close by regardless of what state it was in, but it was nowhere to be found.

Enrico took off his life-jacket to swim under the boat, he came back up again shouting to Giuseppe that I was trapped. Giuseppe swam under the boat but couldn't free me. I had five racers trying to pull me from under the wreckage. The force of the water on rolling the boat had pushed me deep into the footwell of the cockpit underneath the steering wheel, stuffing me tightly into a ball in the tiny space. I had been knocked unconscious, my crash helmet had been ripped off with the force and I had drowned. The guys repeatedly tried to tear me out but couldn't. The life jacket that is there to preserve my life was actually preventing rescue as its buoyancy was pushing me further into the inverted and flooded footwell.

The capsized catamaran now had three men on its upturned hull. There was only one thing left that they could to do, but it was virtually impossible. They all stood on the back of the sponsons to upset the boat's balance, hoping they could turn a boat full of water the right way up. Then something miraculous happened. As the front of the boat lifted higher, one of the rescuers managed to jump up to the centre section and pull it over with his body-weight as the others stayed at the back using their weight as a fulcrum. How they did it no one will ever know – in subsequent TV reconstructions of the crash the rescue had to be altered as it couldn't be mimicked. It was a miracle.

The rescuers now swam next to my righted boat with me still trapped in the footwell. They scrambled back on board to rip me from my watery tomb. I had now been under water for quite sometime. The doctors later said it could only have been four minutes because the textbook states any longer would have resulted in brain damage, but the reality was far different. The rescuers all reported that I was underneath for a minimum of ten minutes or more. It seemed modern medical wisdom had been torn up, but in fairness they have never actually tested it on a human guinea pig. It's all guesswork.

Once my crumpled body was pulled out of the footwell, Giuseppe immediately looked for signs of life, whether breathing, pulse or heartbeat. Nothing. I was totally unresponsive so he swiftly removed my life jacket to start CPR. I was bleeding from my ears, nose and mouth, yet he wiped away the blood and carried on regardless. After a few minutes of unsuccessfully working on me, Mario had shouted to Giuseppe, "You need to leave her, she's dead."

By now the helicopter was overhead and safety boats were on the scene for assistance. Giuseppe continued working on me even when the medics had been lowered down until I eventually puked. I was alive.

They put me in the cradle before being hoisted into the helicopter with the paramedics. While the story was being told to me, my brain activated memories I didn't think I had and vaguely remembered the coldness of the scissors running down my chest as my race overalls were being cut off while being flown to the hospital. All I thought at that moment was 'Oh no, my La Perla bra.' But how did I remember this? They had done this to attach the defibrillator. It was used on me on more than one occasion.

I remember moments of calm shouting as my heartbeat stopped, I remember brightness, peace and tranquillity. I remember being warm and small lights like fireflies guiding me to a nicer place and I remember my journey being interrupted by not being able to breath because of the down-force of the helicopter blades as I came to before drifting back to calmness. I remember trying to leave this place but being pulled back.

When Giuseppe Bevilaqua, the man who gave me back my life, arrived at the hospital to check on me, it was heart wrenching. This man had done CPR and not stopped even when one of them told him to leave me because I was dead. I was also fortunate that he also happened to be a medic and worked on boats in Venice. Mum would always hug him so tightly on his visits and would fuss around him, after all, without him I wouldn't be here and she wouldn't have a daughter. We owed him everything.

I remember Fiona's first words to me, "Never fucking do that again." We both laughed before she recalled the events. Mary had done as asked and made sure the chain of command was in place, with Fiona telling my parents ensuring that the officials didn't contact my mum. Fiona said it was the hardest thing she has ever had to because the hospital said I may not make it through the night. I can't imagine what that did to her as a mother herself, Dad and my brothers. Dad stayed at home with my siblings, trying to hold it together but was struggling to come to terms with the news.

The hospital later called Mum and told her something no mother wants to hear – her daughter was on a life-support machine and they couldn't guarantee survival. She was already preparing to fly out. There was only one problem – she had no idea how to book a flight. Mum had never been on a plane before; the family would always drive to our holiday in France. So Fiona did everything for her. Mum simply picked up a toothbrush, her passport and a change of clothes and left the house, with dad driving her to the airport.

My mum knew of Giovanni but had had never met him. He met her at Venice airport then did everything he possibly could for her. Giovanni had spoken to Mary and then to Fiona and had Mum's flight details. He took Mum immediately to hospital and stayed there throughout and translated everything. He also found Mum a hotel and made sure she ate and he picked her up every day to take her to the hospital and stayed with her. It rained one day and he bought her an umbrella before he even reached the hotel. She treasures it to this day. His mum had also sent me slippers and a gown.

While he was too modest to mention it, I was told that as soon as the race had finished he had noticed my boat hadn't returned so asked who had crashed. He was initially greeted by silence because everyone knew of our close relationship and as I was the only female worldwide that raced, he looked after me like a little sister. Once he was told of my crash he had jumped off his boat without even tying up, he threw the rope to someone else to do it, and didn't even sign off. He just left for the hospital.

Mum said that when she got to the hospital every single Italian racing driver was there. The pits were empty. It wasn't a great victory for the team that won because few racers turned up for the podium, they were all in the waiting room watching the over-bed camera monitoring me on life support in the reanimation room. Mum said that every day it was full of racers waiting for news. It's funny, I always loved the Italians and I still do but to have support like that was incredible. Naturally the British racers couldn't stick around, they all had lives to get back to and transport home to catch. The Royal Yachting Association were useless. Their spokesperson simply released an official statement saying 'there will be investigation into the cause of the accident', but it was all a façade. There was never an investigation. The only reason the RYA made a statement was because the news teams were all over the story and they had to be seen to be taking a proactive stance. The reality was they swept it under the carpet. I was the only female racer, I had just done a Bond movie and it was bad press that the RYA couldn't afford.

The accident hit morning news the day after and many of my friends heard the headline 'James Bond stunt girl and powerboat racer was critical' on Radio 1 and Capital Radio whilst driving to work. It shocked many to the core. From that moment the phone lines rang hot to my parents and my close friends trying to find out what had happened. Flowers poured into the hospital in Venice and so many were sent to my parents' address that my dad joked that it 'looked like a bloody morgue' and there was nowhere to put them all. Eon Productions sent a card signed by everyone from the Bond film, and a huge bunch of flowers. I even had flowers from the USA and Dubai, there was just delivery after delivery from well-wishers across the world.

***

Despite all the attention, laying in bed was hugely frustrating. In between bouts of sedation I would just lie there wanting to get back to my normal routine, to live life and enjoy the outside world.

I eventually pulled the drip out of my arm. Mum glared at me and shot out to get Nadia. Nadia rushed in. I was put back in bed and sedated. When I came round again I insisted on leaving. The staff explained how bad for me this could be, but I didn't care.

I was discharged from hospital and taken to the airport, ironically by boat by Giuseppe and Giovanni, with my mum. Nadia my nurse packed a plastic bag with a load of powerful painkillers and prescriptions of what I needed in the UK. She warned me that as soon as I left hospital that my pain couldn't be monitored and that I should prepare myself for the morphine to wear off. I didn't care, I just wanted to go home.

Giovanni was highly efficient and had already changed the flights, giving my mum all the details of everything I needed including who to contact at the airport as he had called in advance to arrange for a wheelchair and airport assistance both in Venice and Manchester. Leaving him was so utterly heartbreaking for us both, Mum couldn't thank Giovanni and Giuseppe enough and they struggled to break her hug.

I had been given a 'fit to fly' although the reality was far different. I was still covered in blood, and wearing pyjamas, a dressing gown and slippers. My entire wardrobe had been taken back to the UK by the race team and my race overalls were in a bin with my best La Perla bra.

Mum sat me down and looked for British Airways assistance as advised by Giovanni. No one listened, no one helped, no one came and no one wanted to help us. Mum didn't know what to do. I was very ill, my medication was wearing off, I could barely walk, and I couldn't really talk. Mum was at a loss. I managed to murmur, "Hate British Airways," before leaning on mum as we staggered to the British Airways check-in desk drawing stares from Brits returning from their Venice break.

At check-in I didn't look your normal passenger, still covered in blood with black eyes, looking like I had been in a street fight. Yet at no point were we given any assistance. I even hobbled up to some British Airways bastard holding a wheelchair and mumbled if it was for me. Admittedly he may not have understood me but it didn't take a fucking rocket scientist to know that I needed help. They didn't even help me up the stairs onto the plane.

Mum pushed me up the stairs and at the aircraft door the ultra-smiley Cabin Services Director (CSD) pointed mum to business class and me to regular. It seemed the only flight available to Mum at such short notice was business class so Fiona had naturally ignored the expense and booked it. Giovanni rescheduled our return flight unaware Mum was in business.

The flight was virtually empty. The CSD, still smiling with a shit-eating grin didn't offer us to sit together in either class, and said we had to take our designated seats but as it was an empty flight we could move after take-off. Mum who is usually very polite and calm at this point bit back, "Does she look like she can move or sit alone?"

The CSD looked at the manifest and agreed we could sit together – in economy class. Even though business class was empty, and even though

Mum had a business class ticket and even though I was clearly in trauma, she put us in cattle.

It transpired that on the way out, because Mum had never flown before and had concerns about flying, the airhostess had moved Mum out of business class and put her in economy so she was near the galley at the back where the hostess was stationed, so she could check Mum was OK. While this may seem diligent, there is also a galley and cabin crew station at the front in business class. So in effect the whole business class flight that had cost a whopping amount was spent in economy. Thanks BA.

To make matters worse, Mum called the CSD over and mentioned about the prearranged wheelchair upon arrival, as I had recently been on life support and was clearly ill. The CSD stated it had been arranged.

Upon landing, we waited on the plane until the others passenger had alighted. We waited, and we waited and we waited. By this time I was in so much pain I couldn't wait any longer. So stumbled from the plane without any assistance whatsoever. I have never flown British Airways since and would rather stick knitting needles in my eyes that fly with them again.

Dad was at Arrivals waiting for us. I virtually passed out into his arms. I'd never seen Dad cry, he was tougher than sunburnt leather yet here he was with his bloodshot eyes, emotional at being able to hold his baby girl, something he often thought he may never do again. It was simple treasured moments like this that made me realise how much parenthood meant to them.

They got me home and put me on the couch. Dad had arranged everything downstairs so I wanted for nothing. He had even bought a camping toilet so I didn't need to go far. They had thought of everything. My brothers clucked around and the house was already full of flowers. I was just glad I wasn't prone to hay fever.

It wasn't long before the painkillers had totally dispersed from my body and I was constantly wailing like a banshee, much to the distress of my family. It made me yearn for the sterility of Venice hospital and it was a painful realisation of why I should really have listened to the doctors.

I lost all feeling in the lower right quadrant of my face. The nerves severed were both those for movement and feeling and I dribbled when I tried to speak and eating had to be done through a straw but I would still dribble or spill it all down my chin, neck and clothes. I was on a liquid diet for over six months. I went so skinny, my broken clavicle was visible, but it's not a diet

I would advise. Over the months the movement returned, but to this day the lower right hand side of my face is still totally numb – it's certainly an advantage at the dentist.

***

When well enough, albeit I wasn't in a fit state to do anything other than walk and drink liquefied food, I flew to Italy to see Giuseppe, the man that had saved my life. I had bought him a present. He was a smoker so I bought him a stunning lighter from Harrods and had it engraved with 'Thank you for my life'. It remains unused and takes pride of place above his fireplace.

Against the judgement of all those around me I decided it was time to get back into a boat. It was my litmus test to see if I could mentally hack it. Physically I was in no state but at the top level it's the mind that makes a champion not the body. I was back from the dead and the accident was a long way behind me. Mario was there. He was the one that told Giuseppe to leave me because I was dead. He smiled at me as I walked up to him.

"How are you my good friend?" I said with a hug.

"It is beautiful to see you." The relief in his face was a picture.

"I don't look very dead do I?" We both laughed.

In the fall out of the incident I found out it was engineer error causing the engine to shift and unbalance the boat. The engineer responsible approached me. He looked ashamed and didn't know where to look. I grinned at him and gave him a huge hug.

"Saretta, I am so sorry."

"It's OK," I replied. "Shit happens."

After all, I play the game, so therefore I am responsible for my own actions. When we choose to race in the most dangerous sport in the world, where we contend with an unpredictable racing surface, when we run at speeds twice the sensation on land, where if we crash and the crash doesn't kill us we may drown, get hypothermia or die from severe infection, then really who is to blame? We take our chance every time we don the crash helmet. Human error happens, it's part of being human. I am not here to blame anyone for what happened. I chose what path to take and I had no worries about crashing nor being in hospital, nor was I afraid to die competing in a sport I love.

I finally got into the boat to test with Giuseppe. We got the boat to 100 mph on the Venice waters. I knew if we barrel rolled again I wouldn't be as lucky. We raced twice that weekend. We came 3rd in the first race and won the second race. I loved being back on the podium with my friends.

Did it bother me? If it did bother me do you really think a girl like me would admit to it? Would I fuck, I'd suck it up.

Many soldiers say that unless you come close to death, you can't really appreciate life. I know how they feel.

I had been given a second chance. My new life was at year 0 and anything going forward would be AD (After Death). My BC (Before Coma) life had been amazing, I aimed for my AD life to be even better.

Chapter 7

Black ops to podium tops

'Fuck off, you'll run her ragged'

There wasn't even a sea breeze to flutter flaccid flags or give respite to the summer sun that beat down on the water. The only shade was the overly large beer tent in the pit area, or at least that was my excuse for being there.

I was in Cowes on the Isle of Wight for a long bank holiday weekend as it was the inaugural Offshore Powerboat Cowes–Torquay race and part of the British Championships.

More than eighty boats had come in from as far as Dubai and as per normal for these huge events the pits had been secured off with fences and security were all over the place checking passes. Cowes radio had been taken over by the racing fraternity and we had non-stop commentary in the pits, even when the racing wasn't on they had one of the chatterboxes spewing out bollox 24/7, talking about the teams and doing the odd interview with a racer. This was usually where I kept a low profile so interviews wouldn't get in the way of the drinking. After all I was the only female racer amongst about 160 guys and they always wanted to talk to me as if being female made a difference in racing. Yawn…

I was featuring in two races, and had just completed the first. I changed out of my sweaty salt-covered overalls and ran a brush through the bird's nest, that masqueraded as hair, before diving onto my friend's pleasure boat called *Lethal Magic*, berthed in the marina next to all the race boats. It was not a normal boat by any means; it could reach speeds of 100 mph (and for you landlubbers, remember that's the equivalent of 200 mph on land) and had a sister race boat called *Lethal Menace*; it also had another relative, an AC Cobra with the same paint job, of which everyone with no understanding about the exhaust system but wanted a ride was easily spotted with a huge burn on their lower limb. They were all owned by Southampton businessman, the super gregarious Colin Stoneman.

Once aboard *Lethal Magic* we darted across the racecourse to watch from the designated area, which those with sense adhered to, but many yachties, or WAFAs (wind assisted fucking arseholes) as powerboaters affectionately call them, did their own thing. It may be a racecourse but no one actually owns the sea *per se* and safety control can only ask people to steer clear of the course, so if some dickhead wants to cross it then it is not illegal, just highly selfish. Powerboats don't have brakes, it's stupid, and downright dangerous yet cross it the WAFAs often do, travelling at the mighty drifting speed of about 5 mph. I never understood why they do this. We would never cross their racing line, it's just not something we would dream of doing, but day sailors did it to us all the time.

We sat lulling in the designated vantage area, on board music played to the many passengers enjoying the spectacle. In reality the boat was way over-loaded but when gin is on offer no one cares. I stepped onto the sun-drenched deck with beer in hand to sit down with Alistair the boat bitch, to soak up the sun.

Colin the owner shouted Alistair back to the cockpit for something and they decided it would be highly amusing to get *Magic* on the plane travelling at speed with me hanging onto the deck for dear life shouting that if he didn't stop the boat I would fucking kill him if the fall didn't kill me first. For those resting in the bolster seats the ride was added excitement, for me on deck, too much excitement. The beer ended up in the water, I was hanging onto the bowline which ran from the front of the boat into the boat where it was tied off and after much laughing (but not from me), Colin backed off and we sat there lulling again, this time I was like Clarence the Cross-eyed Lion, one eye on the course, one on Colin's right hand to make sure he wasn't touching the throttles. Tosser...

Before the race started I spotted six guys dressed in all black dry suits in a black rigid-hulled inflatable boat (RIB). It was hot already in the boat but my temperature was about to pop the thermometer at the sight of these guys. My red-blooded female eyes couldn't stray from the sight that greeted me. "Who the fuck are they?" I asked the crew.

No one had a clue so Colin gently eased up close to them, me in prime position on deck with them probably wondering what we were doing.

"Hey guys, nice outfits, who are you lot? Milk Tray delivery?" I blurted out.

"Race safety," they answered.

Interesting. I didn't recognise them as our race safety team. We always get people assisting but not hot guys in their late twenties and certainly none that looked that sexy on water.

Of course, it would be ignorant not to offer 'race safety' some refreshments and to climb aboard and have a beer. I loved watching powerboat racing but I thought it my duty to ensure race safety were being taken care of… Banter continued between the boats until they took a radio call. The team leader apologised and said they had been tasked. Bollocks, my soft as a sledgehammer approach hadn't worked. Before they shot off I asked them if they were around later on in the beer tent and if they were race safety on Sunday. I was feathering my nest.

The race finished and *Lethal Magic* soon was moored up in harbour. Chris Bryan, a former career Royal Marine who had become a good friend, came to find me on the pontoon so we could start an early drinking session in the beer tent. At 6'3" and built like two shithouses welded together he cast a large shadow across the pontoon. With his shaved head he looked mean, and from what I hear during his service, he was quite a force to be reckoned with and didn't take shit from anyone, something highly prevalent during the years we raced together. But with me he was a total gentleman, and looked out for me whether I needed it or not.

As we walked along Cowes harbour, my eyes were drawn to the beauty of sun-spangled powerboats bobbing at their moorings. The harbour had been cleared of all its usual berths and now the entire harbour was bow after bow of sleek, glistening fibreglass, all polished and sprayed with exotic paints and vinyl's, reflecting the golden sunshine. Engine hatches were open, engineers were disappearing into the engine bays and the air roared with engines being flushed and tested, sending a delightfully thick pocket of exhaust fumes billowing across my excited nostrils. The thundering noise of 525 HP engines vibrated the pontoons and attracted spectators and teams alike, who were leaning over the railings watching the crane working tirelessly to cradle these stunning boats in and out of the water to prepare for Sunday's race. A powerboat racing wet pits is truly the eighth wonder of the world, mixing colour, glamour and danger. It is my dream world, my passion, my true love and the simplicity of just watching them, never mind being involved in them, are moments that I will treasure for the rest of my life.

The huge carpeted beer tent was situated in the middle of the pits and rammed with racers and engineers cooling off with beer. I stood with Chris and surveyed the scene. With my 'hot guy radar' working splendidly, it wasn't long before my well-trained eye saw the six race safety guys, still dressed in their all-black garb, sitting at a wooden bench.

"I see the SBS boys have caught your eye then?" Chris said whilst spilling beer down his top.

So that's who they were, Special Boat Service. I had a feeling they were military as they were far too sexy, efficient and disciplined to be civvies. I think at this point I dribbled slightly.

"Not wrong Chris. Fuck I wouldn't know which one to choose; just look at them." I wanted to get to know them. All of them.

"If you go and sit yourself right in the middle of them, I'll buy your drinks for the rest of the…"

Too late I was already there. It was going to be an expensive night for Chris as I needed no encouragement. I noticed a small gap between two of the guys nowhere wide enough for a person but crowbarred myself in nonetheless and faced Chris. I took a swig of the nearest beer, whoever that belonged to, and raised it to Chris to say cheers and to motion '*start getting the beers in*'.

"Alright guys? Who are you lot then and what you doing here?"

The Milk Tray boys were still quite bemused I had just pushed my way in and started drinking their beer.

Chris soon walked over to the table and said,

"I see you've met Sarah, what are you all drinking before she drinks all yours?"

The banter went on for a few minutes and it was fairly obvious Chris was pretty close with the lads as they had worked together.

I made myself very comfortable and stayed with the guys for the next few hours. I hooked up with the lads again that evening with the rest of the racers and the drinks flowed. Mid enjoyment I was called over to the racers and was set another task. My new task was to get a black dry suit off one of the SBS lads by the end of the weekend.

Dry suits are not cheap, and the SBS suits I doubt could be bought in any shop as they were specialist, so I bided my time. Alcohol loosens up even the most disciplined special forces operator so I sank a couple of rounds of shots with them and made my move. It was as subtle as a rock through a windscreen. "Those dry suits are great, have you got any spare? One on the lads wants one and I've been tasked or I'll get punished and it won't be pleasant. The last time I lost a task I ended up taped inside a portaloo. And they tipped it up."

"No problem, we'll sort you out." Mission complete and they brought me a dry suit, which I promptly handed over, much to the disbelief of the racers.

The SBS guys asked about my boat and we talked shop for some time. Some were so knowledgeable about boats that it was cool just sat there with them. My engine was a race tuned Merc XR2, and I had two props. One fast, one slow, so to speak, but both weather-dependent and both had specific jobs to do depending on the sea state.

"Who looks after your boat?" one lad asked

"Well I've an engineer but he's not full time."

"Why don't you bring it down to our place and we'll look after it for you and check it over."

"Fuck off, you'll run her ragged, she's not a toy," I laughed.

"No seriously, bring it down and we will give her a top to toe. It's what we do, we've time on our hands and it keeps us up to speed."

I've had some invitations in my time but never one like this. The Special Boat Service looking after my boat? Of course they would test her, they have to, but then again they were the most qualified people to do it and even they would learn from a raceboat as she was a different vessel to what they were used to by way of acceleration and balance. I dropped her off at the base with extra kit, went over the necessities and there she was, nursed by the Milk Tray men. When I collected her she ran smoother than I had ever known and her reliability was second to none on the circuit. They clearly had golden hands as well as golden looks.

It was a chance meeting with the SBS boys but friendships have lasted and I've since had many a night out with them from staying on base to going to summer and Christmas functions. They would often blindfold me and say I wasn't allowed to know where the functions were before being driven into the middle of nowhere. I used to let them have their moments of amusement, as long as I had beer all night I was good!

Cowes beer tent always had fond memories for me, many are blurred but some are as if they happened yesterday. I had bought a new boat and John Cooke was navigating for me. It was a stunning summers day an August bank holiday weekend. The yacht masts were gently swaying and clanking and the seagulls balanced effortlessly on top of them watching for any food they could swoop down on. Cowes dry pit area was in the marina itself surrounding the hub, the beer tent, and is all private property and race weekend it is solely for the race boats and their tow vehicles. All boats are given their spot allowing for length of boat and tow vehicle. Everything has its place in a nice neat row. John and I had arrived some hours earlier and finished our paperwork and equipment checks so hooked the boat up to refuel her and left the pits only to return to a black BMW parked in my designated space.

This car didn't even have a tow hitch on, so what was it even doing here and what the fuck was it doing parked in a space clearly for a race team? I was furious. This is a tight ship and everyone has their place like a complicated multi-sized jigsaw that the organisers have plotted in advance and this couldn't have been a racer's vehicle because no racer would do that. We were now in the pits in everyone's way because we had nowhere to go. I leapt out of the car and checked to see if it was open and if the keys were in. With no joy I walked through the pits asking if anyone owned the annoying black BMW in my space. I still had no joy, so there was only one thing to do. Block the fucker in and teach them a lesson.

I got John to reverse our boat right back until my trailer was almost touching their bumper. We unhooked the boat and John removed his vehicle. The BMW was going nowhere but I was going to the bar. I could have been on my third beer with a group of the guys when three blonde women in badly fitting tight dresses stormed in looking like old sausage meat trussed up and bursting out of ill-fitting skins shouting about being blocked in. So here were the culprits. I ignored it. They bee-lined for a racer, one of the women's boyfriends and a good friend of mine called Richard. She screamed at him to help her get the car out because someone had blocked them in, she was hysterical as were her allies. They all looked like the sort who were moths to candlelight, the sort that hung around rich guys and hoped their looks would get them places, albeit they were knocking on a bit so their clock was ticking. Richard was mid-conversation with his team and wasn't impressed and asked,

"Why did you park there? I said you couldn't park in the pits."

"It's not the point, are you going to do something about it?" she shrilled as her sausage body fought to stay in its skin.

"What boat number is it?" Richard asked.

"C69 right behind this tent!"

At this point Richard nearly spat his drink out as the rest of the team started laughing wide-eyed as his girlfriend demanded what was so amusing. With eyebrows raised he said, "That boat belongs to Sarah Donohue, you're on your own, I told you not to park here I'm not getting involved."

He turned his back on her much to her annoyance and continued with his team as they roared laughing that out of all the people to piss off she had unknowingly picked me, she stormed off marching around the tent asking for Sarah Donohue who had blocked her in. I was stood right there watching but she was blanked by everyone.

It took the three women a further hour to track me down and I wasn't exactly approached in a polite manner. The car owner stormed up to me and demanded, "Are you Sarah Donohue?"

I looked down at my left breast shirt pocket which clearly said my name and I continued to drink my beer with John. By now the entire bar knew what was going on and it went silent as the lads nudged each other for possible fireworks. The woman's language was shocking and I now had three crazy banshees all gesticulating and shouting at me in the bar telling me to move my car immediately. I gestured without words that my beer was still half full. The obvious owner got in my face barking like a rabid hound. I stepped back so as not to contract Hep B with all the spit coming out of her loose lips,

"You came into our pits and parked in my space allocated for my boat. All I wanted to do was refuel, re-park and have a beer and now you are unhappy that you are blocked in. You don't race and secondly you don't tow so get the fuck out of my face because I wont be moving any time soon. Now fuck off."

She screamed that I had scratched her bumper with my trailer and she was going to call the police and sue me. Of course we hadn't and I informed her it was private property where she wasn't even allowed, and it begged the question, "Who the fuck are you anyway?"

By now they were fuming, John doesn't have the resilience I have and he said he would move the trailer to allow her out. As far as I was concerned I was going to leave her blocked in all weekend as I had already checked with the crane that my boat could be lifted directly from its present position. But John was feeling guilty. I banned him from moving for at least another hour just so they could stew a little longer and take note of the consequences of the error of their ways. Eventually the Witches of Eastwick clambered into their car and John moved. I swiftly put a cone in front of them so they couldn't go anywhere before I had patronisingly uttered the words through their window,

"Respect the speed limit in the pits and don't drive off through red mist, in fact don't ever drive in any pits again. You aren't welcome." I removed the cone and off they trundled, a marshal was now walking in front of the car really slowly much to my amusement, leading them out at snail's pace as he turned and winked at me. He had witnessed the whole fracas. They had faces like slapped arses and I never did see them again. I'm also not sure Richard saw them again either. No love lost anywhere that day.

***

Cowes was always guaranteed amusement. The favourite race of the year, the biggie where racers and teams from all over the world congregate and the whole of the sea front and small cobbled high street and all the restaurants are buzzing with teams in brightly coloured matching shirts – some teams you would only see once a year so catching up and sharing past moments was always special. Everyone loves Cowes week, famous for its flamboyant characters and huge boats. The crane lowering the boats in the water and retrieving them seemed like it worked 24/7. You could look over the fence into the wet pits from the dry pits and there was an incredible array of colours, sometimes clouded by exhaust fumes which filled the air with a delightful smell as you inhaled, taking in every moment. The crane quite often could pick the close boats up directly off their trailers in the designated parking spaces, it was all so close and tight. It's the most prestigious event of the year and every event stays in the mind and heart of every racer.

I was post race in the beer tent and a couple of the rescue guys and officials were close by, they beckoned me over so I wandered over and Bob said, "Howard says hello."

"I don't know anyone called Howard."

"You do. Your ex-boyfriend." By now some amusement had set in with the lads as I adamantly denied any knowledge of anyone called Howard. Bob sat resting on a table top with his arms folded grinning at me during the interrogation. I tried to change the subject. My face didn't break. I only knew one Howard and yes that was my ex-boyfriend but Bob couldn't know that because I always kept things quiet and have until writing this book. Howard Donald from boy band Take That but he couldn't possibly know Howard. Could he?

"Howard from Take That," he stated inquisitively with his eyebrows raised as I felt the other guys staring at me as I wanted to be somewhere else but not there having this conversation. .

"Nah, I don't know him Bob, what on earth makes you think I do?"

"Well he knows all about you and he speaks very highly of you, in fact he actually boasted about you and told me all about you before he even knew that I knew you. I think he's still got the hots for you. He was very proud of your achievements." I was now being stared at by all of them and could feel myself becoming flushed.

I had been busted. I quickly thought of denial again but it was futile as the guys burst into a Take That song as I called them a bunch of wankers.

It turned out Howard was looking to buy a pleasure boat and it just so happened that Bob was the on-hand expert assisting him. I had flown back from Germany with Howard only a few months prior and he was telling me his boat buying plans so I knew Bob had met him. I had started my racing career when I was dating Howard, in fact I used to tell the band all my escapades on my hotel visits with them when they were on tour. They always asked for updates for a bit of normality and escapism from their lives of fame and fortune. Howard had excitedly told Bob that his ex-girlfriend raced powerboats. It wasn't rocket science. I was the only female racer so Bob asked, "So you dated Sarah then?"

Howard became excited that he knew me and so the conversation flowed no doubt to Bob's amusement. I always shared the powerboat stories with the band and the only reason Howard and I had split was because the band had got so big that there wasn't enough time to have girlfriends because of the pressure and travel. My skulduggery of keeping the relationship quiet hadn't worked. Howard was blurting it out meanwhile I'm trying to deny it. I even denied it whilst exiting hotels when clearly I was lying hidden under a large peaked cap.

I visited Howard and the lads when I could because I loved them all, especially Gary and Howard and we remained good friends even after we broke up. I was so busy travelling as well it would never have worked. I continued to write to Gary whilst they were on tour for many years. He always wrote on hotel headed paper and I always wrote back to the hotel but under code name 'Mickey Mouse'. I still have my Mickey Mouse titled letters to this day, not for any other reason than I hoard stuff. There was always something happening in the pit area of a powerboat event, I just wasn't expecting that. As I walked back to the bar I asked the lads to keep it under their hats about Howard. I didn't want a reporter getting it and there were loads of them around the pits. That was mine and Howard's private life and life needs privacy and respect, and Take That were the biggest band in the world at that time. I don't agree with selling stories to make a fast buck. Friendship is always more important.

Over time a couple more girls arrived on the powerboat scene. It was speed week at Windermere again and a girl we shall name Carol had joined one of the teams as a driver. It was her birthday that weekend but her boyfriend couldn't join her as he was working. Her nickname (but it must be said in an accent not too dissimilar from Count Dracula's) was 'Le Panther… Vil she strike tonight?' Amusingly Carol always got a bit of thirst on for men after a few drinks so, although gentle and polite by day, by night she prowled.

Carol had left the pits in the later afternoon with an engineer who had flown in from the USA for the week. No questions were asked as they disappeared after having a couple of beers in the back of the truck. Amusing comments were thrown about as well as, 'Vil she strike tonight?' being chanted every few minutes. But nothing had prepared us for the next instalment. As we packed up and walked up to the Low Wood Hotel, a naked man resembling the American engineer ran across the roof clasping his nuts in one hand closely followed by Carol throwing his clothes out of the window after him onto the lawn below as we all stopped and stared. He clambered down the drainpipe big white arse for all to see, grabbed his clothes and disappeared behind the hotel. We all stood there in silence, we had no idea what was going on but we wanted to.

As we ran to the bar to find out finer details from anyone that knew, it seemed that Carol's boyfriend who we shall name Carl had travelled to surprise her, and oh yes this surprised her. She was over 250 miles away from him or so she thought. Bouquet carrying Carl had been spotted at reception by a quick-reacting member of her team who had seen Carol entice the engineer back. Fortunately knowing her room number he shot upstairs and sounded the alarm before heading downstairs to catch Carl at reception and kept him talking for a few minutes. Carol hadn't even given her new mate time to put on his underpants, she opened the windows, kicked him out followed by his clothes as there was a knock on her door. She had already turned the shower on to cover any noise and had dived in to wet her hair wrapping a towel around her head giving her another few seconds to check the surrounding area for anything which shouldn't be there. As she opened the door it was as if it was a total surprise seeing him there. The happy couple soon appeared in the bar arm in arm and we didn't utter a word but we all remember the famous American engineer clutching his tackle running naked across the Low Wood hotel roof and clothes flying through the open window.

Chapter 8

Taking the title

'The pits were buzzing with race crews, journalists and photographers'

There were certain venues across the world that we favoured for racing. Cowes on the Isle of Wight was one and anywhere in Italy was a racers dream. Italy was fun from start to finish and after my accident, the Italians had treated me like a princess, unlike the UK's Royal Yachting Association's powerboat department who were useless so I refused to continue running with a British license. Not only are our licenses the most expensive in the world, but when it comes to value for money, It's like spending Rolex money on a Christmas cracker watch.

The RYA weren't happy with my decision and made it rather difficult for me when I made the decision to have an Italian license. Getting the RYA to communicate with the Italian federation was a bit like using an ashtray on the back of a motorbike. It also meant that I had to go to Italy for a medical and join an Italian racing club all very simple to do but not if the RYA moved at a pace similar to that of a corpse. Eventually I secured my Italian license and I remained racing as an Italian for many years. After all, an Italian had saved my life.

It was the 2 ltr European Championships in Viareggio in Italy. Race teams stay either in hotels or in the pits in their trailers. The dry pits were directly on the other side of the canal from the town and where the trawlers pulled in selling their fish during the days. The whole area was full of bright lights and the smell of delicious cuisine pouring out of the restaurants that line the streets. Myself and my team mate Ricky had opted to book an apartment opposite the marina on the other side of the canal just up from the trawlers right on the corner on the third floor so we could see across to the boats from our balcony. It was a big apartment, lots of dark glossy wood teamed with marble floors and dreadful crocheted dollies draped over almost every flat surface. The only thing missing was the smell of lavender and a rocking chair.

Seven English teams had driven across to Italy all towing boats, many of us in convoy because the trip down is as much fun as the racing. It was always an adventure coordinating the same ferry crossing as the other teams, meeting for a beer in the bar and shooting the breeze on deck.

Three teams had travelled down together – ours, Chris Bryan's and John Cooke's. Upon finally reaching Italy, we decided to pull up for the night in a roadside services so we could put the awning up get some food down our necks and have a drink in the lovely warm night's breeze. John thought it may be too dodgy to stay at a services with so much expensive equipment on board so found a five-star hotel where he could park his vehicle safely and get a good night's sleep. We preferred to slum it and hang out with a crate of cool beers, hungry mosquitos whilst surrounded by truckers and diesel spills.

The morning sun woke us. I love waking up on a warm morning and possibly why I love Italy so much. My teammate Rick cooked a greasy fry up and made coffee and we sat out in the 7 am sunshine on camp chairs waiting for John. We had arranged to meet for breakfast so we waited another twenty minutes before calling him.

"Where are you?" I asked.

"Err, with the police."

My first thoughts were '*What have you done now.*'

"Well you know when I said I was going to a hotel so I could securely park the vehicle as the services were dodgy? Well some bastard broke into my 4x4 and stole all my tools, propellers and a spare engine."

If it wasn't so serious it would have been hilarious but either way we continued to pull his leg about it for the next week. There was nothing we could do so we just arranged to meet him in Viareggio in the pits. It was however a huge issue for John. As soon as you enter the pits, you are under race regulations, and trying to fly in specialist race equipment to a venue when everything is so specific to that particular boat is almost hopeless, when the boat needs to be re-tested and engines ran in and you can only put your boat in the water and test at designated times.

We were just pulling out of the truck park to continue our journey when a young lad walked up to the car and waved. He had a mobile phone for sale. It was a good phone and was unlocked to be used with any sim card. I declined his offer but Rick wanted a look

I told Rick not to look because it must be a con, roadside service car parks are hardly the destination for official phone distributors. Rick couldn't see the issue, and the more the young kid showed him, the more Rick liked it, so much so he pulled out some cash. I told Rick not to but he handed over the equivalent of £80. The lad handed him the phone and disappeared. As Chris followed us, he radioed me to ask what was going on.

"It's nothing just Rick getting fleeced by a scoundrel."

I could see Rick was annoyed at my piss-taking so he pulled over to show me what a bargain it was and to shut me up.

Rick stared at the phone he now held up. "That little twat, this isn't even the same fucking phone, this one doesn't even fucking work. I'm going to fucking kill him!" he bellowed in his thick Welsh accent.

I was thrown into my passenger door as Rick sped off into a U turn to re-enter the services.

I radioed Chris, trying to speak through snaffles of laughter "Mayday Mayday, bald Welshman been ripped off, returning to scene of crime, please follow, over." At this point I didn't dare say, "I fucking told you so."

Rick was boiling over. He parked up and shot into the services café looking for the young hoaxer. His bald head now like a beaming red snooker ball. I had said it would be a fruitless trip and the lad would be long gone but Rick was desperate for revenge and to reclaim a modicum of dignity.

Five minutes later he stormed back red faced. Suddenly no one spoke English in the café and no one could help him. His Welsh accent thickened with every angry word and by now even I couldn't decipher what nonsense it was, it could have been backwards Swahili, but whatever it was I was doubled up in laughter which only enraged him more.

He still hadn't calmed by the time we pulled into the pits some hours later. As soon as we found the other English teams, as all children do, I rushed to tell everyone about Rick falling foul to a con artist who was obviously good with sleight of hand. Rick wasn't impressed, which meant we wouldn't let it drop all week.

John arrived some time later, his window taped up with polythene, cursing and swearing but he was soon over it and busied himself with calls to Mercury to arrange delivery of parts, whilst also begging and borrowing off other racers. Powerboating isn't like other sports, if we can help another team get on the water we will, even if we are in contention for the title against the team, it's good sportsmanship and the right thing to do. Nationality is irrelevant, friendship recognises no borders in the powerboating world.

This was one of the best events I had been to as far as entertainment was concerned. The welcome party at the yacht club was extravagant with limitless food and drinks for all the competitors, with a discotheque later on should we be able to squeeze in any more drinks and canapés.

I travelled to the discotheque with a group of Italians and the English followed on. At this point I'll pretend I'm twelve years old again and call it a disco because the last time I visited a 'niteclub' in Italy with racers, it was full of 'loose' women, which we found out to our detriment only when we were handed a massive bill for drinks and 'company', when a few of the ladies of the night sat with the racers. I did think the girls a bit underdressed for a night out and there were no couples in the bar, just salacious males and chicks with far too much red lipstick. Since then we have avoided anything called a 'niteclub.'

On arrival I was impressed, the disco overlooked the sea and jutted out over the beach on stilts. I had driven there with the Italians and as we parked up and walked in you could hear the sea lapping against the shoreline and all the little fairy lights hung all over the outside of the building which was also covered in flowers. The inside décor was lavish, purple and gold and the venue had many rooms and there was area sectioned off with wicker furniture around and palms lusciously draped everywhere. A lavish buffet dripping of lobster, caviar and wonderful Italian meats awaited us. It was my idea of heaven and a place where a vegetarian would certainly starve. This area also had a champagne waitress welcoming us. It was a delight and I piled straight in with the lobster and caviar. I could eat that stuff until I puke. And I have.

Everyone who entered the venue, although on a guest list, still had to be issued with a payment card. With every drink taken the card is stamped. The card is then handed in upon leaving where the bill is settled. If the card is lost a maximum price is charged so there is no cheating the system.

I had hooked up with Chris Bryan and 'Nasty' Nick, a serving Special Forces operator, they were to be my drinking partners for the rest of the evening. My race partner Ricky soon had way too much to drink as we shot triples after triples until he was comatose. I relished in my victory by taking pictures of him in various states of unconsciousness as he slumped on a wicker sofa with us firstly filling his shirt pocket with pink flowers and then placing flowers behind his ears.

Ricky is well known for taking the piss out of others but he hates people doing it to him, so the further we got with this, the more amusing it became.

The music pumped loudly as the international racers gathered around, eager to see what japes were in store away from the prying eyes of security. We took a small wicker coffee table, placed it on top of him balancing half of it on his belly, the rest over his legs with one of the table legs balancing on an adjacent drinks table. Next came the drinks menus that we managed to stand up on said table and then came the small plate of sandwiches, which took a while to steady, because no one had a steady enough hand as we were laughing so much. It was an unstable yet amusing structure. I swear I laughed so much I wet my pants a little as I stood there crossed-legged, bent over. I took a swig of booze, inhaled with laughter, choked, and Bacardi flew out of my nose and down and my cleavage, the rest landed on Chris which only exasperated an already hilarious situation. To finish off the masterpiece Nick found a 'reserved' sign and balanced it on Rick's shiny bald head. Ricky flinched not one iota.

We took a picture, paused and without a second thought, all just shouted "RICKY" at the same time. He shot bolt upright. Tables, sandwiches and signs flew everywhere.

"What the fuck? What's going on? You fucking cunts."

I was surely going to wee again. Chris had already walked off denying all responsibility. Rick, totally paralytic and clueless as to what had just happened, slumped back down after uttering more obscenities and swiftly passed out again amongst the carnage.

At closing time it was time to leave. Nick had the biggest bill, he was confused as to why there was a million stamps on his card, Chris and I feigning similar confusion yet knowing it was us that were responsible for most of them.

I had lost my card. They say with power comes responsibility and I'd also add the same goes for having a big cleavage. So I have a responsibility to use my cleavage to get me out of trouble on occasion. It worked, the security guys only mildly questioned me and believed I never had a card. Of course Italy is a country of gentlemen and the chances of me having even the smallest of tab was slim as men tend to buy the drinks.

I left the club with Brian Peedell and his wife, Pat. We had got one of the few taxis available and were dropped off just across the canal from the pits.

It was soon realised that the footbridge over the canal closed at 12 am and to cross over the regular bridge was a mile walk and there were no taxis in sight.

The water shimmered under a full moon. I swore it whispered my name.

"Fuck walking," I said, and immediately took off my clothes down to my G-string and bra. "I'm swimming, who's joining me? Come on Brian get your kit off."

I gave my clothes to the unimpressed Pat. Brian laughed and undressed. We both jumped in. This canal only served the trawlers and fishermen to sell their catch every morning. It was absolutely freezing and stunk of dead fish and diesel. It actually felt like diesel as well. It was nothing like the hotel pool. I had certainly had better ideas in my time but the thought of having to walk two miles was out of the question. I could float, but not walk at this stage of inebriation.

We slowly scrambled our way through the oily and slippery canal to the other side where there wasn't a clear point of exit. We clung onto the side of an old boat so decrepit it was a miracle it was still afloat. We looked for anything that resembled a ladder. Nothing. We were stuck.

"You didn't think this through did you?" howled Brian.

"I was more concerned with the walk than with getting out the other side," I managed to say whilst drinking diesel-filled salt water. I tried pulling myself up the side of the boat to at least get out of the water but it was covered in silt and oil. We were both in fits of laughter which didn't do us any favours because the more we laughed, the harder it was to hold on, and the harder it was to hold on, the more we laughed.

Just as we settled into the seriousness of our predicament, we heard someone stumbling about above us. It was Pat with a couple of racers. "Will you take a look at yourselves. Idiots, the pair of you," she said somewhat amused, still with our clothes in hand.

After giggling like a schoolgirl, Brian asked, "How the fuck have you got there?"

"As soon as you jumped in, funny old thing a taxi turned up. Now get out."

A couple of the racing lads hoisted me out no issues. Brian, being a bit of a lump, was more of an issue. As they struggled with Brian I sat shivering on the side laughing at him while he continued his cockney one-liners mostly calling me a prick.

After being yanked out, Brian grabbed a towel from his trailer and invited me and the lads to have another drink. Sensibly, Pat had gone to bed but we hadn't finished our night. We were joined by a few Italians and enjoyed the frivolous nature of them as they plied us with grappa. From there everything else was a blank. All I remember is waking up in the awning still damp and covered in diesel. I stunk to high heaven. My hair was matted, my makeup was halfway down my face and I was tattooed green from a form of plankton that covered me.

The last time I had woken up in such a state was in Poole, Dorset. Rick and I had been out on the lash with the lads during race weekend and as we got back to the hotel, which for some reason had checked us in as man and wife, I unsuccessfully tried to joyride a mobility scooter parked outside as it was still plugged in so it wouldn't move more than a foot no matter how much welly I gave it. Rick lifted me from it and threw me in the badly maintained goldfish pond at the front of the hotel to sober me up. He was a gentleman bastard though – he put me to bed, fully clothed and covered in plankton.

Brian walked in to the awning, fully clothed but dripping wet.

"Have you been for another swim?" I asked.

"Nah, I couldn't make the ten yards to my trailer and comfy bed. I fell asleep on the grass outside. Some wanker turned the sprinkler system on and woke me up. Farking 'ell girl you look like a zombie."

He wasn't wrong. I think death had been known to look better.

Just as the sun was beating down beyond Brian's wet, slimy back, Chris' boat canopy flicked open and out popped Chris' head. We approached Chris who was sat cramped in the tight driving position in his boat.

"You didn't sleep in there did ya?" Brian asked.

"Yeh," came the reply. I locked myself out of the camper and was too pissed to find the keys so I just slept here."

"How did you get back?" I asked.

"Well I came out of the club and you were gone." said Chris. He pointed to an old rusty bike bent on the grass where Brian had slept. "I couldn't get a taxi so I had to ride that fucking thing back!"

The bike had a bent frame, two punctures, and without a saddle. He had peddled that piece of shit for ten miles and then locked himself out and had slept in a racing seat. Needless to say he had a sore arse.

Totally emotionless he climbed out shook his head like a wet dog. "Jeez Sarah, you look rough. What happened to Nick?"

There was that hesitation of silence when we realised that one of us was missing. We were all big and ugly enough to look after ourselves but we knew we had all been so drunk anything could happen.

Rick then appeared from inside the camper. "Keep the fucking noise down will you. Fuckin' hell Sar' you look like shit."

"Yep, cheers Rick. I think it's common knowledge. I look like shit."

Nick eventually appeared as we all sat around Brian's trailer awning drinking coffee. It seemed he had decided he wasn't going to pay the bar bill so had locked himself in a toilet cubicle and attempted to climb out of a window that was way too small for a big unit like Nick. Bearing in mind he was a Special Forces operator who could break into top secret facilities anywhere in the world, he had managed to get stuck halfway through a toilet window trying to escape from a disco. It took him twenty minutes to get out, nearly dislocating most of his body in doing so. He eventually fell out of the window, rolled down the banking into some unfriendly shrubbery, and almost made the whole ten-mile trip back to the pits, still drunk as a skunk. I say almost – he woke up half in the sea half on the beach 200 metres from where we now sat.

The pits were quiet that morning. It wasn't race day so all nationalities had drank way too much. Engineers were tinkering, mithering the drivers who were more interested in sobering up with a hearty breakfast or at least the ones that could stomach one. Normally I'm a good happy drinker but the canal had taken me a step too far. I threw up in the shower as I tried to rid myself of all the grime I had gathered. Steaming water excited all the putrid smells attached to me, plankton and diesel enveloped me in a mist of rotten eggs, and I used nearly a container of shower gel to cut through the diesel. It was possibly the most horrendous shower I had ever had, and my hangover wasn't helped by the day that just got hotter and hotter. I went to the beach just so I didn't have to talk to anyone and could sleep off the day.

It was race day. We had prepared well but Chris and I still had one major admin task to complete. We had been shopping and bought some stickers of Homer Simpson. On the side of everyone's boat is their name in vinyl. We stuck the Homer stickers next to Rick's name because he had a bald head and a bit of a pot belly, indeed had he suffered from jaundice he would be Homer's double. When Rick saw them he went mad, he never did find out it was us. But karma is a bastard sometimes and someone had decided to change the graphics on Chris' boat whilst in a drunken state. Chris' boat was called *Genus Group*, but by the time the mystery culprit had finished with a Stanley knife and a bottle of vodka it had changed to *Penis Group*. As the race was being televised, Chris was severely pissed off and ready to kill someone. He never found out who did it. There are always a few days before a race to prep so always better to get the fun and games out of the way before the hard work and concentration is needed.

It was going to be a day of rough racing as we woke up and noticed the flags were rippling in the wind as the sun beat down on the pits and the sea was full of little white horses giving the game away that is was going to be a bumpy ride. The whistle blew, meaning that you had to get your arses in gear to leave the pits and follow the start boat out to the milling area. The boats would all mill in an anticlockwise direction just pottering until the two minute smoke flare went off when you would begin to look for the position on the start line you would prefer to take, bearing in mind that most people want the same place so how you go about it is trial and error, timing and a bit of luck as to where you are in your milling circle as you all peel off to line up. As usual I felt stressed and sick, normal for me on race day. My blood pressure goes sky high and until I'm clear of the messy fucked-up water that is the start chute then I don't settle. We accelerated quickly and popped up onto the water with ease due to a great choice of propeller and were straight up with the front three boats, stable and out of the aerated water being thrown about by so many boats running at similar speeds. The front three all went into the first mark at the same time, all of us perfectly banking at the same time and chasing down to the next mark. We were flying and the sea state was perfect for us.

The second turn mark approached and the other two boats took a different angle and veered off in a different direction to mine; the rest of the fleet who were not too far behind took the same route and Ricky screamed at me that I had taken the wrong line. I shouted to him to shut the fuck up and do as he was told and my line was fucking perfect and we were heading for the lighthouse that I had plotted on my written map the days previous, and which I had stuck to my dash for reference in a waterproof casing. If we were to head to the lighthouse we would hit the turn mark head on. We continued to argue for a couple of minutes as I told him to get fucked and do his own job. Soon enough we hit the turn mark and as we took her through an almost 180 degree turn we saw the other boats heading towards us but they could have been a mile behind. Every single boat had gone the wrong way apart from us, they had followed each other instead of trusting their own navigation. Racing is stressful and sometimes it is easy to follow because navigation can be so complicated in European races, however you should never follow.

It's the first rule. I always had drawings of the course taped to my dash. Like a child I used coloured felt tip pens so I knew what colour which buoy was and what to look out for. I coloured the headlands brown, the beaches yellow and drew lighthouses or masts on the mainland for lines of reference as they are much bigger and easier to see than a small turn mark bobbing up and down in the water. I also had tape on the dash, a piece of tape for each lap completed so I could rip them off one by one. I didn't always remember and sometimes it wasn't possible but I certainly tried.

As we headed back up the coast with the beaches to our right, the other boats were simply miles away. We were one of the quickest boats in the fleet so unless we broke down we had this in the bag and the beauty about being so far ahead was that you don't actually need to go balls out, causing possible damaged by over pushing. In fact by the time we were half a mile off the chequered flag we slowed right down because we simply had no need to go at breakneck speed. Rick was over the moon and I slapped him hard on his crash helmet and called him a twat for not trusting my decision. We did the whole podium thing trophies and medals but it was far from over. The main podium was not for another two days when the event would be over and the European Champions would be crowned. We still had another race to do and we knew it was going to be tough. The good news was that the longest race is always the first race and although points are the same for placings then if two boats have the same points, it's the boat that wins the longest race who takes the main prize.

It didn't take long again for race day. We changed the propeller as the water was much flatter. Our boat was quick but not as quick as the Swedes, whose boat was built for water like this. They would be running at least 4 mph quicker than us if it remained flat, but we turned quicker. We simply hoped it would blow up a bit and knew as we got offshore it wouldn't quite be as flat, and that's how the race went. On the offshore legs we caught up and overtook them, as we turned in land sheltered by the cliffs, the sea flattened off and they overtook us like we were stood still. We needed to stay ahead of the team running in third place and if we took second to the Swedes we would win the European Championships so we weren't too bothered about them, just more concerned about the team close behind us, as the Swedes had taken a second place in the first race so points were crucial. We probably took more risks during that race than we had taken before. We spoke all the way around checking on each other making sure we were both happy and did one or the other think we could do anything to get more out of the boat, these weren't deep conversation, these were short questions requiring one word answers.

The race was tough. It was one of the most stressful races I had done purely because we were so close to taking the title but anything can go wrong with boat racing, after all it's the roughest racing surface in the world, electrics and water don't mix and there can be added complications in the water causing issues, from lobster nets to the odd plank of wood. It doesn't take much to stop a race boat in its tracks. All the boats this day were running so quickly and we really had to push hard to stay up at the front. We had less than a mile to the chequered flag and the boat behind was closing on us. We were running along the bay where the water was calm and the boat behind favoured flat water. We gave everything we had as she bit at our heels and the boat was running so light and so flighty than any rogue wave would ruin us but we didn't have a choice, it was all or nothing. I could see them coming alongside but we were just a nose in front as the chequered flag was waved at us and we had taken a second place to the Swedes, and just in front of the team who had been chasing us for the entire race. We were ecstatic. We knew that we had taken the European Championship title. In 1999 I had crashed in Italy and had been on a life-support machine. It was 2001 and I was back in Italy and I was European Champion with Ricky in a fleet of only men, exactly where I like to be. Me and Rick spent the next few minutes hitting each other on our crash helmets and head butting, punching the air, waving to the helicopters above and the big spectator boat who would have had commentary for the entire event. As the other boats crossed the line and turned into the centre of the course where we all safely congregated until the race was over all the teams as usual showed their respect to each other for a safe race with no accidents and to us for a championship well earned.

There are two podiums on the final race. One for the race itself as an individual event and one for the combined effort for the overall European Championship title. The podium is always in the pits and the pits were buzzing with race crews, journalists and photographers. The crane worked nonstop lifting the boats out with the top four boats lifted out first to be weighed and checked against rulebook measurements. Meanwhile as points were calculated and other boats cleaned and put away the music started up and the podium celebration got underway. Rick and I were grinning like a couple of Cheshire cats as we clambered off the first podium call-out holding our massive trophies. Third then second place were called for the European Championship title.

As the music built up, I stood there with my face aching. I was covered in salt, my skin dry and white, my suit wet with sweat and saltwater and my hair made me look like I'd been dragged through a hedge backwards, but I didn't give a shit. A podium is not always a glamorous place, and no matter how rough we look the rewards of being handed the champagne and trophies are beyond any magical feeling. Our names were called out and we were helped up onto the top position. Punching the air and grinning from ear to ear with the national anthem playing as we stood there joyously loving every moment. Half way though the British national anthem the music abruptly changed into 'Il Canto Degli Italiani', the Italian national anthem, the Italian's all cheered as the English realised what had just happened. I had won the championship as an Italian not as an English racer. Life just got better, it was a two-finger salute at the Royal Yachting Association, a brilliant moment for me and proof that life after death is certainly sweet. As they say, 'Italian's do it better.'

My amazing family taken in the 80s

All grown up with my dad and brothers

On the Bond set with
Maria Grazia Cucinotta

Courtesy of 007 Magazine. Bond Girls L-R, Molly Peters (Thunderball) Martine Beswick and Jan Williams (Russia With Love) and me. Alongside 007 Editor Graham Rye

Driving the 007 stunt coordinators and directors down the Thames

Pearce in the jet boat hence the on-board camera

Petrol Dump explosion

Petrol Dump explosion aftermath

Speeding past the Houses of Parliament

Launching the new James Bond exhibit by abseiling into London's Trocadero

On the set with Gary Powell stuntman and co-ordinator

At the Raymond Revuebar in Soho
with the backstage crew

1993 My first year with Charles Burnett III

My first little 1.3ltr, 16ft Phantom
powerboat from CBIII

1st race, 4th place, Italy – European
Championships

Powerboat awards shenanigans. Pat
Mohan, Ian Cutler, me, Alan Layton and
Deborah Cottrell

With my teammate Deborah taking 3rd
after a tough battle around the Isle of Wight

My second boat from Pat Mohan

My third little race boat

My fourth boat 'Penthouse' given to me by
Max Walker to race for the season in 2ltr

British Nautical Awards with Nigel Mansell

Granada TV's Men & Motors Girls with Jo Guest

Presenting from the race pits for L!VE TV

Signing autographs at Capital Radio alongside Katie Richmond and
Jo Guest for Granada's Men & Motors TV show

Sky Sports interview

The boat I crashed in, 1999
with Enrico Buccerio

Racing with Giuseppe Bevilaqua,
the man that saved my life

On the podium with Giuseppe

Taking the title. European Champions

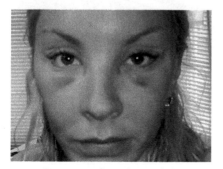

Recovering from the accident

Winning the European
Championships in Italy

Champions 2001, time to relax

Martin Lai teammate

Tom Williams-Hawkes, Martin Lai,
podium placing at Cowes, IOW

Trophy 2001 – Italy

The 41ft Pantera in the wet pits,
Cowes 2010

Powerboat P1 racing with
Italians Al & Al

Racing with Nigel Hook in Lucas Oil, USA

With teammate Karen Benson in the USA

Driving Sheikh Hassan's Class 1 in Dubai with Luca Nicolini on throttles

With Luca Nicolini in Dubai

The infamous bum shot for ZZ Top

For Soldier Magazine shot in
Marbella by Gary Tapp

Fundraising with the Royal Navy

The real James Bond, Royal Navy armourer

Adrenaline Junkie – Explaining the dunker drill

Filming Adrenaline Junkie in Dubai, Jack Osbourne,
Jesse Metcalf, me, Joanna Page, Reggie Yates

My very first winners shot in 2012 courtesy
of Kwoklyn Wan for
'Galaxy Universe Organisation'

The Galaxy Games, Europe's first ever
functional fitness pageant at the
K2 Track in Crawley

First ever Galaxy Training camp at Hooks Gym, London, 2011. Myself
and awesome Gladiator Saracen

My first Galaxy Nova
Competition in Tampa

I loved assault courses

Me and my girls in 2013, 'Miss Galaxy Universe'

Final winners shot with pyrotechnics and confetti. The best stage in the industry

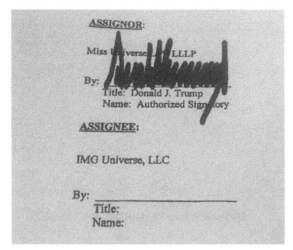

Trump suing me

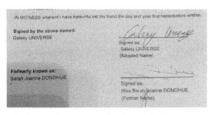

I changed my name by Deed Poll just to
irritate the other side

My abusers started soon after this post.
Poppy ironically studied psychology

Claire Bird

On the subject of DonoWHO. All the girls she leads are fucked up,
but not at fucked up as her. She professes to help women achieve
there goals but she is a c*** Im glad JH is out of there. Onwards and
upwards and she deserves everything she gets. Taking a title off a
young girl just because she won't promote your show. disgusting!!!

One of my abusers. If you don't want the
world to see it, don't write it

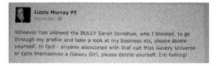

Another abuser. Her sister and
father are famous actors

Paul Corkery
19 January

If you hated someone (I'm talking hatred in capital letters, dripping in
blood, smeared with faeces and sprinkled with hundreds and thousands)
and you wanted to be a gremlin in their lives by being mischievous but
non-incriminating, what cunning ideas would YOU come up with?

Sent to prison for sexual assault in 2016
and put on the sex offenders register

Married to a police officer. Doyle ironically
started the SFN Sisterhood at Glasgow's SFN
Expo the year following abusing me – it's for
'inspiring' women. Unbelievable. Now the
truth is out showing her true colours

Super-grande
@Jason_Latham   +☺

@JodieMarsh @GoldenRivet1 @TheGalaxyGirls_ I thought u were against bullying? S. donahue is a fucking bully?!

Never even met this coward

Claire Bird
Sorry I'm not mentioning any names otherwise this post will be removed! Or I will be threatened with legal action like anyone else who has spoken up! Or someone will phone the police about FB status' - yes this really did happen! What a waste of police time!!!!!

Not mentioning someone's name is not a defence in defamation law

CJ Swaby I think it was Plato who once said, "Hell hath no fury like a Hooton scorned." – But then again I could be making that up. x
34 minutes ago · Like

Jacqueline Hooton CJ this isn't about me, this is about all the victims who were isolated, discredited and frightened. No more victims x
31 minutes ago · Like · 👍 5

Everyone knew what
Jacqueline Hooton was up to

Jacqueline Hooton with **Claire Bird** and **12 others**
38 minutes ago

This is what you get for messing with my daughter

And this is atonement for everyone I may have wronged when I believed the lies

This and more is what she orchestrated

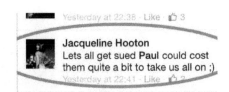

Yesterday at 22:38 · Like · 👍 3

Jacqueline Hooton
Lets all get sued Paul could cost them quite a bit to take us all on ;)
Yesterday at 22:41 · Like · 👍 3

Hooton's calculated attack and yes she DID get sued

Lucy C Doyle
As I have always said, bullies always get found out in the end
Yesterday at 22:52 · Like · 👍 3

Paul Corkery
Sued for telling the truth? Bring it on. (Y)
Yesterday at 22:54 · Like · 👍 3

Doyle and Corkery were the worst

Billy Murray   ⚙   Follow
@BillyAMurray

Look at my daughters(lizzie Murray) enterprize on f/book,'Self Defence Federation london & south East'So proud of her,its so worthwhile.

Lizzie Murray's celebrity dad

Julia Hubbard
August 15, 2013

I have to say i think Sarah Donohue has done more im one year to encourage women to enjoy a fitness lifestyle and improve confidence and self esteem and compete with healthy attitude and sportsmanship than any person or organisation i can think of- in just one year! Its a galaxy revolution im so proud to be part of. X just saying ...

Like · Comment · 👍 44 💬 22

What people actually thought of me. I have 100s of messages of thanks for helping women achieve their goals

After show flowers from the girls

My invite to 'Woman of the Year' in
London as a 'Woman of Achievement'
for helping 100s of women achieve
their goals and build confidence

Miss Galaxy Universe calendar shoot in Ibiza, villa
courtesy of Miles Jennings powerboat champion

Wedding day, Julie, Talisa, me, Averil and Vickie

A blissful moment. Three weeks after
Hooton flailed into submission

I was given away by powerboat racer and
good friend Matteo Nicolini

L-R Andy, Lowell, best man Craig and my husband in the wedding villa

With CBIII at his 60th Birthday in Colorado

Day 1 CBIII's, 60th in the especially built
cowboy town Saloon

Louise Anne Noeth better known as Land Speed Louise
alongside her husband, me and Lee at CBIII's 60th

The launch of the Asia Powerboat Series. Hong Kong September 2017
with Charlotte Camsey and the film crew

CBIII's Gorgeous Newtown Park

At CBIII's Newtown Park
with the Red Arrows

The Happy Couple

Chapter 9

Portugal – The second time I nearly died

'When did you realise I had no steering?'

It was around 2008 and I was still racing powerboats and also getting chased by magazines and newspapers for features because of being a female in a man's sport – it was unreal. Everyone wanted to interview me and photograph me and it did in all honesty sometimes get in the way of racing because it's nice to be left alone.

At this time I was racing Powerboat P1. This was a series where all the boats were big Mother Hubbards, most over 40-ft in length powered by over 1000 hp, weighing around five tons travelling from all over Europe. The P1 series back then was probably the most glamorous race series on the water with the most amazing race village set up consisting of huge marquees and hospitality units, silver service dining and champagne tents for sponsors, VIPs and racers. Models wearing very little strolled around looking utterly delightful and there were glam parties, fashion shows and everything else you would expect from a millionaires playground as it was owned by Asif Rangoonwala. It was rumoured he was the 'baker' of all bakers and supplied a major international fast food restaurant with all their buns, a far cry from the gourmet food served at a P1 event. On arrival the professionalism was second to none and it was beyond spectacular.

While I was always happy to promote the sport that had given me so much, on occasion being the only female in a man's sport was the downside to my success. When preparing for a race focus is key, so having a camera thrust in the face at every conceivable moment and having to be interviewed every two minutes could take me off my game and when it became too much I'd hide away spewing forth language my mother wouldn't approve of. I understood why – I'd been the one holding the microphone for many years but I always tried to be mindful of the racers mindset at any particular moment as I'd been there. On the glamorous P1 circuit publicity was even more intense due to sponsors liking their names spread around as much media as possible. The P1 was an amazing race series. We travelled all over the world and the event village was alive with big parties and wonderful dinners. I was racing with Martin Lai. Martin and I really worked well together and I got on really well with all the team hanging out in the pits with them and bringing them food and drink if they needed it. If they had work to do and couldn't make the evening functions, I didn't disappear, I often just stayed with the lads in my scruffs joining the party later when the lads had finished.

Our boat was a 5-ton, 41-ft monohull propelled by two 525 hp engines. She was a beast and lovely to race although with Martin on the throttles she could be hard to handle. We always had a TV crew with us as Martin was the only Chinese offshore racing driver and a big name back home.

As a female in a series as big as P1, and because of my stunt work and modelling, I was always chosen to be one of the 'lucky boats' lumbered with an on-board camera for filming. Portugal was no different; however, in addition we both had microphones slotted inside our crash helmets. Cameras are great for sponsors but we were already sorted as Martin's own crew and channel were on top of media, allowing us to concentrate on driving and not PR.

What really got on my tits here in Portugal was the new idea of microphones in the crash helmet. We already had an intercom system to communicate in the boat, which was temperamental at best, due to the extreme sea conditions. To have someone else come along to try and fit yet another piece of equipment inside the snugness of a bespoke helmet was not only uncomfortable but immensely irritating, especially when a sound guy would rip out the inside of your crash helmet to insert it as if it doesn't matter. I hate people touching my kit, so would sit there silently seething as someone rooted around in my bash hat. Positioning of the equipment is key. There's hardly a lot of room so we didn't want to eat an intercom or lose teeth during a race – it's already like doing twelve rounds with Mike Tyson. I've broken my nose thrice and just had to shrug it off, now I have a tendency to snore like a trooper because of my breathing. Yep this racing thing that people think is glamorous – ask my husband his thoughts when he is often kept awake due to my nasal thunderstorm.

The organisers had a 'hit' list on who they wanted to film and our contract with the race series gave them *carte blanche* to film whatever they wanted and now, instead of just filming us, they thought it might be interesting for the viewer to listen to how the crew speak.

'*Sod that*' I thought, '*You ain't listening to the shit that goes on in our boat.*' So I played hide and seek around the pits like a child to avoid them. I heard the producer asking pit crews if they had seen me. All denied knowledge, aware I was avoiding cameras like the plague. But eventually they caught up with me and I was taken to our boat. We had the basic interview of, 'How are you feeling?' 'How do you think the race will go?' 'What speeds are we likely to see?' This last question no racer answers truthfully. Firstly we don't want other teams knowing what speeds we can hit, and secondly it's all sea state dependent. The TV companies know this so it's a pointless question used only for effect.

After my short interview they pulled out a small blue bag containing a lip-stick cam for the deck mount, wires and microphones for our crash helmets. I frowned as the sound guy climbed on the boat still donning footwear.

"Oi, shoes," I growled. "We've spent all morning polishing that."

He apologised and kicked them off. We had a non-slip pad running down the deck as it was so highly polished that standing up on the deck would give you cartoon fast legs resulting in a visit to the hospital after falling 15 feet from it. You could use the deck as a shaving mirror it was so polished.

After attaching the abomination lip cam to the boat and having a cable tied and duck taped up the grab rail that ran central from bow to cockpit, our clean and pretty boat looked awful, like a myopic electrical apprentice's first electrocution. The lead fed into an electric box, that rarely lasted an entire race and no one but the racers seem to understand the force of nature and just how dangerous something can be should it become loose.

My engineer had just fitted my intercom, but we had to then hand over our helmets so microphones could also be fitted. I took Martin aside and asked him if he was OK with me disconnecting the microphones once on the water. Martin also didn't want anyone listening to us so it was agreed. I was sweating as I could see the sound guy removing sections of my crash helmet, designed for protection.

It was all getting too much. I had to vanish to get a coffee from one of the Italian hospitality units. Thankfully the coffee was good or I would probably have thrown it in the sound guy's face as I watched him further destroy my helmet.

"OK all done, try it on and see how it feels."

"It feels fucking awful, it's going to take my teeth out." I was getting incredibly annoyed. I'm not known for my mild manner before a race. I get high blood pressure prior to racing, so much so that in America they gave me an hour to calm down or they couldn't let me race. I get very excited, bad tempered, irritable and I can't sit still. By now I could feel the hair standing up on the back of my neck, trying my best not to burst with anger. All I wanted to do was get our kit sorted and launch the boat. Finally both our helmets fitted OK but on checking the intercom system, we found that whatever the sound guy had done, our intercom was now down and we were starting to run precariously late. We both dived inside our helmets to check for any loose connections. The sound guy stood there without a care in the world, why would he? His microphone worked, I don't suppose the safety of the drivers worried him. My engineer grabbed my arm just as I was about to explode.

By the time all camera and sound systems had been methodically checked it was all systems go. I had calmed down but was now race stressed. We did the usual radio through to safety control communications check just before being craned into the water and were awaiting for the whistle to leave the docks when, as if by magic, the sound guy walked over, leaned into the boat, down the side of my legs and flicked his system switch on I was hoping he would forget.

Right now every single word that Martin and I said was being recorded, and seriously people had no idea the shit that we talk about in a boat. Some of it isn't even about racing. If we are milling, broken down, delayed the last thing we wanted was to be recorded, after all, some of our ire was directed at the P1 organisers, some of whom we weren't keen on.

I told Martin I was due to pull the microphone connection after the third mark once the fleet had separated. It wasn't going to be easy and would be dangerous to pull it any sooner.

The whistle blew and the teams steered their brightly coloured, highly tuned, temperamental beasts away from the moorings, we idled out of the marina to the milling area following the start boat's yellow flag.

By now we all had donned our life vests and crash helmets, this was mandatory or we risked a fine or disqualification. Those with canopies had them open, those with open cockpits were still securing their lines and fenders under the relentless sun. Being covered head to foot in race overalls made of three layers of fire retardant fabric called Nomex plus a huge life vest we were all boil-in-the-bag racers.

As we left the harbour a big lulling swell hit us, the type that if we could stay on top of, we'd fly from one crest to the next and probably need to inform air traffic control. The sea state can make a race incredibly uncomfortable and catch a wave wrong it's a back breaker as water floods over and into the cockpit whilst feeling like it's ripping your head off. Either way, five tons of steel and fibreglass are being tossed like a light salad. It's natural to tense the entire body awaiting that massive slam as the boat again hits the water. The shock goes up through the spine, into the ribs and batters the internal organs. What's worse are continuous back-to-back swells, there is zero recovery time and not only is it painful but breathing becomes an issue as the lungs have just had all their spare air shunted out of them. This type of landing is often accompanied by a squeal, dropping the F bomb and the necessity of the world's best sports bra.

There was no doubt our initial racing water was going to be a back breaker, but because the water is an unpredictable racing surface that changes and moves – what we had right now was not what we may have the next moment. A following sea is a whole new game of cat and mouse, it's often softer but much wetter, it can be forgiving with the boat balanced correctly but if caught incorrectly it could submerge you, rip off a part of the boat and take the boat out of the game.

We turned out of the milling area and lined up as best we could. We went down the start chute hell for leather when the green flag dropped and Martin isn't one for backing off, so it's about keeping my line and hoping for the best because that guy either has a screw loose or massive balls and even racing with him for years I never knew which, but people always used to comment that I seemed to be the only person Martin would listen to in a boat, but that was probably because I'd raced longer and I would bollock him if he applied so much power that I couldn't corner accurately for the next course mark. We all attack the course and turn marks in different ways and the crew need to set their boat up prior to that turn mark for the next heading, and if Martin was running too quickly as we came into a turn it would fuck up my positioning. Not getting this bang on the money can really alter race positions and it's not just about lining yourself up, there are other boats and the sea state that need to be taken into account. Even in the water there can driftwood, lobster pots, ropes or nets which can damage the boat or wrap around the propeller. Racing isn't the same as hiring a ski boat or personal watercraft on holiday. It's way more complicated.

Racers can even pump fuel around the boat, weighting it differently dependant on sea state as well as shifting water around in the ballast tanks.

The first mark of the course is always the most dangerous. You are all running around the same speed going for a similar line. It's always very close and you can almost reach out and touch the boat next to you. On an unpredictable racing surface anything can happen and there is no saying that the line you are planning on keeping will stay where it is. I've raced in what I thought flat conditions and then a big fucking hole has opened up and I've nosedived right into it. You have to admire the water, it covers 70% of the earth and it's the most powerful element in the world.

We turned the first mark and headed to the second and by the third the fleet had split and we were on a long leg which gave me time to rip out the wires without damaging our own intercom. I had already inspected it first, it's just that running at 90 mph on rough water made everything much more challenging, a bit like having a cup of tea on a rollercoaster. I reached to the side of my helmet and disconnected it, and reached to the side of the boat and ripped the wires out – it wasn't a clean job by any means, I had butchered their neat work but at last Martin and I could go back to work. I also have a habit of swearing a lot in a boat and it's not something my parents would be proud of nor could it be aired, so I was doing everyone a favour. But although racing for a team is a job and part of that job is the media and everything that surrounds it, sometimes you just want a break, you don't want to be watched and listened to all the time, and I hated people touching my crash helmet, I'd fractured my skull before whilst racing, I was now precious with my safety gear.

The race was on one of the roughest seas I'd encountered. Martin and I were running in the top three. The long leg towards the port entrance was on a massive head sea, these huge waves were coming towards us. The turn we were heading towards was really sharp, close to 45 degrees, so we had to either slow and take it tight, which was preferable as we were close to shallow water, or take it wide and fast. On the approach my steering suddenly became extremely heavy. It felt like it had locked out but it hadn't. I was now holding five tons of boat in a rough sea without the hydraulic steering.

Just as I was about to tell Martin of this major catastrophe the intercom went down. *Seriously?* This wasn't good. The sea state was so punishing that damage of some kind was inevitable if not unavoidable. All teams understand that if the intercom goes down – and it happens more frequently than one would think – we communicate without words. It's not easy and depending on the boat's set-up, it can be made increasingly complicated and ours wasn't a minor communication issue where the boat was fine. We were travelling at speed about two miles to a tight turn and I wanted Martin to back off into it so I could throw the boat round the mark with him piling on the power to pull us out of it as I straightened up. Without power steering I was struggling to hold her in a straight line. I had about two miles to sort this. Yes, I could pull the engine kill, but that was a last resort and with boats up my arse, it was extremely dangerous. I was shouting at Martin but he had no chance of hearing me. I held the wheel tightly with one hand and banged on Martin's hand on the throttle for a millisecond to get his attention but all I got was Martin inanely grinning at me through his visor and giving me a thumbs up. He was having a great time. Holy fucking shit – something was telling me this wasn't going to turn out well.

I tried banging again and again but he was in the zone and hydraulic steering never faults so why would he think I had a steering issue? Any other issue would be shown on our gauges or felt in the boat, yet she was running like a dream. We now had less than a mile to the next mark and I was running out of ideas. Another team came up on our inside, we still had right of way but they were running close. Martin ran her faster and lighter which in this situation was not good. I banged on Martin's hand again but he still didn't get it. I couldn't do more than bang because our bodies were being thrown all over the place in rough water and any limbs not attached to the boat are thrown around like leaves in a gale force wind.

The other team backed off, crossed our wash and came around on our outside. This was worse, much worse, given the dangerous situation we were in, and potentially deadly. They came alongside within touching distance, which meant by the time we got to the mark, they could well have right of way. They tried to push us off course slightly to allow them a better line for the turn mark. Even with every muscle in my body I could hardly move the wheel and the five-ton boat seemed to get heavier and heavier and I had half a mile at best to do something as I fought like Frodo protecting his ring just to keep her in a straight line and not hook. Hooking is the boat equivalent of a politician performing a drastic policy U-turn – the boat violently switches direction 180 degrees and goes from 100 mph to 0 mph in a split second, usually resulting in the crew being catapulted into the sea like so many disillusioned voters.

Those who have the right of way always dictate a turn and even then drivers trust each other to turn at the same time even when running rubber to rubber. As soon as the boat on our outside would start to bank and turn, the expectation is that we naturally bank and corner with them. If we didn't we'd crash and someone could be seriously hurt, it's that simple. Every muscle in my body was straining.

As we came up to the mark where Martin would expect me to set her up and I would be usually shouting to him to back off whilst I threw her around the mark, I was helpless and I could do nothing other than clench my body tightly bracing for impact making myself a small target in preparation of a devastating high speed crash, much bigger than the one that had put me on a life-support machine a few years earlier and one that I surely would not survive. I shrank into my bolster gritting my teeth with the grim expectation of the impending collision, sure-fire hospitalisation or a one-way trip to the morgue.

Both boats closed into the turn mark at speed, the other boat was now ahead and had right of way. I shut one eye and waited for impact and ultimately death. I wasn't scared, I just thought, *if the crash doesn't kill me, mum will!*

I inhaled deeply, squinted and waited for impact as we were upon the mark. All of a sudden the boat felt like it was in mid-air and it then came to a halt just outside the course. '*What happened?*' I ripped open my visor, and looked at Martin to see where we were, my eyes were like saucers. Martin, his hand still on the throttles, had his visor open, wearing a big grin. We were about twenty metres from the turn mark in a straight line from where we should have turned.

I had escaped death a second time. I could see Martin giggling. I just burst into fits of laughter and couldn't recover, it was a nervous yet raucous laugh of disbelief. At the final nanosecond Martin backed off the throttle and momentum coupled with the sea state catapulted us over the top of the other boat as they turned directly underneath us and looked up at our hull as we flew overhead. The helicopter footage even made it onto one of those world's most amazing near miss TV shows. How the fuck we didn't kill ourselves and the other team I have no idea.

I banged the steering wheel whilst doing a cut-throat sign language to Martin to tell him we had no steering. He shrugged. We needed points so there was only one option – continue. I tried to tell Martin that five tons is heavy by flexing my Nomex covered biceps and pointing to the wheel. He nodded. We both knew the risks. I pointed forward onto the course. He was about to bang down the throttles for a high speed start when I leaned over and slapped his helmet hard to sign language that if I hit his throttle hand it meant slow down because I couldn't take the corner. He gave a thumbs up and hit me back on the helmet twice as hard for good measure.

We returned to the race. Many boats had broken down, offshore racing is often about enduring the race and simply finishing. We were back on the line and Martin floored it, clearly with no idea how heavy five tons of dead boat is. I signalled to him to back off as I needed to take her to the port a few degrees. As long as I could keep Martin on track and watch the gauges to make sure we didn't sustain any more problems we were ready for the final lap.

I must have slapped Martin's hand about twenty times. Martin ran with no fear and he didn't realise that the entire steering system had gone, he just thought it was a little bit heavy. Eventually we crossed the finish line and turned into the middle of the course. I radioed for immediate assistance and I put the boat under tow. I told Martin to switch off and I climbed onto the deck and got the ropes out as the safety boat came over and threw us a line. I radioed that both crew members were fine but we had no steering and couldn't safely make it back to the Marina.

As we reached the wet pits in the marina we were glad to be back. Martin and I removed our safety gear and gave each other a huge hug. Neither of us said much other than "That was tough."

As the situation had occurred close to the entrance of the port our team had watched on binoculars and couldn't work out what had happened but were there waiting to find out.

"We had no fucking steering." I blurted. "I thought we were going to die."

The crew chief said, "You did that last lap with no power steering?"

"Yes."

He shook his head. "I have no idea how you even held onto her, never mind steer."

My biceps were so pumped I could barely hold anything, I just silently thanked heaven that I was much stronger than I looked due to so much weight lifting.

Martin and I stood knackered on the pontoon grinning at each other. We hadn't yet managed to speak about what had happened.

I said, "When did you know my steering had gone?"

"Just as the other boat turned in and you didn't go to turn with her. We were about to T-bone her so I knocked the throttle off and the size of the wash that kicked back actually threw us over the top of them."

The guys in the other boat came up and spoke to us afterwards. Both were laughing and said they actually saw the entire bottom of our boat and propellers as it leaped over them. They thought we were going to land on top of them but with them moving so quickly and with the sheer momentum of the water we went straight over the top. To say it was a close shave was an understatement. They came to our truck for a few post race beers wiping the sweat off their brows and counting their lucky stars. Anything can happen in offshore.

Chapter 10

Oh to dance with ZZ Top

'Fuck off. No fucking way.'

Whilst writing this book I've had many emotional moments, bringing back memories and reminiscing about the past. I've always been a firm believer in grabbing opportunities and seizing the moment and whilst some have worked out, there are more that haven't, but I've shrugged things off and moved on. One I will never forget and it changed the way I dealt with whatever life throws at me and makes me take every opportunity no matter what. It's my only regret in life.

It was back in my early 20s. I had moved in with my boyfriend Michael who I'd met a couple of years previously at the celeb drenched Midem Festival – the music industry's equivalent of the Cannes Film Festival – when I had been working for Square One Studios in Manchester with Derek Brandwood who worked with Stock, Aitken and Waterman. It was an exciting time of my life and allowed me the luxury of meeting so many people. Michael worked for ASCAP in London (American Society of Composers, Authors and Publishers) He was a couple of years older than me, super intelligent and quick-witted. Michael was second in command to a portly pompous gay guy who rolled around on a six-figure salary looking like a red snooker ball after a few drinks with his Rudolph-esque nose and bald shiny head. Both had huge expense accounts that they squandered on wining and dining music industry professionals and musicians, whilst speaking bollox over long lunches. I ended up moving in with him albeit looking back I wished I hadn't. There was no talking on Sunday mornings whilst the entire *Sunday Telegraph* was viewed over perfectly ground coffee. It was like dating a pensioner minus the smell of lavender and bedpans.

It was actually a pretty cool life with Michael and having the job I had at the Raymond Revue. I went to all the big parties in the west end, especially the Christmas functions for BMI Records, Sony Music. I was backstage at gigs hanging out with huge names and even had coffee on occasion with Paul McCartney and his daughter Mary. I became so well known on the circuit I didn't need Michael to get invited to things; I was out most nights of the week from Groucho club to Soho House mixing with everyone from George Michael to Annie Lennox, I can't ever remember not being near a free bar in those days as everyone's expense accounts and open bar tabs allowed those chosen few to lead a carefree existence. I turned on the radio and heard that ZZ Top were looking for dancers for their upcoming tour through a competition ran by *The Sun* newspaper. I bought the paper to see what it was all about. Michael wasn't at home which was handy because he didn't allow trash newspapers in the house and if I bought anything he considered wouldn't nourish my little grey cells he just threw it in the bin.

The Sun's request was for girls to send in a photograph and their CV of where they had danced, their training experience and why they would be great as a ZZ Top dancer. If you lied you were royally fucked and would simply embarrass yourself and there would always be someone to step in your shoes. I thought I'd be perfect for ZZ Top, a go-go dancer, strong body, fit and loved being scantily clad on stage, it's what I did day in day out. It was the Recycler Tour and the first gig would be Milton Keynes.

I wrote a fairly amusing letter, and searched for a picture that I knew would blow their socks off as these guys wouldn't even read the letter unless they liked the photograph. Bingo! I found the perfect shot and started to giggle. This was either going to make or break it but it was the best to get their attention.

Most girls would send a head shot to show how pretty they were, or a full length swimsuit shot maybe or a dance shot. Not me. I sent them a photo of my arse. The shot caught the bottom of my long curly hair down to a high waist G-string and was cropped from just above the waist down to the mid thigh. The bottom line (excuse the pun) was ZZ Top was 'all about the arse'. If they didn't like it then there was little I could do. I sealed it and posted it recorded delivery. I didn't tell Michael. It was a bit of fun and no way was I going to be one of the four girls chosen from thousands across the UK, so my days carried on as normal.

Two weeks later I had just got out of the shower when the doorbell rang. It wasn't the postman, it was man wearing a peaked cap and gloves standing in front of a luxury car. He checked my name, and handed me an envelope before driving off. I put the envelope down on the living room table and continued with my morning routine. When I finally sat down I realised I still had to open the envelope on the table. I opened the envelope having forgotten that I had even entered the competition. I sat there dumbfounded as the words ZZ Top jumped off the page and hit me on the end of the nose. My eyes widened like a rabbit in the headlamps. Shivers ran through my body, my hairs stood on end as if someone had walked over my grave and I became flushed. I felt a little bit sick and I'm sure I felt the blood drain away from my limbs making them weak as my heart pounded so fast I thought I was going to have a heart attack. Holy fuck. I had been picked as one of ZZ Tops dancers for their tour *'Fuck off. No fucking way.'* I don't know how long I sat stunned for but when I went to drink my coffee it was tepid. I was to call the number to say I had received the letter. I would be picked up by car a couple of days later and taken into central London to a hotel where myself and three other girls would do a publicity shoot with ZZ Top for *The Sun* newspaper and from then we would be given other information and rehearsal details. I was fucking dreaming. I wanted someone to come in and punch me or at the very least hit me with something until I woke up. I didn't move for several minutes. I would have moved but my legs didn't work as the blood was still surging to my heart giving me palpations.

I phoned my mum to tell her, she was dumbfounded and said I deserved it as I was one of life's grafters. I wanted to tell Michael but he was at work, so not being able to contain the excitement I called him and arranged to meet for lunch at Café Fish my favourite restaurant on the Haymarket. Bubbling over I didn't even wait until we had ordered as I just spewed the great news to him. I expecting him to have a huge smile and be happy for me. After all, it's every dancers dream to hit the big stage. Michael just looked at me and asked in a telling way,

"You're obviously not considering it are you?"

"Of course I am, this is just amazing."

"Don't be ridiculous. It's embarrassing. I'm not having my girlfriend gyrating on stage with ZZ Top when I know their manager. It's embarrassing for me."

"This isn't about you it's about me and I thought you would be happy?"

"Ugh, preposterous," he said with disgust. "You need to think long and hard about this because if you do it then we are over."

I was devastated. What sort of cocksucker gives his girlfriend that sort of ultimatum? It was a very sombre lunch and I was very sad, I couldn't even speak. He changed the conversation as if he hadn't even heard my news in the first place. I didn't listen and was too busy trying to decide if to just get up and leave. As I got home I phoned my mum very upset. She told me to do it regardless as I may never get the chance again, I was even more confused. I look back now and I remember 'young love', I presumed it really was love but it was preparation for true love and a lesson on how to cope with the many mistakes and choices good or bad that come our way. He returned home and asked me if I had made a decision and warned me again it would be over and I could pack my bags. For the first time in my life I didn't know what to do. The next couple of days I walked around like a zombie and had a feeling that I may have to kiss a few more frogs before I found my prince.

The big day came. I hadn't slept. I was sad and the life had drained out of me. I had done my hair and make up and I was sat waiting for the driver to pick me up. I was still confused. This was the biggest thing that had ever happened to me and could map out the rest of my career. A photo shoot with the biggest band in the world and then rehearsals. There was a knock on the door. I felt sick. I was frozen to the spot. There was another knock at the door and a few moments later the phone rang. I was shaking and desperately trying not to cry because of my makeup. I didn't answer it. I sat on the stairs staring at the door knowing that on the other side was a world I wanted to be in, but at the same time I would have lost a man I thought I loved. I sat on those stairs for hours motionless, I was numb, the life sucked out of me like a wispy corpse. My head had been leaning against the wall for so long there was a perfect profile print of my face against the once brilliant white paint.

When Michael arrived home I knew right there and then I didn't want him anymore and that I had made the biggest mistake of my life. I picked up a copy of *The Sun* newspaper the following day and there it was, ZZ Top and three girls in hot pants. The fourth was missing, she was heartbroken wanting to turn back time but couldn't. To this day it haunts me, but it taught me a valuable lesson in life and I take every opportunity life throws at me and I will never allow anyone to dictate my future. If someone loves you, they should love unconditionally. This single experience taught me more about love, life and opportunity than anything. Every day is a school day. No one should hold us back from our dreams. If someone truly loves you, they will set you free and know you will return.

***

I'm fortunate that grabbing so many opportunities has led me to some awesome moments. It is about accepting that the rough comes with the smooth, the good comes with the bad and all life experiences make us strong.

It was way back in my 30s I heard through an internal source at Shine Productions that *Gladiators* was making a comeback. My friend who worked at Shine had given me a heads up knowing I was perfect for the show so I called my manager Steve Markbride at Big Bang Management and Steve knew that without any shadow of a doubt there was no one more suited. The open search wasn't to go live for a few weeks but it was said to get my info over asap. At this point in my life I had already won a world fitness title in the USA and was on the way to nab another. Obstacle courses, muscle endurance tests and games that put stress on the body were key to my enjoyment, competitions and lifestyle and I was still modelling full time. I was made for this.

This is my version of events. Accurately remembering audition numbers, who joined in at what process of the audition period and in what order we did things within the audition process I can't precisely say. Only that it was a long six-week process.

I went in to the Shine offices and spoke to reception. The receptionist looked somewhat confused when I asked to speak to either a researcher on *Gladiators* or the producer. She disappeared and someone came out and asked how I knew that *Gladiators* was in pre-production. I didn't give away my source and politely handed her my file. I was ready. Makeup, big hair, a screaming tan, tall, blonde, pearly white teeth, big tits and athletic-looking with a massive smile, gregarious personality, confident, polite and lively, what more did they need? Admittedly my only downfall throughout my career so far was that everyone always said I was almost too Americanised for mainstream UK TV. Even legendary NASCAR driver Dick Trickle on interviewing him at Daytona Raceway asked if I was England's answer to Jenny McCarthy. That said it all really, the biggest compliment I'd ever had, but no doubt I would have got more work in the UK if my personality didn't resemble a firecracker and my looks were more demure. I always felt more at home in the States than the UK, the girls were simply buffer and louder.

I thanked Shine and disappeared onto the streets of Notting Hill where colourful characters waltzed down the streets, often so stoned they lived in cloud cuckoo land or under a haze of fairy dust, and the others sat there playing their phallic looking didgeridoos expecting passers-by to drop some loose change in their cap.

Several months later the call came through to my manager Steve. I had got through the initial clear out of pointless applicants, many I imagine with the muscle endurance of slug. There were thousands that had applied and they had narrowed it down to about sixty of us and the audition was at the military base in Greenwich. On arrival and looking around at my competition all seated on wooden chairs in a hall, there was a lack of colour and personality in the room. Spending so much time in the USA I was used to a different type of girl, none of whom were there, so this was the best of an ever-so-British looking bunch. I mean no disrespect to Brits but competing in some of the most physically demanding tests against thousands of girls from across America, there is a distinct difference in all that they are and I'm used to going up against bionic bombshells and being nervous just looking at them.

I did however notice a very good friend. She was a professional boxer and packed a powerful punch in a small pretty package. We had worked together on two separate TV shows and had a lot of fun. BBC's *Can't Cook Won't Cook* and *a Diet Doctors* special for CH4 alongside four Olympic athletes.

During the initial audition we had paperwork to do and were told all about *Gladiators* and the process we would be going through over the coming weeks. We would be narrowed down in numbers over the coming six weeks and four of us would make the cut. We also had a very short and simple fitness test but as there were so many of us it lasted all day. The six weeks all blended into one but from a hazy memory, about thirty girls were sent packing and about thirty of us went through to the next audition. I kept in contact with Steve continuously because we knew from the get go I had this in the bag. It wasn't overconfidence but we all know our own strengths and weaknesses we have developed over the years and there is no harm in 'knowing' who you are. This was an audition which embraced all my key strengths and absolutely zero of my weaknesses. That would be eating cockroaches and sitting still.

Every girl had turned up looking fairly dull in black and dark blues, I had turned up in my favourite bright Bebe Sport kit leaving little to the imagination, and I was functional unlike many girls in the fitness industry that think they are just because they look athletic. So I knew I was the entire package. I had been built by Mark Jarvis, one of the UK's best conditioning coaches famous for coaching MMA fighters, Hollywood celebs and boy band One Direction.

I loved fitness tests and running assault courses. I'd even gone head to head with sections of the American military and ran military assault courses here in the UK. I worked for Granada as a TV presenter so my camera work was on point and I was also an entertainer. I was happy and ready.

The auditions were filmed, with the second audition being gym-based fitness tests and a mini assault course. We were split into two teams of about fifteen running the course with one from each team running together. We were timed individually and as a team. I was the fastest with the strongest plyometric ability as our times and reps were recorded. Plyometric work is a discipline lacking in the majority of people that do any and all gym work. Plyometric work is high impact work so think repetitive hopping, jumping, etc. People avoid this type of work unless they are actually training for a sport because it is simply tiring and tough using the biggest muscle groups in the body continuously over and over. But plyos are the best form of exercise for many things from burning fat, increasing the heart rate, stamina and endurance, shaping the glutes and legs. There simply is no downside to plyos apart from the fact they are fucking tough when done repetitively. Most of my plyometric work was weighted so at the audition, my heart rate barely moved.

I also supported my team members and ran round the course with the weaker ones pushing them as all teammates should. Or at least we did that in the USA.

I knew I would be at the next audition. I phoned Steve and told him I was through 100%. Self-belief is everything. The next audition came and it was narrowed down again to about twenty of us all taking a drug test urinating into a container which was then split into two containers, signed and sealed by us and sent off. We filled in a form on the current medication, or energy drinks we were taking which could possibly ring alarm bells and then at this audition we had the filmed interview. I enjoyed this process because I did this every day as a career. One of my favourite jobs was working with TV presenter Nick Knowles for Meridian TV's *H2O Show* based in Southampton. Sometimes I laughed so much with Nick I couldn't even get my lines out. I once had to ask that when we spoke on camera he didn't look me directly in the eye or I'd just fall apart. It happened when presenting at the London Boat Show. Even the producer and crew started to laugh as the crowds gathered to see what was happening. Nothing was happening, there were just two presenters sat on top of a 'Batboat' that simply had the giggles for an astounding ten minutes.

***

Other girls in the room looked nervous, not everyone loves the camera. I filed my perfectly manicured talons and wore very little, although it screamed with colour. My mane of blonde curled hair cascading down, teamed with immaculate makeup. I was pulling out all the stops. I had gone in looking as a Gladiator would for the TV show. Why let them imagine me in the role when I can turn up and show them?

The final audition came and there were about ten of us. Four were going to become Gladiators and one reserve. Although my memory is slightly hazy from so long ago, by the time we got to the last audition there were about three girls who had appeared along the way having not done the entire six week process which raised eyebrows. They hadn't completed all stages and we were told categorically at the first audition that four girls from that very room would become Gladiators. It's not easy to remember every face at every audition but between the top girls we were aware of who was who. These six weeks had been tough.

But who were these new and chosen girls? We knew that these girls had been dropped in and this was a mere formality for them, it isn't unusual in media as everyone knows. I've worked in the business long enough to know that. But regardless I soldiered on. I was bound to be better so my aim was to go in hard during the next task.

There were three circles drawn on the wooden floor of the old military gymnasium which looked like it needed some tender love and care and a repaint. The annoyingly new number of around twelvish now partnered up into pairs. The game was for each pair to stand in the middle of the circle, grab each other and on the whistle push the other out of the ring. Like a sumo but without the fat gut and nappy. Out of the girls I was asked to take on maybe six of them.

The first girl got in with me, two seconds later she was out of that circle. The TV crew presumed she wasn't ready so asked us to go again. She felt so light I just cast her aside like a rag doll. The other circles the girls were fighting it out and after sixty seconds unless someone was out the whistle blew. I watched the others unimpressively battle it out. Some of them lasted the entire sixty seconds and with this amount of energy expended unless they conserved it they would all be knackered very soon. I hadn't broken a sweat. Mark had built me for staying power.

The next girl faced me, she was out within two seconds again. It was the first time we had all gone head to head as everything else was exercise focused. By the time I got to the fourth girl the sound guy was laughing albeit quietly as it was funny. Finally the last girl got in the ring. She was one of the new girls and my last challenge. She was blonde like me, there were only three blondes, two of us bright blonde and as far as I could see it, they would only be taking one blonde through and my issue was that most of us by now had a sneaky feeling it was rigged.

I had one aim. To prove that I was stronger and fitter in every aspect. We stood in the middle and grabbed each other both with full weight on the other getting ready for the whistle.

The whistle blew, my legs bent making me stand fast, a small target and every bit of power in me was exerted through my upper torso as I pulled her towards me to put her off balance and threw her past me to the side. The blonde bounced across the floor and landed about four metres away from the ring, most of her time spent in the air before crashing down on the hard wooden floor. She yelped in pain as her coccyx hit the ground sending shivers up her spine. Whoops. She was about the same height as me but didn't carry my depth of muscle or weight. She grabbed her back in pain and I suddenly realised we had been told not to hurt each other so I rushed to her side with a look of concern on my face, maybe she should have upped her game and not come in at the last minute. It felt like I was tossing a papier-mâché doll through the air. I apologised to the production team.

"I'm so sorry I didn't realise she was so light."

First round over, second round was holding onto a broomstick and pushing or pulling your partner out of the circle. The only girl that gave me any trouble was the black girl, she towered over me and was much bigger, she was a seriously gorgeous Amazonian type girl so I really had my work cut out with her. I hadn't been teamed with her in the first round. We were both still in the ring when the final whistle blew. It was the first real competition I had had in six weeks although she flailed behind on fitness and endurance which for success is key on many events. But she was very good and had been with us since day one.

The audition process had now come to an end. I phoned Steve to tell him the good news about how the final audition had gone and that the only way I couldn't get on was if it was rigged, Steve agreed with me, after all he's my manager and knew me better than anyone. I had gone over on my ankle right at the very end of the day but fortunately it was time to sit and wait. Getting this wasn't just about ability although that was key, it was about looking right for the part, not being shy and being confident in front of the camera. I ticked all those boxes. The moment of truth arrived.

Steve phoned Shine and a member of the team came on the phone and said, "Unfortunately not this time." Normally a manager would take that on the chin, win some lose some and so would I, and my trainer. But Steve didn't because it was almost impossible. He requested an explanation but had no joy. I had the right look, body, skill level, strength, power, endurance, the ability to perform at any level under pressure and on TV. I looked like one of the American Gladiators and I had out performed everyone with control and professionalism. I was never outspoken and always polite and respectful. I had the full package.

This was the first time I had ever questioned losing a job after an audition. I had been in theatre since age 11 and been to thousands of castings as a model. Sometimes not getting an audition or modelling job we ask, "Is there anything I can focus on next time?" or we simply ask for pointers, but I NEVER complain or question. But this was very odd and my boxer friend who also auditioned called me once she had seen the 'Gladiators' chosen and asked what was going on. We both only recognised one girl from day one. It could have been great make-up and hair dye but either way, only one girl was up to my standard or even my friends and she was on the show, the rest we seriously didn't recognise from having been there from the very first day, we could have been mistaken of course and there are many reasons people don't get through castings, but this was different.

I hadn't told anyone I was auditioning at the time and a few days later a gym regular Josh casually asked how training was. I didn't even have time to answer before Mark swept in and said about *Gladiators*. Josh wide-eyed said he was one of the set builders on both the original and new *Gladiators*. He said he wished he had known I was going for it because he would have told me not to focus all my energy on it because they already had ideas on who they wanted.

It was apparently part of a deal of having a well-known face back on the show which had happened at some point during the six week process. That person wanted a say in who became Gladiators. We weren't surprised. The TV world has always been part casting couch, part set up and part real deal, I shrugged it off. I'd met some amazing people. I had trained none stop for six weeks and loved it so all was good. Naturally I was disappointed but that's showbiz.

My manager Steve threw Shine a curveball. When they were advertising for contestants. Steve phoned them and put me forward. Shine wouldn't even audition me. Steve asked why, after all, they knew I made good TV and they knew I would be a good contestant without even needing to audition me and I looked good. They didn't offer him an explanation. Steve told me they were never going to allow me on *Gladiators* as a contestant because it could be embarrassing having seen what I was capable of. When I told Mark my trainer they turned me down as a contestant, he grinned and laughed, "Take it as a compliment."

Always look at things on the bright side. It was the biggest compliment I had ever had.

Chapter 11

What? This much fun with my clothes on?

'Like a cheap German prostitute – packed full of seamen.'

The British Armed Forces are widely considered to be the finest in the world. They are unique in many respects; from their professionalism in the field to their ability to arbitrarily strip naked in a bar and drink until their eyes fall out, you would be hard pressed to find a more consummate and loyal bunch of individuals. Ask any serving or former member of Her Majesty's finest a seemingly simple question and you will undoubtedly be subjected to a creeping barrage of sarcasm and insults more suited to a front row roasting at a Frankie Boyle show than a casual conversation in a bus queue. But, if you want someone by your side in a sticky situation then look no further. Far from being a social repellent, it was these endearing qualities which cemented my staunch and on-going support for our nation's paragon of altruism, integrity and hard drinking.

The military has always had its mascots and the pinup has long been a mainstay of forces life; from the buxom beauties adorning the noses of aircraft to the saucy posters garnishing immaculate bed spaces and lockers, the pinup has a distinguished service record as a beacon of beauty in an otherwise grotesque sea of bombs, bullets and blood. The propaganda posters of WW2 encouraged everyone to 'Do Your Bit', so this led to my appearing several times as a pinup in *Soldier Magazine* – the official periodical of the Armed Forces. I'd also spent time with SSVC Forces Entertainment (think *It Ain't Half Hot Mum* on steroids) and graced the airwaves on BFBS radio – probably more Terry & June than Terry Wogan but God loves a trier. As my involvement on the Home Front grew, so did my passion for our guys and girls serving Queen and Country. I loved fundraising for different military charities such as 'Combat Stress' and being involved in any and all things military that a humble, albeit ample breasted, civilian could assist with.

During my years of racing boats and working alongside the Armed Forces at various events, I spent time at different bases getting involved in all manner of different things and it was always lovely to get an invitation to wherever it was. On one occasion, I was very fortunate to be invited to an event in Gibraltar – that 6.8 square kilometre piece of British headland dominated by the infamous Rock and serving as a regular stop-off point for British servicemen and women on their way to warmer waters. It was also to do with Offshore Powerboat Racing as we were having our World Championships out there later that year so I was flown out to meet 'VIPs' and enjoy everything Gibraltar had to offer. Now, if you were to ask any member of the Armed Forces about these offerings, they would regale you with tales of enforced runs up the Rock, being assaulted by the indigenous Barbary Macaques and losing their clothes in one of Gibraltar's many drinking taverns – although not necessarily in that order. I, however, was new to the potential delights that this jewel in Britain's overseas crown had to offer so was, for the moment, blissfully optimistic. Wayne Warwick was my main point of contact. He was a clean cut, square jawed Clark Kent lookalike standing about 6'4" with tanned skin and short cropped dark hair. He wore glasses (although a monocle would have been far more fitting) and had a big, perfect Steeplechase Face smile which reflected a keen and witty sense of humour.

Having a racing event in Gibraltar was unusual to say the least especially as the Gibraltar Straits were infamous for drug-running between Spain and Morocco. Consequently there were enforced speed limits everywhere with police patrolling the harbours and open seas as best they could. Under the circumstances, it had taken a lot of work on Wayne's side to organise and get this event authorised, owing to the obvious complications involved. The speed limit had to be lifted for the event however this meant that testing times were strict and under no circumstances could you deviate from the testing area – one lapse of concentration by your navigator could result in the unexpected addition of flying bullets to the menu of obstacles that the open water had to offer.

As I stepped off the plane at the modest airport of Gibraltar the heat hit me like a hammer and I was so happy to be away from grey, bleak UK climate. I was privileged to be greeted by a military guard of honour including Wayne himself, several officers with chests adorned with medals and a very large bouquet of flowers. I felt like royalty as I was shown to a car and chauffeur-driven to my hotel. I was due to stay around four days and it promised to be an action packed stay for sure as I was given my itinerary. First stop was the hotel to check in, a change of clothes and then I was to meet Wayne in the lobby. I was taken on a fascinating historical tour of Gibraltar and, as I hadn't been before, I loved every minute. The first stop was HMS *Tireless,* a damaged nuclear submarine that belied its name as it languished, inoperable, in the harbour. The closest I had been to a submarine before was watching *The Hunt for Red October* so the sheer scale of the vessel coupled with the cramped working and living quarters was a real eye-opener. Unfortunately, Sean Connery wasn't on board but you can't have everything.

Next we moved onto the caves and the underground theatre. Now without turning this into an impromptu Alan Wickeresque tourist guide I won't go into too much boring detail. Suffice it to say that they were impressive and need to be seen to be believed. I was taken down a desolate road with Wayne and a couple of smartly uniformed soldiers. In front of us loomed a dark arched opening into the rock but it was gated off and padlocked as are most of the tunnels.

One of the soldiers briskly hopped out and unlocked the gates, pulled them back and, as we drove through, he locked the gates again with us seemingly imprisoned inside the dark cold rock. The temperature difference changed dramatically and instantly (like being hit with another, slightly colder hammer) as I put my hoodie on for a bit of warmth. As we drove slowly but deliberately through the dark tunnel, my attention was drawn to an emergency type of lighting dimly illuminating the rough rock floors and arched tunnel around us, forming a network of ominous shapes in the shadows. As we went deeper into the rock, the shadows began to take on different, more familiar manmade shapes. As my eyes adjusted to the light it was evident that these shapes were boats, stacked either side of the make shift road in some places three high. It was a haunting menagerie of seemingly abandoned seafaring vessels; from large craft to ski boats, jet skis and engines in abundance piled up for miles all along the side of the road like a maritime elephant's graveyard. I got the guys to stop and I jumped out of the open-top jeep and stood there trying to comprehend the almost surreal sight before me. There must have been hundreds of powerboats and engines littered around the tunnel. This bizarre spectacle rendered me almost speechless although I still managed to ask what the fuck all the boats were doing in here piled up like a giant game of Jenga. It became apparent that all these boats were not abandoned, but had been confiscated by the Military Police because they either belonged to drug runners or were captured breaking the speed limit. Not only was there a speed limit but the engine size was restricted and, if you had a boat with a big engine and you ran it in the Straits then it would simply be stopped, boarded and confiscated. So this underground tomb was the result of years and years of boats breaking the law; speeding, smuggling drugs and arms or simply being deemed too powerful, they all ended up here. My eyes were wide open and my mind was uncharacteristically working on overdrive. I was looking at all the engines and, although many of them would be useless, there were many Mercury XR2's (the chosen engine of the Class III racer across Europe) and whether they were in working condition or not, they had parts in them which would be worth a considerable amount back in the UK. So without thinking I just blurted out,

"If these aren't used for anything then it's such a waste. If I arrange a container or way of shipping, can I take all the XR2's back to the UK?"

Clearly I had not engaged my brain that morning. It was swiftly pointed out to me that the Ministry of Defence owned everything in the tunnels and they could not be removed let alone shipped anywhere; indeed they were, as my previous analogy alluded to, left there to rust in their nautical necropolis. Desperate to cash in on this veritable Aladdin's cave I even offered to split the profits but that went down like a fat child on a seesaw. I jumped back in the jeep still dreaming about what might have been if I could have shipped them all back, the pound signs in my eyes fading swiftly away.

Our next stop was (yet another) gate. We were now getting even deeper into the rock and it continued to drip with both water and history. The walls themselves were festooned with holes where the cannons and other guns that protected the rock had once stood. Further on we reached an area where the rock opened up into a concert hall. It was a grand theatre hidden inside which had a full complement of seats and different levels, specialist lighting, lit areas of the wall, but essentially we were just inside a big cave; no heating, no carpets no home comforts just a beautiful grotto decked out like a concert hall. As I didn't know anything about the inside of the rock, it was even more of a surprise for me as my jaw fell open. We were the only ones in there as it wasn't the normal tourist season so I enjoyed my private look around and I bounced around all the levels and off the walls, drinking in the majesty of this underground auditorium. It was probably one of the most wonderful experiences of the trip because I simply was not expecting anything so grand inside the heart of a rock. As we emerged out of the tunnels, locking all gates behind us we made our way back to the hotel where I was to get dressed for dinner.

I was collected later that evening and taken onto the military base and was received by several dashing young men in uniform, then escorted into the wardroom where I was led to a table surrounded by six uniformed gentlemen. They all politely stood up as I entered, introduced themselves and showed me to my seat. My eyes almost popped out of their sockets at this point; after all, what lady doesn't love to be surrounded by men in uniform?

We were the only people in the wardroom. It was closed off for us and I wish I'd worn my sunglasses as there was more gold braid on show than a royal garden party. There were the same amount of waiters as there were dining guests and the table was laid to a standard higher than any Michelin starred restaurant I had ever visited. It's also fair to say that the food was on a par, if not better than some of the finest restaurants I have had the privilege to dine in – the standard of food served that evening was really outstanding. The food was only matched by the company. I had been seated next to a naval 'Sea Lord'; quite the honour considering his high status which, it turned out, isn't the equivalent of Poseidon releasing the Kraken, but an exceptional Admiral – and not the insurance company although he did smell faintly of halibut but that may have been the fish course. It had been my first day on the rock and it had been mind blowing. The dinner lasted a couple of hours. We drank coffee, port, rum, shared jokes and enjoyed each other's company. I loved listening to their conversation and it was a shame when it ended. I could have stayed up drinking with them all night, but I had a busy day the next day and needed my sleep – besides, I had no intention of falling off my chair, doing my best Ruprecht impression with a fork and a cork, and being unceremoniously carted back to the hotel in a shopping trolley.

As sunrise burnt bright orange over my balcony I started to prepare for the day ahead. The car picked me up and took me back to the military base where I hooked up with Wayne. It was to be a morning of scuba diving as I donned a wetsuit and off I went with the Royal Navy divers to discover the coastline; I certainly wasn't going to turn my nose up at five men in rubber! I had done my PADI rescue diver course so all went seamlessly and I loved it. It had been a year since I'd been in the water so discovering sea-life all over again was exciting although, and to my lasting regret, the divine Sea Lord didn't make an appearance to hold back the Clashing Rocks despite the still lingering smell of halibut.

A shower and hot drink later, I said thank you to the dive team and off we went to a special Field Gun display; two teams of brawny seamen re-enacting the relief of Ladysmith during the Boer War by wrestling a twelve-pounder field gun and its limbers over a series of obstacles. Seasoned Field Gunners often find it difficult to count to ten owning to the dangerous nature of the gun run, where it's not unusual for team members to lose their fingers during this highly competitive event. The teams were preparing for the annual Field Gun competition at the Royal Tournament and the day's event had been put on for their special guest, who happened to be me. I was a little surprised my visit had been so planned with so much taking place with so many experiences but I wasn't complaining. I was queen of fuck all for the day and loving it. As the battle commenced the two teams fought it out with screams of encouragement being shouted to each other and from the side-lines. It was sheer excitement watching and understanding just how heavy this equipment was and just how fit you had to be to be in the team. With no loss of fingers or any other limbs, I met the teams, had my picture taken with them for the *Gibraltar News* and shot the breeze with them for a good ten minutes, where I was asked if I wanted to join them for the Rock Run. Of course I accepted (after I asked Wayne about my schedule) and with a big smile of inclusiveness a few of us went for lunch. I have to admit, as a hot-blooded female I was now on my second day surrounded by really fit military men; it did cross my mind if a move to Gibraltar or even an extended holiday was in order. I was in uniform heaven.

The rest of my second day was somewhat relaxing as I was shown up the mountain to take in Gibraltar's wildlife namely the infamous and aforementioned Barbary macaques who have been resident on the Rock since before Gibraltar was captured by the British in 1704. These mischievous monkeys are everywhere, baring their buttocks with gay abandon and with a penchant for rifling through tourist's handbags. These cheeky little rascals are pure enjoyment and very friendly.

The first time up the Rock was somewhat relaxing, sharing my time with nature and being mugged by monkeys but when morning came again I had arranged to be at the barracks bright and early for my second visit. With hair scraped back, no makeup, a pair of shorts, top and trainers it was time for the famous 'Rock Run'; 2.7 miles, some of which at a 1:4 gradient. There were some mighty fit guys running that day on a route that has remained the same for many years. The run is famous with the Royal Marines and the Royal

Navy, testing every inch of the body to its limit. Reaching the top was tough but the view was worth every graze on my knee and every carrot of vomit I coughed up en route. I'm sure I could have been a front runner but the fact that this was my only chance to watch a considerable amount of young men wearing very short shorts run in front of me with contracting buttock muscles, bulging thighs and nicely toned calves then I was happy bringing up their rear, that was most certainly the best view a girl could ever have.

With the Rock Run over I had some food back on base with the lads and went back to bed for a couple of hours – unfortunately not on base but back at the hotel all on my lonesome with strict instructions not to bother applying makeup or to style my hair as they had something else in store for me later that day. I had got to know a lot of the guys really well during my few days there and had shared a few drinks with some of them. Word had got around that I was pretty much game for most action coming my way so I had been asked to join the lads of one of the Gibraltar Squadron Boats for a bit of a jolly out on the water before being taken out by the Military Police on a patrol boat. I was now in my fantasy land.

As we went out onto the Straits one of the guys gave me a rundown about the types of boats used by the police and the military in Gibraltar. I think he had his eye on me rather than being my guided tour operator but he was blond-haired, blue-eyed and easy on the eye, had a nice arse and stood over 6ft tall so I had no complaints. He then asked me out of the blue if I water-skied. Mildly confused I replied that I had tried it in the past but was by no means an expert. My next question was "Why?" However my question was swiftly greeted with a pair of water-skis, a rash vest and a spare pair of board shorts. Surely they were joking? This wasn't a ski boat, this was a huge patrol boat; it had to be around eighteen metres in length and weighed over twenty-five tonnes. It kicked up enough wash to drown most sea mammals so how the fuck did they expect me to water-ski off the back of this let alone get down into the water? It wasn't for me to question so I swapped my top for the rash vest, my trousers for the board shorts and I was given a life preserver. I expected nothing less than to be pushed over the side of this massive vessel with them throwing the skis in after me and then the ski rope. Wayne had joined me on my adventure and found it highly amusing as I was dragged behind a huge patrol boat on a pair of sticks holding onto a bit of string in a wash so big that drowning was high up on the list of possibilities. I was dragged over twice and face planted, engulfed in something which felt like a tsunami and breathing became difficult but drowning and being put out of my misery at this point suddenly seemed appealing.

By now the entire crew were on deck watching me get dragged through huge swells holding onto a rope for dear life. On about my third go I managed to get to grips with it and sat back on my skis, let the boat do the work and up I got as the boat accelerated, kicked up a mammoth wash, which I'm unsure if I jumped over or ploughed through. I stayed up for a few turns and then face planted. The hot blond then jumped off the back, swam towards me, checked if I was OK and took me back to the boat where I was lifted out. I was handed a towel, a hot drink and we stayed out on the water for a while longer shooting the breeze. I think I had a crush on just about every military guy on the Rock and even the divine Sea Lord with his giant fish tail made me hot and sweaty under the collar (despite the ever present whiff of halibut).

The day wasn't even over as I was taken for lunch with the lads and later introduced to the Military Police. MPs or 'Red Caps' are probably the most popular branch of the British Armed Forces where the only entry requirements are to have been born out of wedlock and be able to eat a crayon. Potential candidates who can write their own name are considered overqualified and usually go on to become proper soldiers. I was suitably dressed in my Helly Hansen light wet weather gear as I had been pre-warned as to what was going on but nothing had prepared me for the excitement to follow. I was introduced to the crew of the rib. Basically it has a hard V-shaped hull for cutting through the water, surrounded by a rubber ring. They are incredibly safe in all weather types and are easy to moor up and come alongside another boat due to the rubber so nothing will get damaged. This was the police boat and the only boat with a higher-powered engine. It was around twelve metres in length and had a centre console and around two rows of four jockey seats. I jumped on board making us a crew of four and the driver opened up the throttle. After all, they were the only boats allowed to go at speed and it was a stunning day as they took me down the Strait and spoke to me about drug running, how they operate, what they look out for and how they track the drug runners. The driver stepped aside and asked me if I'd like a go at the helm. "Fuck yes," I said as I stepped in, eased the throttle forward as he pointed me in the direction of travel.

It was noisy with the sound of the engine singing and barking as she skipped out of the water every now and again and the warm wind hitting me in the face along with refreshingly salty ocean spray but we could still hear each other talk as I had my eye on a buoy we were heading to. Suddenly a call came over the radio. I backed right off so he could hear the transmission and, although a lot of their talk was coded, it was clear a potential smuggler had been spotted. I instinctively handed the helm back to him without even asking and he stepped in and told me to sit down and hang on. I was joined on the seats by the other two police as it was explained to me that a possible smuggler had been spotted because the radar had picked up a vessel travelling at considerable speed across the Strait. I had already been given a bulletproof vest, which wasn't exactly the comfiest fit I have ever had over my ample bosom, but nonetheless I was ready to go – the MPs with their fully loaded weapons and me with my sharp wit. A second patrol boat had been deployed to join us and I was told it was because the main boat had me on board which made it complicated for them to which I replied,

"Oh fuck that, don't mind me this is awesome, floor it!"

This was the best thing that had ever happened to me. I could feel my eyes becoming huge saucers and my heart was pounding as if I was on the start chute of a race.

"Oh, we will regardless," said the driver as he pushed the throttles down on being given the coordinates.

It was exhilarating as we shot off at high speed on a mission. I felt like Tom Cruise, only not so short and my nose wasn't as big. The rib bounced off every wave as we thundered through the water with spray showering us as we closed in on the mark. I could see to my starboard side the other patrol boat which had been launched carrying four guys, all tooled up. Oh man this was the best day of my life, we were gong to catch me some smugglers. All of a sudden I felt like I was in the movies (again) but this was for real. Transmissions were made over the radio which I wasn't party to but, if I was, I could feel a *Smokey and the Bandit* moment coming on. One of the crew pointed to a blip on the horizon. It was moving at speed kicking up a small white plume. That was our target and we headed towards them balls out. This was the most fun I'd had with my clothes on. Both ribs closed together taking the same line heading towards the mark. This was incredible. All we needed was a clapper-board to slam shut and some one to say "Take 2 and action" as we ploughed through the water. We got within a short distance and our boat slowed right down and the other carried on.

"What the fuck. How comes we've stopped?" my sad emotional face said to them.

"Because we have you on board so we can't go in any further at this point," came the reply.

I was gutted. A real mission with real guns and real superheroes and bad guys. My heart sank. Cops and robbers, cowboys and Indians, smugglers and us. I was probably more upset for the crew because these guys train for these moments and drug running across the Straits is simply not as commonplace as it was in the sixties. So when the opportunity to get some action crops up, it's a big deal and I felt I'd ruined it for them. It's their passion and I know if I were them I would want to be getting amongst it, wrestling the baddies to the deck and fighting off crocodiles.

The other crew had caught up and pulled alongside both still running at speed. I was passed a pair of binoculars to soften the blow and the crew got the boat to stop and took control.

I was jabbering "What's happening? What's going on? What are they doing? Tell me, tell me", like a small child pestering for an ice cream. As far as I was aware they weren't running drugs however, even if they were, I wouldn't be privy to that information. So I chose to stop the line of incessant questioning because it was simply not my business but this trip was just getting better and better. My Milk Tray men dropped me off back at base where Wayne was waiting for me. He had heard everything going on as he had been listening to the transmission on the radio.

"You had fun out there then?" he grinned at me.

I was pretty speechless at this point. All these heroes and uniforms and weapons and testosterone in the air. I didn't know if I was going to implode or explode. I had the pleasure of everyone's time experiencing their life and I was truly honoured to get an insight into the life of military personnel at this level. Of course not every day is like being in the movies for these guys. I married a Royal Marine so am well aware but regardless of the what, when, whys and ifs, they made me feel really welcome and it's a memory that will live with me a lifetime.

The following day I had managed to climb down from the ceiling and was taken for some chill out time around the shops and for a coffee to see Gibraltar as a tourist would. It made a nice change from the whirlwind I had been in for the past two days and, as the afternoon came, we jumped in the car and for some reason made a trip to the airport where we were again greeted by military personnel and taken up to air traffic control. This was really cool. Of course Gibraltar has a tiny airport but it was so interesting as they explained how everything worked. The Sea Lord made an appearance again surrounded by a few other handsome looking officers and the faint aroma of halibut and I was handed a set of overalls to put on. It was a flight suit.

"Ooooh, what's this for?" I asked.

"We have two fighter jets coming in and we thought that you would like to be taken up in one if that's OK with you. Not scared of flying are you?" one of the officers grinned.

This was way above my pay grade. A fucking fighter jet landing here and taking me for a quick shifty up there at a million miles an hour. I nearly shit my pants. Fuck me I was back in the movies but this time it was *Top Gun*. I was back on that powerboat start chute again feeling excited, sick and nervous and I couldn't even speak. Those overalls went on me like a tramp on chips. I was ready, I had never been more ready for anything in my life.

"What time do they arrive?" I asked; hands sweating, heart pumping and nearly wetting myself with excitement like a puppy dog with her tongue hanging out.

I was given a precise time down to the second and, sure enough, what sounded like thunder filled the air. My hair stood on end, the tower trembled and the two jets landed. This wasn't happening, I was just blown away. We made our way down to the runway where the pilot was due to take me to one side for a quick chat before I climbed aboard with him. But before I had chance to drool over his flight suit and undress him with my eyes whilst caressing a lean mean fighter jet, a transmission came through. The crew darted and there were a lot of instructions being shouted. Amidst the mayhem, I seem to recall something being mentioned about the pilot's hotel running out of pink gin which sparked a panic although I may have been mistaken. My chance of getting in a fighter jet had just been dashed so the closest I got was stood next to one wearing a flight suit. I have to say I didn't mind. Yes, it would have been the most mind-blowing experience but the trip had delivered so many treats already that I was beginning to think I was actually asleep and just dreaming. I really felt like I was in the middle of a superhero movie. Apologies were given to which I just grinned and said that merely the offer of flying was excitement enough. As I handed my flight suit back with a smile, they offered to make it up to me. I was invited back to the wardroom for dinner that evening.

***

It wasn't long before I was back in Gibraltar but in a racing capacity for the World Championships. Our hotel, the Caleta, was beautiful and over-looked the sea on the edge of the cliff top. My two favourite memories of the event didn't even involve racing. Cliff and Mark in their 4 ltr catamaran *Tub Humping* needed to run their engine in after blowing one earlier that day. The problem being that in Gibraltar it wasn't possible outside of testing times because of speed restrictions in the straits due to drug runners smuggling between Morocco and Spain. A new engine has to have running time on it before it is abused by trials of racing. There was simply no way around it apart from doing it and risking the consequences. Both Cliff and Mark were big characters in racing, both funny guys and more concerned about their engine than the consequences of spending the night in jail. So, with that in mind, I went down to the pits along with a group of the guys to help out, act as look out and, more to the point, to watch with much amusement as they decided that the lay day of racing (rest day between championship races) they were going to get that engine ran in.

The military radar system is watching 24/7 for boats going above a certain speed so for a set time they would be running within the limit. No one would know they were out there because naturally the officials were on a day off so why disturb them to ask special permission and get refused, but at some point they would have to take it up a notch. This is when all hell would break loose and I wouldn't have missed this gaff for the world.

As the late afternoon sun hit the water, the lads had already switched engines in preparation and they started up their boat, powered by two Mercury XR2s and off their rumbled hoping their bright yellow boat wouldn't be spotted by anyone. The race boats were all moored in the 'basin', an area of enclosed water used mainly for mooring, working and military vessels and now a temporary home to our boats, affectionately known as the 'wet pits'. This was separated from the sea by a large concrete 'breakwater' so, for landlubbers, it's essentially a big wall in the middle of the water which stops the waves from crashing into the basin making it wave free and mostly calm. Attached to this breakwater was stationed a police boat on 24/7 call.

Me and the guys sat on the side drinking beer and watched *Tub Humping* pass the breakwater and disappear into the great expanse of cool clear water. Forty-five minutes passed and we heard them turn it up a notch. If we heard them, then it meant the harbour master did. It also meant they were over the speed limit and would be in serious trouble if caught. We all watched with bated breath as the breakwater suddenly woke up. The police boat was actioned, their flashing light was switched on and off it shot out of the basin into the open water on the hunt for the rogue powerboat.

At this point a call was made to racing safety Flipper and Boff who were close by and they were instructed to get whoever was on the water back before they were either arrested or shot. It was so funny we were doubled up laughing as Flipper and Boff shot out of the basin in their rib on the hunt for Cliff and Mark.

The boys at this point had been out a while and had got the boat up to speed. The water was perfect, there was a mild chop, just enough to lift the boat allowing air underneath making it light and fast. This was perfect testing water and in true Cliff and Mark style they went for it at full tilt up the straits hitting 100 mph.

We were on the harbour wall pissing ourselves laughing whilst cracking open more beers. This was the best entertainment of the week. We could hear the bark of an engine in the distance as Cliff and Mark had picked up speed. We could see the police boat dancing across the water desperately seeking them out. Off-duty race safety, who like the lads had to stick to the laws of the land, were situated in a position where they could be spotted by Cliff and Mark and they were waving furiously at them, letting them know that they had to curtail testing. Cliff had already turned the boat around for another run on that perfect water and shot past the safety guys at speed and wouldn't stop because the boat was performing excellently, reaching speeds he hadn't seen before so off they shot towards Spain past the airport now engaging the Spanish patrol.

As their speed crept up and they jollied up the Straits they had a call on the radio that hot on their tail was a gunboat, the Civil Guard had been launched and had spotted them on their radar system. They were now in Spanish waters, its attack crew, guns at the ready preparing. Cliff didn't give a shit, he was seeing speeds not seen before and just wanted another minute at full tilt telling Mark, "Fuck em, they won't catch us." The large gun on the front hadn't made him bat an eyelid as he reached maximum and headed back in, Flipper and Boff still manically waving at them.

As they reached the breakwater another boat chased them at speed so like cat and mouse they disappeared again to shake them off their tail, there was a hot pursuit going on, it was a like live comedy sketch as Cliff disappeared behind the breakwater the Gibraltarian police unsure of their position hesitant on their next move. We all looked at each other wondering what the fuck was going on. Then the cat and mouse game really picked up as *Tub Humping* slowly crept around the left side of the wall into the basin. This was most certainly the funniest thing we had ever seen, with the police still out on the open water.

We sat there in silence. The land crew prepped. Ropes and fenders were at the ready, a second set of cowlings (engine covers) were ready to replace the ones on the boat which would now be warm giving the game away as to which boat had been running if the police were to check.

As the boat closed in, Mark was already on deck prepping the ropes. I fended off alongside the other racers and it was a quicker turnaround than an F1 pit stop. Fenders down, boat glided in place, engine off, ropes secured, engines covers changed, boat cover thrown over and tied down. We pegged it up to the Caleta, the warm engine covers now safely locked in their truck. The lads were showered, changed and back in the bar within minutes as if nothing had happened. The following day the police paid the race officials a visit and at briefing the race fraternity were questioned on the previous evenings illegal activities. Funnily enough no one knew anything.

Cliff's fun didn't stop there. On the way back he decided to fill the entire boat up with cigarettes – that's a lot of fucking cigarettes. He was stopped at customs, the boat was checked and he arrested along with his wife who knew nothing of Cliff's hoard of cigarettes, Cliff didn't even smoke. They spent six hours in a police cell before being let out and the contraband confiscated. Cliff's wife then refused to speak to him for the entire journey from Gibraltar to France still annoyed for his stupidity and her having to endure a police cell for something she knew nothing about.

They live for the now and like most of the racers, make the world a funnier and better place.

***

The night of race day came upon us and it just so happened that six Royal Naval boats had come in to port. A couple of Royal Marines I had met at Cowes powerboating knew I was in town so tracked me down to the Caleta and came to the bar to take me out for the evening. I was drinking with

Chris Bryan who gave the lads a stiff warning to bring me back in one piece or he would 'hunt them down and kill them.' Chris didn't want me to go out because six ships full of sailors who had been at sea a while probably meant trouble and he didn't want me in the middle of it, especially as he said that long blonde hair and big tits would be like throwing a lamb to the slaughter. He gave me a stiff talking to about not getting gobby with anyone and to be back before midnight. "Yes, Dad," I muttered before exiting with the two heavenly Royal Marines.

Chris knew his business well as it didn't take long for me to end up in shit creek. We had been in the infamous Charles' Hole in T'Wall and it was packed. The whole of Gibraltar was like a cheap German prostitute – packed full of seamen as the crews from the six ships piled off and into the bars and clubs. It was a veritable sea of sailors all thirsty for cold beer and warm women. It didn't take long for me to get a few comments, all cheeky but complimentary and, as I always like to give as good as I get, it escalated fairly quickly. Bob told me to pipe down because, although I was used to dealing with men, this was an uncontrollable number as everyone's eyes fell on my ample cleavage. The guys suggested we move bars, I said I would nip to the toilets and be right back. Bob offered to walk me to the toilets; I thought it a little overprotective and politely said I'd be OK. Just as I was about to come out of the cubicle, I heard the main door burst open and in poured a rabble of drunken men. I remained inside. A fraction of a second went by when I heard the door burst open again and it kicked off right outside my cubicle. 'What the fuck?' I thought, the short argument was clearly about me as someone was thrown against my door and then moments later it went silent as the altercation disappeared.

I stayed in the cubicle for another couple of minutes to gather my thoughts and then exited. My two trusty marines were now guarding the female toilet door and were waiting for me. "What the fuck was that about?"

"The dickheads at the bar you were bantering with had followed you to the toilets, so we followed them." Bob glared at me, took me to another bar and then swiftly delivered me back to Chris at the hotel bar ahead of schedule.

"It kicked off, didn't it?" Chris asked knowingly.

"Yep it sure did," the Marines answered in unison.

They stopped for a quick drink and headed off into the night apologising for not taking me with them, but they simply wanted a quieter night and having me around was way too exciting for them.

Chapter 12

Jack Osbourne: Adrenaline Flunkie

'I deeply inhaled the pleasure of exhaust fumes.'

Jack Osbourne: Adrenaline Junkie was in its fifth series. It had been a successful reality show documenting physical challenges Jack had to face, ranging from climbing El Capitan mountain in Yosemite National park through cattle drives in Mongolia to diving in shark-infested waters. I'd liked the show in so much as it reminded me of my days getting paid for having shitloads of fun. While any such show had to have an element of jeopardy there was very much a feathered health and safety nest – death, while great for viewing figures isn't great for a TV production company's future and as such every challenge would have been carefully chosen and manipulated to mitigate the chances of a corpse being the star turn.

Someone from ITV2 rang me to say they were considering a powerboat racing challenge in Dubai and asked my thoughts on whether it could it be organised. The organising wasn't a problem; it was the fact that this was a step up from anything they'd previously done – people died powerboating. I wouldn't miss this for the world. Everything in TV is sugar-coated, so to see how people outside of racing reacted to the extreme pressures of a race boat made me curious.

They chose Dubai for the challenge, which made perfect sense. It is glorious place to race; the seas are warm and reflect the brilliant blues of the sky, the pits are modern yet beautiful and everything is so clean and colourful.

When I began my career I thought racing in the UK was awesome, but once you raced around the globe you never wanted to touch the British seas again. I'm happy to admit I'm a sunshine kinda girl and so the dull greys and crappy weather of the UK aren't my bag. Even when walking round the pits of the UK round of Powerboat P1, which was highly glamorous like F1 motor racing, you'd walk around the dull grey pits in a rain mac trying to shelter from the wind and rain, and even the bright international racing colours would be subdued unless there was a rare sunny day.

Once you start racing globally, you soon become spoiled. I only have to reminisce about racing in Sardinia and I dream of returning, so revisiting Dubai was a rather exciting proposition.

All the Arabs I had met were just divine and so wonderfully helpful and generous. The set-up is remarkable, not too dissimilar to Sardinia and the other events with the hospitality units set up in a line. All the teams have their own chefs and staff and everyone is always welcome in everyone else's unit. It's totally glorious. Everyone in powerboating is so friendly and nice. Like everything in Dubai there is a sense of detachment from the realities of life, and while many criticise the city for its plastic culture, I found the place full of deeply intelligent people who get shit done.

The Dubai International Marine Club (DIMC) hosts all races, so my first stop was to speak to them prior and check the state of play. Their officials organise everything by the book so when they gave the green light, I knew the challenge would be a success.

I arrived a few days early to see friends and finalise arrangements with Rory Power the UIM Commissioner. Rory was there for the big international races and ultimately in charge of everything to do with power boating; having his baby shown to a new audience was obviously a risk so he needed to ensure everything was perfect. I had raced with Rory in the years previously and what he didn't know could be written on the back of a stamp. Beaches and all airspace in and around the course were closed; onshore medics and an emergency helicopter were booked. We also needed to book timekeepers and a safety official for every mark of the course. Finally, we needed to look after the film crew.

I found it amazing that the whole crew didn't understand the complications of filming on water. There is no steady platform from which to film – the racer is in a boat and the film crew are on a boat. They expected it to take the same length of time it took to film other adrenaline sports, but I had informed them that powerboat racing is just not that simple. From my experience it could take three times as long.

Jack Osborne finally arrived at the DIMC with the film crew along with Reggie Yates, Radio1 DJ; Joanna Page from TV's *Gavin & Stacey*; and Jesse Metcalfe the supposed heartthrob from *Desperate Housewives*. After the initial introductions I took them into a side room to privately brief them without the cameras intruding. Rory Power stood to my right along with a few racers and our safety guys. I had already spoken to the racers so they knew they would be piloting a 'made for TV' race – a full speed professional-type race would not only be irresponsible but potentially fatal.

I let the celebrities know that this challenge would be like nothing they'd ever done and they shouldn't expect it to be a walk in the park. "Once I've teamed you up with a teammate, it's very important you do everything they tell you. They're not here to put you in danger and you won't be going at normal race speeds."

I could see that none of the guys were even interested in any of what I was saying. Only Joanna took notice of everything. They seemed to have the attitude of 'let's just get in the boat and go'.

I finished by saying, "Of course, before you are even allowed into a boat you will have to successfully complete a dunk test that we've arranged for tomorrow afternoon."

I explained the dunk test, what it was, why we did it and where it would be done. I then handed over to the safety guys in charge of the dunk to run through it in detail.

"Fear not, we'll be closing off the beaches, the sea around the course and the airspace above it for the medical evacuation helicopter."

Life seemed to drain from the celebrity faces; apathy had turned to fear as the enormity of their task set in.

"Yes guys, this isn't a game like bungee jumping."

They didn't seem to understand that every single thing in powerboats is covered and nothing is left to chance. That on the water there isn't just the possibility of an accident to cope with but also drowning. Rory Power the UIM Commissioner then took over from me to go through anything I may have missed and to reiterate the important parts.

I then introduced them to their teammates. I knew all the lads who were racing the X-Cats – very fast boats with an incredible power-to-weight ratio. The celebrity would drive and the racer would be in charge of the throttle and everything else. All had been picked carefully knowing each other's personalities and they were ready to rumble.

I thought it important to put Jack with one of the top UAE guys so I teamed him up with Ahmed who was always a lot of fun. His boat was the most beautiful on the circuit with an incredibly stunning paint job in burnt orange. He was very Westernised in many ways but always wore a traditional dishdash around the pits before changing into race overalls.

172

For Joanna I chose a very old friend of mine Ian Blacker who I loved to bits, having known him since I started racing. Incredibly experienced, he was a really tough racer, had balls of steel and took shit from no one. He was safe, yet raced on the edge and I trusted him completely to look after Jo.

I put Reggie with the adorable Italian Kristian Rivolta, another racer who was like brother to me. He lived with Giovanni Carpitella the Italian who had looked after me and Mum after my crash. He came from a very wealthy family and he was just adorable, quite a few years younger than me with glacial blue eyes that women swooned over. He was a total petrol-head having started his race career on bike but he was safe and knew his stuff.

Jessie was teamed up with fellow American Gary Baloo whom I had known for several years when I raced in the USA. Gary was a true 'Golden Balls', succeeding in everything he touched, winning many championships in every type of boat. Just to add to his perfection Gary was in his 40s yet always looked much younger.

The briefing as concluded with a request to meet again at 8 am the following morning for a weather briefing. As everyone cleared the room I called the celebs over for a quick chat in private. I explained that the racers were doing *them* a favour, as they would actually be competing in a championship race in three days time. With a huge amount of money at stake, the most important thing to the racers was their boat and the championship, the celebs came very low down their list of priorities, and I'd had to sweet talk my boys into doing the gig. It was clear the celebs and TV crew didn't quite understand my point.

Powerboat racers aren't interested in the celeb culture. Royalty and celebs alike have raced so it's nothing special. Giovanni's teammate for example is Luca Fendi, and every woman in the world knows the Fendi brand. It's the norm for racers to either pay for their own racing or cut deals with rich friends businesses. So to take some unknown foreign celebrity out for a TV show they've probably never heard of doesn't do them any favours, all it does is put excess time on an engine and means re-measuring fuel. It's actually a total pain in the ass.

I also warned the celebs that the dunk wasn't a nice experience. As I started to go through it again, Jack and Jesse said, "Yeah it'll be fine," and left.

Reggie soon followed, but Joanna stayed. I've always found girls to be the best listeners, we're the most likely to be sensible and follow instruction because we are thinkers. She asked me several question as she was determined to get it right. I had no concerns about Joanna, although I told her to get the test out of the way first because if one of the guys panicked, it may put her off.

Racers, pilots and the military use the dunker test. It's about how to escape from a cockpit if you land in water and, worst-case scenario, you end upside down. Some dunkers are enclosed so it's an actual cockpit, some are a roll cage so have no sides, but irrespective of design you are only allowed in and out of one place to pass the test. The feeling of being strapped into somewhere alien, disorientated and under water isn't that glamorous and has been known to weaken the resolve of the strongest man.

The dunker for the celebs was in the marina against the dockside. Divers swam around to watch and pull anyone free should they panic or get into difficulty.

The guy in charge of the dunker went through everything again, with the celebs stood in their overalls on the dockside. When he asked who was going first I butted in and said "Jo."

She looked at me a bit concerned but I reassured her it was a piece of cake. "So Jo, this is the order: as they kick you over, take a massive breath. When you're upside down don't panic. You'll feel your sinuses fill. This is the worst bit; deal with it. Count to three until you settle and relax. Above all remember you're being watched like a hawk and you're safe. You will be strapped in with your five-point harness so you won't go anywhere. As soon as you have settled upside down it becomes easy. The divers will tap you when they are ready for you to exit. Reach above your head and feel the latch, it's in a direct line above your head. The latch will release and open the canopy. With the same hand reach down to your harness and pull the release catch. As you release yourself as long as you don't panic you can reach up and just pull yourself out in a straight line and once clear swim to the side and come to the surface. Don't release the harness before you release the latch on the hatch, which is why I've told you to use the same hand or you will be in a mess as you wont be able to get out."

Jo offered a huge smile and gave me the thumbs-up before entering the dunker with the camera crew pointing at her. I checked her life jacket, helmet strap and pulled her harness tight. She took a deep breath and was kicked over.

Fifteen seconds later a cherubic smiley face popped out of the water, blonde hair wrapped around her face. We looked across to the diver who would give a Gladiatorial thumbs up or down as to a fail or a pass. It was a thumbs up. She made it look easy. Jo was always going to do it first time.

Next was Jesse, I went to fasten his safety gear on him and secure his helmet and asked if he was OK – he was up his own arse for sure, not sure about OK. I knew this was going to be a fail before he even got in. Someone's attitude to safety tells you a lot about the person and this was going to be a long afternoon as the only one that seemed to care was Jo, it was as if because the others were men it was going to be a walk in the park, because power-boats are a man's domain not a woman's.

Jesse got in the dunker, the diver tightened his harness, he took a deep breath and was kicked over. Within seconds he was out. Thumbs down. He had panicked, unfastened his harness immediately and bolted out of the side, he was now hanging onto the pontoon breathing heavily. Shocked eyes were the windows into his fear. We checked if he was OK and asked if he was ready to go again, he took about five minutes before he nervously re-entered the dunker went again. Being tightly strapped into something so you can't move upside down in water isn't natural, so we all must understand that some people never get used to it. It's a necessity that all racers must do to get their license then pray it never happens for real.

Jesse went again with the same action and reaction. A big thumbs-down again. He was hyperventilating, clinging to the side in panic. After another two fails we allowed him to rest, but with implicit instructions that he had to pass or he couldn't race.

Both Jack and Reggie were now nervously looking at Jessie sat like a drowned rat on the pontoon not looking quite as cock sure of himself. I tightened Jack's harness and did my final brief as I had with Joanna. He too had the attitude of "Yep I'll be fine."

I thought *what the fuck is it about all you guys saying 'yes I'll be fine,' obviously you're not*. It was almost that because I was a woman it was demeaning for them to be going through this shit with me. He had a count down, took a breath and was kicked over. He was out as quick as Jesse coughing and spluttering. This was a guy who had a show named *Adrenaline Junkie*. I could only think of brown adrenaline running down is legs in this case.

After a five minutes rest he went again. This time he took too long and we were all on the side thinking *where the fuck is he?* A diver pulled him up. Thumbs down. We had no idea what had gone but by the snot and fear on his face it obviously wasn't enjoyable. He failed on his next go as well so we let him rest.

At this point Reggie Yates was backing off. He wasn't a strong swimmer and clearly worried. We reassured him that he was incredibly safe. He asked me to go through it one more time. I took him through everything and sorted his kit out. I reminded him that the most important thing was to relax going over and once upside down stay composed.

Reggie was such a nice, gentle guy, but was no fan of water. His face drained to the colour of a corpse as he climbed slowly into the cockpit. He wouldn't let them kick the dunker over until he'd composed himself. When he gave the signal to kick, he'd undone his harness and was out before it had even turned over. He clung to the pontoon and wouldn't move.

We made it abundantly clear to everyone that unless the guys successfully completed this they would not be allowed inside a boat. They didn't have the choice, it was the dunk or they didn't film. A film crew member even had the audacity to ask if the celebs could skip the dunker drill. They clearly failed to see that we didn't do this for TV or because it looked good on camera or because we liked doing it. It was for the racers' own safety and absolutely mandatory. The dunker team had been brought in solely for the celebs at the cost of the DIMC to satisfy industry rules. This drill could save a life. No exceptions.

Reggie agreed to do it again. On his third attempt he came up with the diver. He clung to the side still shaking and then quickly turned to the diver and asked, "Did I do it? Did I do it?"

Thumbs up. The look of relief on his face was outstanding and his smile was so bright I'm surprised it didn't blind the divers. It took an immense amount of bravery for him to pass. I always admire those who overcome abject fear far more than those who fear little, no matter how irrelevant or illogical the phobia may be, so I was so chuffed as nuts he had passed.

We still had Jesse and Jack to pass. Neither of them were chomping at the bit to go; I'd seen people with rabies with more inclination to jump in water.

They asked if they could do it the following day. They were told in no uncertain terms they had to test now.

This time they both managed it. Thank fuck these guys didn't have to do it three times like in the UK where to pass students have to go over three times. I'd still be here on the pontoon frying in 40°C degrees of sun. I'd look like a raisin.

***

Everyone had been told that testing would commence an hour after the dunker. The boats were fuelled and the teams were ready to rock and roll.

I radioed for everyone to come to the pits where the boats were and the TV crew went to gather up the celebs. Only Joanna was present. The three guys had gone back to the hotel.

I took the producer to the side and asked, "Why aren't they here? The DIMC and all its employees are doing all of this as a favour, they don't get paid overtime and the racers certainly don't get paid to hang around in 40 degrees when they'd sooner have themselves and their engines under shade. They're keeping forty people waiting and it's massively discourteous to the Arabs because they've organised this and left nothing to chance. It's just embarrassing."

He made a call. "They're staying at the hotel and they'll see us in the morning and test then."

My answer to that was, "Like fuck they will. Get their arses down here or it's off. This is humiliating and the DIMC is being incredibly hospitable and if they won't test it's being pulled." The producer called them back.

I turned to Blacker who was with Joanna and asked were they all set to go. Joanna gave me a massive grin and thumbs-up. I knew she was going to love it because she climbed in whilst giggling excitedly.

The roar of the twin 2.5s vibrated through the air and I deeply inhaled the pleasure of exhaust fumes bringing back sweet memories of a life on the water.

The other teams were not happy and asked what was happening because they didn't have the time for this shit. A few minutes later Reggie arrived in his race gear. I took Kristian to the side and said to be even more aware because Reggie was nervous. He was a DJ not an extreme sports addict. I knew Kristian would look after him. The racers wanted the celebs to enjoy the experience and of course they had a major race within days so the health of the boat was priority.

I explained to Reggie the feeling he would have as the boat planed and the noise from the engines, the fact they bark and that the sensation of speed on water is twice or more than on land. "Enjoy it and don't be nervous."

Where were Jack and Jesse? One of the producers said that Jack and Jesse's managers had said they weren't allowed to get in the boat for testing. Rory, the UIM officer and I exchanged glances. I had worked in media and I'd never heard such a pile of shit. We now had so many people hanging around doing nothing in over 40 degrees of sun.

"That's nonsense. We're shooting an extreme sports programme and surely racing had been researched prior to coming out? They know what they're doing. Even if the managers don't like it they could only advise and not stop them. They're obviously scared shitless of the boats." I just thought it better to say it how it was.

We understood that racing wasn't for everyone, it can be frightening even for a racer and we've all had some really close experiences, but this was supposed to be fun. Being in a boat with the world's best offshore drivers was the ultimate experience. They could never experience a full on race; this was a fun event.

I gave the final ultimatum. "They either get their arses down here or we cancel everything."

Funnily enough, they both turned up and seemed willing. As we got Jack and Jesse prepped, Kris and Reggie pulled back into the pontoon. They had only been out a few moments so I presumed there was a tech issue.

The crew opened Reggie's hatch and unfastened him, he climbed out ashen faced and walked to the end of the pontoon where he sat with his head in his hands.

"Kris, what's happened?"

"I haven't done anything to scare him but as we left the harbour Reggie started to panic. As I accelerated to plane the boat and the engines roared Reggie started screaming, "Slow down, please slow down, I don't want to die, I don't want to die!" I tried to tell him that he was OK and he was safe.

"How fast were you going?"

"Only about 30 mph, said Kris"

Boats need to plane, and to plane Kris had to accelerate; he could then drop the speed again, think of it like an aircraft taking off.

I sat with Reggie on the end of the pontoon. He was shaking and was very open about being scared. I talked him through why Kris had to accelerate to plane and the noise of the engines working to get her on top of the water.

I gave Reggie and hug and said I understood and it's not for everyone, but Kris was the best and he was also one of my best friends. Reggie to my surprise looked at me and said, "Right let's do this. Is it OK if I go again? Will Kris be OK?"

I grinned and dragged him over to Kris. They shook hands and off they went. Twenty minutes later they returned. Reggie was ecstatic and grinning ear to ear and wanted to stay out there.

It just took a bit of TLC. For the second time that day it took real balls to overcome such fear. I loved Reggie for it and hoped it was a great lesson for him in overcoming different obstacles in life.

Joanna had come in a few minutes prior and was as excited as Reggie. She had been saying to Blacker, "Faster! Faster! Can we go faster?"

Blacker said she was a good driver who listened and understood the water.

Jesse and Jack went out. They looked as though they were heading to the gallows rather than a powerboat. Upon their return it was obvious they were pleased to be back on dry land, and far more subdued than Reggie and Joanna. Gary and Ahmed had kept the speeds down because they knew they boys were nervous and both stated that the guys were fairly quiet in the boat, but had at least listened and been OK.

We returned to the hotel and I gave a quick reminder for us all to reconvene the following morning.

As we broke off a loud northern voice shouted, "Ooh, you're off the telly!"

Presuming she was talking about one of the other celebs we continued to walk until she grabbed my arm and said, "I recognise you, you race boats. Fancy seeing you all the way in Dubai."

I chatted to the woman for a few seconds before making my apologies to leave. It was a priceless moment. I'm stood there with these celebs and I'm the only person she recognised.

***

The race boats were ready, the air and sea space cleared. The helicopter was ready to go and so were we. I stood with Rory and the cameraman in the start boat as we wanted to conduct a proper race start.

The boats lined up alongside us. As the yellow flag raised, we started to move off. Once up to a good speed we dropped the yellow and raised the green flag. They were off! The start of a professional race is a bar fight with everyone jostling for position. This was a dumbed-down version but would have been a real sphincter clencher for the celebs.

Although it was a race of sorts it was apparent when a celeb was getting nervous as their boat would slow right down, especially on turn mark which freaks many out. They did six laps of a marked out course jostling position all the way. On the final lap Jack and Joanna took the lead, with Joanna and Blacker just pipping Jack and Ahmed to the chequered flag.

Joanna was ecstatic at taking a win for the girls. She even climbed out of the boat on the water and waved the flag she was handed like a true pro.

Despite the difficulties, it had been a fabulous couple of days and the *Adrenaline Junkie* team invited us to watch the London screening, which was a nice touch. Offshore racing is an elite sport and not something anyone can do. Watching it on TV gives a false sense of security; you can't just rock up and expect to drive. There are so many rules and regulations and safety directions to follow. While the celebs all had different characters – Jack certainly wasn't the adrenaline junkie he professed to be in the title of the show, Jesse rather cocky at times, Reggie humble and was beautiful inside and out and Joanna just simply adorable – racing boats opened their eyes a little to real adrenaline and something they hadn't experienced before. Everything else in prior shows had been child's play. I hope they learned a lot and took away the importance of safety and professionalism. Joanna; however, has an open invite to test with Blacker any time. She was a superstar!

Chapter 13

Top Trump

'It's all shits and giggles until someone giggles and shits.'

I started Miss Galaxy Universe because in June 2011 I was invited to be a judge for a fitness show in London and was furious when they fixed the results.

I had thought it odd when we sat at the judging desk without any judging sheets. On asking for some, the organiser told me, "Just get yourself a drink, sit down and enjoy the show, we've got it all in hand, you're just here to look professional."

I exchanged a nervous giggle with Demar Martin, a former TV Gladiator and fellow judge before we realised it wasn't a joke. I grabbed a handful of nearby judging sheets and handed them to the other judges on my table because that's what I was there for – to judge fairly.

I handed all our finished scores to the show organiser, only for her to bat away my hand. I called up the other judges for some back up and followed her backstage. As we huddled in the female toilets, all the other judges but Demar stood silently. It was clear these people kept quiet or took backhanders to get ahead and because this was a big show their egos overran their job description so didn't give two shits who won.

The organiser sat on the sinks swinging her legs nonchalantly and asked me, "Well, who do you think should win?"

"The judging sheets will tell you if you bother to read them." I knew it was a waste of time; it was like talking to a plank of wood. She did, however, allow one of the girls we had judged well to place (albeit not in the position we had put her). Of those who actually placed, none of us even remembered seeing on stage they were so nondescript. I nearly spat my drink everywhere when one of the class winners collected her trophy – with a steroid infused square jaw she looked like some cheap hooker bending over to show us what she had for breakfast and had so many fillers and lip plumping she had a face like Bo Selecta after a night on the piss. When the little shop of horrors walked over to collect her prize I left the building cursing and swearing to Sam Parkhouse, my friend and freelance financial journalist who was as equally annoyed.

I'm happy to confront and toss aside etiquette in the quest for respect and truth so I collared Miss Selecta on the gym floor as I noticed we shared the same space and asked how much she'd paid to place. Needless to say she denied everything, and stated she felt incredibly insulted at my accusations. She has ignored me ever since.

It was later revealed that Bo Selecta *had* paid to place as it was the only way she could get exposure in a certain magazine, and as a personal trainer it would help increase her client base. It was the world's worst kept secret, she couldn't have placed on her own merit no matter what, unless in a 'face only a mother could love' competition…

So founding Miss Galaxy Universe was my clarion call to offer women of all ages, shapes and sizes a safe and fair place to compete and give confidence to achieve goals and a better way of life. I knew that a well-run show would build lasting friendships and unite people of all backgrounds.

Miss Galaxy Universe would combine the elegance of modelling in a bikini and evening wear onstage with hardcore fitness tests that same day to test functionality, strength and agility. It always amazed me that no one in the UK had ever even thought of it, but looking back at when we started, we were in fact the leaders in so many things in the fitness show world. The UK have always fallen behind the Americans in so many things but I came from a theatrical and a sporting background so all this to me was a no brainer.

The first show was performed in May 2012 at the NEC during the *Martial Arts Show* and was a runaway success, far exceeding my expectations. It was Gok Wan's brother Kwoklyn who had contacted me to ask if I needed a helping hand getting my show on the road. He had heard a rumour that I was trying to pull off a show like no other and offered us a huge floor area at his expo and a stage all for free. After all, I was trying to pull a show together on favours and passion with no backers. So Kwok's generous offer was just amazing and without him I would have struggled. Miss Galaxy Universe was off to a flying start.

The name Miss Galaxy Universe originated from my days as a Galaxy Girl from the USA's Galaxy Nova competition and 'Universe' is synonymous with bodybuilding and fitness competitions, so it seemed obvious to put my competition heritage together with a word that had it's home in fitness. I'd already spoken to US Galaxy Nova show organiser David Newingham out of goodwill, and he was OK with it.

I registered the trademark 'Galaxy Universe Organisation' in 2011 but because my figurine logo was hand-drawn, its design couldn't be printed in vinyl for promotion on my car as it needed to be in an exact format, so I agreed for my designer to find me one similar on Shutterstock royalty free images. He found me an image I liked so we used it on my car, I also used it for a new trademark as it was crisper and because the girls had started calling the show Miss Galaxy Universe rather than Galaxy Universe, I simply trademarked the new figurine and registered the name Miss Galaxy Universe in 2012 without a second thought. This sparked off a chain of events that would take four years of my life...

Using the figurine from Shutterstock was a huge mistake. Shutterstock images are royalty free but cannot be used as trademarks which I didn't realise. Yup I didn't read the small print and I simply took it as 'royalty free' period. What a huge boo boo I had made. I phoned Shutterstock and asked to buy the image. It was £10,000 so I simply withdrew my trademark because it wasn't legal. Andy Screen, a former Royal Marine, great artist and fantastic graphic designer designed me another logo and it was amazing. For me it was business as usual but I didn't bother trademarking anything. I simply couldn't be bothered. But the chain of events had started as the second registration, although withdrawn, had sparked unwanted interest.

It was July 2012. I'd gone to meet Lee, my now husband at the Commando Training Centre (CTC) in Lympstone Devon, where if you're lucky you'll see lots of handsome young commando recruits running out of the gate or if luck isn't on your side, returning back, limping, dishevelled and covered in mud.

As we walked to the car park opposite CTC in readiness for one of our epic weekends, an email came through on my phone. Being self-employed I'm always on the clock so immediately checked. It was from a law firm with an attachment headed 'Universe LLC New York', I presumed it was either sent to the wrong person or it was more junk as I often receive emails asking if I want a larger penis.

On second glance it included my name, so I speed read the covering letter that contained the usual solicitor's drivel before opening the attachment on my phone as we both climbed into the car.

It stopped me in my tracks. "What the fuck?" It was all I could muster.

"What's wrong now?" said Lee accustomed to the many oddities that crossed my bow.

I told him. He laughed, and asked to read it just in case my eyes were playing tricks.

"Yup, it's true."

Highly amused by the prospect that once again I'd outdone myself, I speed read the first paragraph, I simply couldn't be arsed reading the other seventy-one pages, let's face it, if the first paragraph is total tosh, then the rest of it would continue as inane garbage that would suck away my soul. Reading something that long and intense could well take a couple of hours that, in the bigger scheme of things, wouldn't be added to my existence in my old age, so I refused to have my time stolen when it could be better spent on doing something useful – like enjoying an evening with friends. I pushed the phone back in my bag, threw it on the back seat of the car and set off to the 'Bamboo' Chinese restaurant in Exmouth to eat and meet with friends, old teammates and some of the area's powerboat racers.

I couldn't wait to announce the news to the group. I was like a kid the night before Christmas. I excitedly withheld any announcement until everyone had drunk a fair bit before I stood up wearing a big grin. The wine jumped from my glass while I gesticulated wildly as I became more and more excitable, my red wine smile exaggerated like Heath Ledger's Joker. "I had an email through earlier on. I'm getting my arse sued." There was a fairly loud cheer before I added, "You'll never guesses who by." Cue stupid answers:

"Ozzy Osbourne?"

"Kermit the Frog?"

"Darth Vader?"

"Getting close," I added.

My eyes met Martin Lai's, the restaurant owner, whose big grin widened in time with my own. "Who?"

The table went silent, "Donald… Fucking… Trump!"

The table remained silent for a few seconds.

"Is that his middle name?" asked Martin.

Laughter roared through the restaurant. On sitting down I told them it was some bollocks about the name 'Universe', as if it's a word Trump has copyright over.

"If he has, Steven Hawking better watch out," someone shouted, adding "It could only happen to you."

Throughout the evening the jokes and one-liners flowed like the endless wine as it had amused everyone that knew me well, until it was asked in a totally non-serious way, "What are you going to do about it?"

My reply was simple. "Fuck all."

***

Registering the new Miss Galaxy Universe trademark in 2012 seemed to have sparked off the Trump clan going via the Intellectual Property Office to stop me from using the name, however a trademark doesn't stop anyone from using a name unless there has been a lawsuit and many companies run without trademarks. It's sensible to register one but not a necessity.

This first seventy-one-page letter I ignored. Ultimately, when you're up against a bottomless money pit what's the point in fighting? I'd never beat a billionaire by playing by the rulebook and, in truth, I thought it pathetic. The only way I could beat Donald Trump was by being a bigger dick than him. I remembered that the law can't deal with unreasonable people so the more unreasonable I was by not instructing a lawyer or playing by their rules, the harder they would find it to deal with me. To me it was a game. I had nothing to lose and everything to gain. It gave me a sick kind of amusement.

Another email arrived a few months later, followed shortly by a hard copy thick enough to have destroyed half the Amazon rain forest. I greeted both with the same attitude as the initial email. It would be increasingly time-wasting should I get involved but I read the papers anyway, admittedly not all of them because it was mega-boring, but laughed at the annexe that outlined an 'undertaking' – basically their document 'from me to them' with a line for my signature to say that *In consideration of you agreeing not to take legal action against me in relation to…* blah blah *I undertake on behalf of myself, my servants, agents, employees…* blah blah *will cease and refrain from infringing your rights which requires me to do at least the following…* it then listed a whole length of demands that boiled down to them wanting me to change the name of my show, hand over my domain names and remove all links to the name referring to either 'Miss' or 'Universe'. I could use one name or the other but not both in the same title, so my show 'Miss Galaxy

Universe' they said infringed on their copyright. I could use 'Miss Galaxy' or 'Galaxy Universe', but not all three words together.

They also told me I couldn't use Mr, Master or Mrs Universe. This left me confused as Mr and Miss Universe are famously bodybuilding shows – Arnold Schwarzenegger is 2 x Mr Universe and there are a whole host of Miss Universe fitness shows. These pages of nonsense were best read over several glasses of wine whilst half-watching a movie. Of course, I didn't sign it. I wasn't interested in their petty games. I eventually gave no more than five minutes to the whole thing before I opened up the ring binder over the bin and let the papers fall out – reading legal documents bores me at the best of times, but wasting my eyes on this trash was taking the biscuit. I kept the ring binders though, as they had a rather nice velvet covering.

Throughout this period, the racers would often ask me what my next move was. My answer was always the same, "They can go fuck themselves." And that was that. I mean, let's get real. He has an infinite wallet, I don't; he's big I'm small. I can't compete on any dimension so I didn't even entertain it. As far as I was concerned if they cared enough they would just issue papers and shut me down so I gave them enough rope to do that. Even something like that would take around a year so I had no immediate worries, not that I had any.

I got so bored of the Trump lawyers' heavy-handed tactics, I changed my name by deed poll to 'Galaxy Universe'. By default I became Miss Universe. I was just being a twat really, it was just another thorn in their side and it amused me somewhat. As the saying goes – 'It's all shits and giggles until someone giggles and shits.' I knew I was taking a big risk but in the world of risks, it's hardly skating over a sea at 100 mph.

A couple of months later I received another email from Universe LLC New York chasing up their original emails. Wow, this was getting really tiresome, but credited them with their judiciousness in wasting money. By now they had sent many screenshots of my own website and features in newspapers of my show in a rather pointless exercise of showing me stuff I already knew – I was more than aware of the contents of the website – I owned it. But with every print their lawyers would add a hefty price tag so I left them to their own devices running up bills to add to their fortunes. I imagined them sitting in the office rubbing their hands together like a Christmas Scrooge.

I could honestly worry if the accusation levelled had any credence, after all we all know when we're guilty of being wrong, yet the poppycock they accused me of started to anger me because I'd like to think I'm one of life's genuinely honest people and have always put others before myself, so reading their drivel only strengthened my resolve to hold my head high and not back down – I'd sooner gouge my eyes out with a rusty spoon. Gen.

I understood that legal terminology isn't personal and that I should remain emotionless, but Miss Galaxy Universe was my baby, it was my passion and gave a home to the many competitors it attracted. It helped women discover themselves and reach new heights – there was no way some twat from thousands of miles away was going to force me to change that especially when amongst their accusations were:

'Miss Galaxy Universe and Miss Universe were in competition with each other'.
And? Even if we were similar, there is no monopoly on fitness competitions.

The services are identical or similar
As a pageant, of which there are thousands across the world, they don't offer our services and the differences are numerous:

- In his show the girls must be under 27 years old. Most of our girls couldn't even qualify for Miss Universe as our average age of competitor is 34. My show is open to women of all ages.
- Their competition has only one class and competitors cannot be married or have children. Ours has different categories for different body shapes and sizes including 'Yummy Mummy'.
- Their show has heats before the finals. Ours doesn't have heats, we want all our competitors to have the limelight at the one big event that features an athletics track and a magnificent stage phase.
- Ultimately theirs is a beauty pageant, ours is a sports based show where the girls have 60% of their overall score based on fitness/athletics. We help the girls with diet and nutrition, fitness and we also run bikini confidence and posing classes and also provide amazing team building weekends ran by former Royal Marines Commandos. To ensconce the girls within our family and enhance our bond, we also do summer and Christmas parties that are always well attended. While competitors, many of the girls become lifelong friends and often help each other with their preparation – something that makes me immensely proud.

Our trademark is similar/that we would take unfair advantage or be detrimental to the distinctive character or repute of the opponent's trademark

Regardless of the fact I would never knowingly take advantage of anyone or anything, as I have not been brought up that way, the respective figurines in the trademarks are entirely different. Phonetically the names don't even sound the same, such as ours has seven syllables and theirs four. Their font is different, the way the font and figurine is set out is different. Every female pageant in the world is 'Miss'. They kept banging on about our figurine, equally befuddling as nearly every pageant uses either a figurine or a tiara or both.

The figurative mark is the same or similar

Namely: appertaining to their figurine known as the 'Lady with the Stars'.

The 'Lady of the Stars' wears a long dress. Fail: Our figurine is naked – it's like charging a woman in a raincoat with indecent exposure as nakedness is 'similar' to being fully clothed.

- She has stars above her head – Ours doesn't – it's like the US taking issue with the Malaysian flag
- She has a line above her head – Ours doesn't – similarly, a subtraction sign could take issue with an equal sign (as in the famous Equal vs Subtraction case of 1903).
- Her arm points up in similar fashion to the Statue of Liberty (who hasn't taken them to court as far as I'm aware) – Ours points down – so in reality the only commonality is that our ladies have two arms. Unless I use an amputee or an octopus, then sorry Donald, we ain't changing. However, more importantly we certainly encourage amputees to compete, as our show was a gift to all women to celebrate all women. We had the gorgeous thirty-eight-year-old mum Joan Steel who had to have her arm sewn back on after a near fatal car crash. Her scars and skin grafts gave her character yet limited movement for which we gave an allowance to, yet didn't stop her later becoming our compere. We have also had Erin, who suffered over 50% body burns in a house fire. The show did wonders for her confidence, she even won a 1940s-style calendar shoot with our partner 'Golden Rivet'.
- Their lady wears a tiara – Ours doesn't – so no commonality, therefore

logic dictates that their issue is that our figurine has a head. I'm not 100% but I'm pretty sure if we used a decapitated body as our logo it wouldn't be as attractive.

- Their lady is in a statuesque pose – Ours is diving – if you tried to stand like our logo you'd break your back and toes.
- Their lady has her hair up – Ours is down and flowing to add to the image of movement

Basically their argument is that our dog is the same as their cat because both have four legs and shit in the garden.

That my website deliberately mimicked the look and feel of the opponent's website with style/fonts/colours

Until I read this I had never even been on their website. I would never have had a need to look it. Our website is a kaleidoscope of colour in contrast to their dull grey. They couldn't be more different. But then again my web creator is a very talented graphic designer and their UK site, in my opinion, looks like it's derived from a website template used by plastic moulding firms or fabrication workshops – far too much wordage and not enough on the girls – the most important people of the whole competition.

There is an economic connection

I have no idea what they were on about here other than we fund our shows using money and not magic beans.

There is a likelihood of confusion/link association with the public

This is one of the 21st century ideas that patronises humanity and gives oxygen to winners of the Darwin awards – those idiots who need a warning that the hot coffee they hold is actually hot. Our show isn't even watched by the general public but by friends and family and personal trainers of the competing girls Everyone knows they are watching a fitness show. Not one person has ever come to our show thinking it's Miss Universe nor was there ever a girl entering our show thinking she was entering Miss Universe.

We would unfairly benefit from the opponent

Trump's show truly has nothing that we would ever want. I don't see how or where we could benefit, this was really annoying as it was clear they were scraping the barrel for as much smeg as they could muster. If they'd spent more time doing research instead of dreaming up fantastical accusations they would have known that our show was not for profit in total contrast to Miss Universe where it's all presumably about the bottom line.

We are free riding or exploiting goodwill and faith, that we are passing off and that they could suffer damage to their goodwill and reputation

This was really starting to piss me off. Free riding? Passing off? What a load of horse shit. Being called a free rider was so insulting. If I had his money, our show would be even more mind-blowing. Their UK show could do with free riding off mine to be honest.

But what really got my goat here was their suggestion that I needed them; that I had gravitated to the Miss Universe name because apparently it's a big name and I could hang onto their coat tails. But why would I? None of our organisers even knew their UK show existed as it is simply isn't that big. They weren't even the first show called Universe. Universe was used by NABBA bodybuilding four years prior to Trump's show and is still used to this day for Miss and Mr Universe. There are numerous shows with exactly the same name. Why on earth would I try and be linked to Trump when I have my own respected background well-known in my industry?

I didn't need Trump's coat tails in the health and fitness industry, my name stands up on its own – I've won two world fitness titles, and had my own TV shows, what could I gain from pretending to be anything or anyone else? The further I read the more I began to think that their lawyers lived in cloud cuckoo land and other than checking my website, hadn't bothered to do any due diligence on me.

We would give the impression that the services or events are of comparable quality, thus potentially damaging the opponent's image

Cheeky fuckers. For me, it's like a Skoda dealer getting pissed off that a Ferrari garage has rocked up next door. I'm a former Moulin Rouge and Vegas showgirl, so have a degree of experience on how shows are run and the intricacies of staging something beautiful. We use a professional theatre using a twenty-one metre wide stage. Our show is as much a state-of-the-art theatrical event as a fitness competition, with professional lighting and pyrotechnics to showcase the glitz and glamour these girls deserve, it truly looks amazing with so many colours within each theme.

Miss Universe GB holds heats in such illuminating venues as the Birmingham Town Hall. With no disrespect to that venue, but it's a town hall – more suitable for a pensioners' tea dance than an extravagant show and harks back to the days of holiday camp beauty contests judged by chain smoking perverts. The Miss Universe GB grand final, which I didn't even know existed until these events unfolded, uses a business hotel as a venue. Their show is hamstrung by corporate convention and therefore presumably accountancy departments run the show so it's cheaper to run, less visually appealing and does nothing to enhance the girls who give 100% only to be let down by the show itself. Of course, they are welcome to hire me should they wish to benefit from my theatrical knowledge, but should a poxy accountant tell me I need to back down from a show's aesthetics then he'll be shitting till roll for a year.

That I made a calculated attempt to profit from the goodwill and reputation of two established UK pageants

This totally confused me. Two? I had not received any communication from any party other than Trump's lawyers and why would they be bothered about any other organisation?

Then it all made sense…

I received an email from the Miss Galaxy Pageant UK that read virtually exactly the same as the Miss Universe lawsuit. The girl that ran the Miss Galaxy Pageant UK is about half my age, and had no real background of holding such events yet had the temerity to go head to head against me saying I was trying to profit from her 'reputation'. I would have laughed my cock off had I have had one.

What really annoyed me was that I didn't even know a Miss Galaxy Pageant UK of any kind existed, why would I? I don't run beauty pageants and the only Galaxy I knew was my own, I flew off the handle at Miss Galaxy Pageant UK's lawyers. I told them in no uncertain terms to 'fuck off' and that my show had nothing to do with theirs. I contacted my old friend and organiser of Miss Galaxy Nova USA David Newingham again. He said that Trump had tried to buy him out and when he wouldn't be bought he had also tried to sue him. David wasn't surprised when I told him what was going on and added I must be doing something right and, like him, been seen as a threat. I should have been flattered.

Eventually I found myself compelled to answer Trump's lawyers at Universe LLC New York using the same Socratic logic as these Harvard-trained lawyers, if only to digest my anger and offer salutary responses to their accusations. I wrote them a lengthy letter, keeping it honest and open, as integrity and discipline were the cornerstones of my childhood. The claimants replied with typical legal subterfuge, not answering any of my concerns and just repeated their order for me to sign the undertaking by a certain date. In response I told them I wouldn't 'bend over and take one for the team' and there wasn't a chance I would do as they requested no matter how big their wallet was. I wasn't interested and to 'poke it'. It's always preferable to be more polite in official correspondence; however, their arrogance insulted my intelligence and although emotion shouldn't get in the way, they were simply irritating me so I fucked them off. As far as I was concerned, if they wanted me they could come and get me. I had done nothing wrong.

All this legal bollocks went back and forth for a few years. One day I would receive an email from Trump's lot and the next an email from Miss Galaxy Pageants UK. The timing of each other's paperwork was impeccable; even containing identical extracts. I'm not a great believer in coincidence in these matters so was absolutely convinced that the Miss Universe people had contacted Miss Galaxy Pageants UK to inform them about my show and by them also starting a lawsuit against me it would overwhelm me into submission.

I don't think either of them realised that I actually enjoyed the heavy workload it generated. I thrive on stress, it focuses my mind and helps me relax, and I adore writing, especially long letters and rants. It amused me that it was going this way, and enjoyed learning all about copyright and trademark law. Lee always found it weird that I revelled in such drama, but just let me get on with it, as he liked to see me getting my teeth into issues.

They also wouldn't have known that Miss Galaxy Universe was my sole job, so spending time on the lawsuits was no problem at all – it was just another part of running a successful show.

After chewing up and spitting out the mediocre Miss Galaxy Pageants UK, they got back in their box and I didn't hear another word from them, although recently they used one of my beautiful show pictures on their social media page so it amused me to be able to email them and tell them to remove it or I would sue them as they were passing off as my big stage show. The organiser apologised and removed it instantly. I was quite surprised the

Trump lot were continuing but like the Miss Galaxy Pageants UK lot, I enjoyed seeing how much money they were wasting.

On 17 October 2013 Trump's Oompa Loompa lawyers sent me another 'undertaking'. This one was slightly more amusing and included their bank details for me to pay them a contribution towards their legal expenses within seven days. It was a laugh out loud moment. I couldn't believe their audacity. If I wasn't willing to alter the name of the show under their instruction, why would I give them any money? I would love to have been a fly on the wall of their office, just to watch this variety of human in their natural blundering habitat.

I emailed them with a personal invite for Donald Trump to sit on my panel of judges so he could see the difference in the shows. He declined the offer. I'm glad in a way – he'd have used up our allocation of fake tan.

The correspondence continued; each letter received amazed me. In my eyes they knew there was no case yet carried on just not to lose face. Had they not heard of Northern grit? There was no way I would back down, the harder they pushed the harder I pushed back. My bookshelf is a host of law books ranging from defamation to fire investigation and while this doesn't make me a lawyer, I've grasped a good understanding of how cases work, especially when reading case files and the longer Trump's lawyers continued the more I learned, so in effect they were giving me a free law education. The further I dug my heels the more fascinating I found it and wondered if being a barrister would have been my true vocation in life.

Like barristers, my issue is that I don't like being beaten, especially if I know I'm right. Unlike barristers, if I'm in the wrong I am the first to hold up my hands and apologise. But in this case I was like a dog with a bone, and I honestly thought the Universe case against me was a pile of bollocks. While I hated the legal terms they used to describe my actions it amused me because they were so off the mark.

Chapter 14

Appearances can be deceiving

'One of the most vitriolic abusers was
married to a Met police officer.'

I was being taken to court by one of the world's most powerful men. Yet my issues with Donald Trump's corporation were irrelevances compared to a group of keyboard warriors getting together on social media.

Social media has flattened hierarchy and empowered faceless people to offer opinion in debates. This is amazing and truly a step forward for the littler person to have a voice. Yet social media can also be used to form alliances far stronger than one powerful entity – people using numbers to push an agenda, this truly is democratic yet it can be abused. People may jump on bandwagons just to feel part of something they don't really understand or join just because their social media friends do. In certain circumstances, people band together not to discuss or debate but to form kangaroo courts to publicly bully and destroy people whether they deserve it or not

When we see a victim of bullying, it's easy to see them having a weakness of sorts; someone easily manipulated who can easily be dominated. We may think of children or teenagers or people who stand out from the crowd – the low achievers, those with body issues, the poor, the nerdy geek or others with poor social skills. Someone who stands out from the crowd for whatever reason but someone whom others deem to have a personality 'flaw'.

With the two lives I have led I may be the last person someone may think of as a victim of bullying. When studying fashion design at Southport College I did have such an experience. I was picked on for being more qualified than the rest of the students and self-confidence can sometimes come at a cost, especially from those who seek to drag others down to their swamp of self-pity rather than aspire themselves to greatness. Yet that was when I was eighteen and put some of it down to immaturity of others, but due to this period I have grown up despising bullies. At the age of forty-three my hate for them still burned strongly. I've chewed up and spit out people who have gone down that road with others as I've always tried to protect and look after people no matter the situation and thankfully, since college I'd never been targeted. Then in late 2013 my life changed and it wouldn't be the same until three weeks before my wedding in May 2015.

I first met Jacqueline Hooton in 2012 when I started my Miss Galaxy Universe show. As we opened show entry we noticed an application from a mother and daughter duo Jacqueline and Poppy Hooton from Bognor Regis. Jacqueline was around forty-nine, the oldest applicant and Poppy would be our youngest competitor at eighteen. We immediately hit it off and as they were a unique combination with a hunger for press and a need for adoration I phoned a couple of journalist friends to team the Hooton's up with the *Sun* newspaper, *Woman*, *Bella* and *UltraFIT Magazine* and later I got Jacqueline on BBC1's *The One Show*. While I never took any fee, the pair were paid quite handsomely and got some fantastic pictures and PR out of it and I was genuinely happy for them. Although I did find it rather odd that Jacqueline confided that Poppy wasn't good enough for *UltraFIT Magazine*'s model search and had only been shortlisted as I knew the editor having myself been a cover model and current article writer as the resident fitness expert. Jacqueline had gladly featured in the magazine several months earlier because of my connection, so I wondered whether the glory she sought was more for her than her daughter.

Nevertheless, the Hooton's seemed very grateful with everything I did for them and liked my energy and positivity. In fact, Jacqueline sang my praises to everyone on my work for female empowerment and helping women achieve their goals. I really appreciated her words; I was a strong, independent woman having never had any assistance to achieve my success, it had all been done by working my ass off. I wanted to offer others what I had never had myself – a helping hand, an easier path.

I decided to host two Miss Galaxy Universe shows a year, and organising them alone I found myself swamped, yet I didn't mind being drowned – in the words of Charles Bukowski, 'Find what you love and let it kill you', something I had taken too literally when powerboating – as I thrive on stress and doing it myself meant it would all be done to my own exacting standard, and it paid off – the competition was so popular that entries flooded in and the show was always full within a matter of days.

After the first show Jacqueline offered to assist organising the next due to her stepping down from competing. I genuinely wanted her to continue but she competed for the final time in October 2012 before stepping down. While I enjoyed the workload I accepted her offer to assist organising the next show in June 2013. She loved what Galaxy stood for – teamwork and female empowerment.

As we started to build up to the June 2013 show Jacqueline helped me with the secret all-female Facebook page established to answer any questions, put to bed any worries and in general mother any girls who needed help regardless of it being personal or show related. As organisers we put ourselves in the firing line for everything and as time would tell, the feeding hand I offered would soon be bitten.

Poppy entered again and it was nice to have her back. She had just started studying psychology at Swansea University so she was also busy, but competing would give her a positive physical outlet away from academia.

At this point Andy Screen, who had served in the Royal Marines with Lee, had joined us. Andy is a super guy and a creative genius. He owns a printing and graphic design company 'Golden Rivet' and while too humble to admit it, he is a world renowned pinup artist and has worked for companies such as Coca Cola and Marvel comics – if you want a superhero drawn, this is your man. This tattooed former commando and boxing champion even designed Barbie boxes for Mattel and his artwork and ability to put things together is second to none, so I was chuffed he agreed to design our artwork, graphics and website.

We thought it would be nice for Andy to have a 'Miss Golden Rivet' section of the show where he would choose a girl to represent his brand for the coming year. Utilising Lowell Mason, our amazing photographer, they would shoot a 40s Forces Sweetheart pinup-style calendar and Andy would draw the winner her very own pinup portrait in addition to untold promotion. It was an amazing prize and we were also shooting a calendar for the show so we could tie the products together.

The June 2013 show was amazing, with over a hundred beautiful girls on stage enhanced by colourful lighting to entrance the lively audience. We had many classes to suit the many body types and ages, including 'Bikini Diva' for the Size 6–8, these girls were born tiny and are the Victoria's Secret-type girls. We had 'Fitness Model' for those women more muscular but who still retained femininity and also 'Beach Body' for the girl next door look. There were age categories within these classes and we also had other titles such as Best Newcomer, Best Dressed, Perfect 10, 3 Amazing Achievers, Miss Congeniality, Best Smile and Best Bum. We also have a whole range of tough fitness tests to really bring out the athletic ability of all the girls. We always brought all the girls onstage for the awards, rounded off by a stunning finale of pyrotechnics and confetti.

Poppy won the Beach Body title and also walked away with the Golden Rivet prize – an amazing achievement. Andy was won over by Poppy's genius idea of asking a uniformed Royal Marine, we just so happened to have helping with security, onstage whilst she performed her 'Showgirl' rollerblading routine to the song 'Candy Man'.

Some people aren't born to win or lose, they are simply born not to compete as they have no understanding how things work. A winner requires a degree of humility – they could not be in their position without others help. Even the most selfish sportsperson requires a team ethic. The abuse I would subsequently receive was born from her winning.

Poppy did a great job when shooting the Golden Rivet calendar assisted by Lowell's photography and Andy's artwork. The other Galaxy Girls were flying out to Ibiza to shoot our calendar hosted by my powerboating friend of twenty years Miles Jennings at his four-storey villa with infinity pool overlooking the magical islet of Es Vedra, in an area usually taken by the likes of P Diddy and Kylie Minogue at a cost of $50,000 a week. Renowned for its mystical beauty as it rises majestically 400 metres from the crystal clear Mediterranean, Es Vedra is shrouded in myth and legend. One legend states it to be the tip of the sunken city of Atlantis, other myths suggest it was the home of sirens and sea nymphs who tried to lure Ulysses from his ship in Homer's *Odyssey*. Many have claimed to see UFOs hovering above the islet and while we never saw anything that could be considered a UFO, the sunrises and sunsets at this spot are beyond anything you could imagine. The calendar shoot here was truly memorable and the all girls loved the experience.

Andy designed the Golden Rivet and Miss Galaxy Universe calendars and each displayed each other's logos so there was mutual benefit. All title winners become Galaxy ambassadors and we'd give them as much media coverage as we could to promote their careers. Everyone would naturally promote the calendars on social media, and Poppy, as a winner in two categories, was obliged to promote both. Poppy had won over £500 cash plus many prizes and I had already put Poppy in several publications and opened many doors for her and I had asked for nothing in return. But becoming an ambassador is different. We would expect at least one social media post every couple of weeks, especially in the run up to Christmas so timing was important. Posting on social media is not taxing, we all do it every day so we weren't asking for much. But trouble would soon rear its ugly head.

Jacqueline helped with organising the October 2013 show and Poppy came to sign her calendars. We also had the Galaxy calendars on display promoted by the gorgeous Bikini Diva champion Maz Marrison.

Things had already become a little strange in the run up to the event. I had booked and paid for Jacqueline's hotel room for both the Friday and Saturday night at the Gatwick Central Travelodge as I do for the judges and those who assist with running the show, but she insisted on staying in a different hotel and picking up her own bill, using the excuse that it was too hot and the windows wouldn't open at the Travelodge. This simply was the oddest thing I had ever heard as hotel windows rarely open wide which is why there is air con. But she was insistent, I said I could get a refund and rebook her new accommodation but she was insistent on dealing with it herself and said it was more expensive.

During the event I was even more confused as to why backstage we had the owner of a diverse model agency attempting to poach my acts screaming like a banshee around the dressing rooms, "I'm an agent, I'm an agent," and some old bloke wannabe model who we shall name Freddie alongside her, because I never allow men backstage apart from organisers. He reminded me of Flash Harry from the original *St Trinian's* film and every time I saw him I expected the music to play so we named him Freddy Four-fingers as it seemed most apt. Boy, did he love himself. Unbeknown to me, Jacqueline had invited them both free of charge and without my knowledge taken them backstage. Jacqueline was gushing all over Freddy Four-fingers, hanging off him like a half scraped leech. Maybe it's just that fake 'lovey' shit that theatrical people do, but I had so much to deal with I paid little attention to it.

After the show we returned to the Travelodge, so I was surprised to see Jacqueline there, after all the palaver of her wanting a different hotel, the hotel next to the theatre some five miles away. Her presence became clearer when she started hovering embarrassingly over Freddy Four-fingers, it was hardly covert and quite sickly. She had done several photo-shoots with Freddy and it was obvious she had become quite attached. Like an unwanted wart.

A couple of hours and a few drinks later I was summoned with my good friend Averil into the toilets by Jacqueline where she poured out her 'connection' with Freddy Four- fingers. Alas, he was ignoring her, being surrounded as he was by the many girls her junior. This was somewhat different to the scenario Averil and I had witnessed – all we had seen was Freddy annoying the girls clambering for their attention. Then the penny dropped as to the reality of why she didn't want to be in the same hotel as all of us and the competitors. She was in no position to warrant sympathy and I had little time for her whining. She soon stormed from the toilets with a face like thunder. Her last night with Galaxy was not a happy one. She didn't even say goodbye to Mr Four-fingers or a single one of the girls.

Jacqueline stopped working with Galaxy three days later. She wrote an open letter to the organisers explaining that her husband had complained about her being away from home so much. She stated that she had enjoyed her time and thanked me by name for helping to build her profile, but she needed time out with family. It was fair enough, we all have lives to lead.

I wrote her a lovely message back saying 'Don't be a stranger'. As I was taking Lee my fiancé to Rome for a few days, I asked her if she minded holding the fort. She replied that of course she would and restored my belief that even after the Freddytoiletgate incident our relationship was still strong,

A few weeks passed and Poppy had been decidedly quiet on social media in regards to promoting calendars nor her awards and cash prizes. As an ambassador it's a part of the contract. Just in case she had forgotten, I posted the Galaxy calendar alongside her Golden Rivet calendar to her Facebook wall and complimented her, as all show organisers do, on what a great competitor she was. When I checked back my post had been deleted, so I reposted it. The same thing happened again. I asked her if she was OK, but received no reply.

Another organiser messaged her and Poppy replied that as her mum no longer worked for Galaxy she didn't need to do anything apart from promote her own Golden Rivet calendar, so she wouldn't promote our calendar or the show. She wrote something pretty abusive about me back to the organiser then lied in writing that I had been disrespectful to her mum.

Andy phoned Poppy and politely explained that the calendars cost a lot of time and money to produce and that as an ambassador she needed to promote both calendars equally because that was the deal. If she didn't, it put him in an untenable position with Galaxy because we were linked. Andy explained that without the show Poppy wouldn't even have a calendar to shoot and all the exposure and every prize she had won was ultimately down to Galaxy.

Poppy refused to accept that, stating that I had never done anything for her and she owed me nothing. She added that I was awful and her mum didn't like me. This really hurt as I had taken her under my wing. She had often come to me and asked for advice when she couldn't speak to her mum, both over messenger in writing and on the phone. For her to say this was just spiteful behaviour. I've gone over time and time again the messages between us where I have looked out for her and always, without fail, protected her and given advice. And this was how I was being treated. I was just amazed that a nineteen-year-old psychology student could act this way.

Andy had to ask her if, bottom line, she was willing to promote the Galaxy calendar. If she wasn't then it became awkward for him and he would no longer be able to work with her going forward. Poppy refused to do one promotional post so ultimately she dropped herself from the position.

Andy phoned me and told me of the conversation.

"Fuck me, this is awkward," I said. "Why the fuck has all this happened?" The whole thing was just bizarre, and in all of this, where was Jacqueline and why wasn't she speaking to her daughter and making all this OK?

I realised that I had to speak with Poppy to see how she wanted to progress, because to retain her Beach Body title she still needed to act as an ambassador.

I simply asked Poppy if she would be willing to continue. I wanted to give her another chance to say yes and of course Andy was in total agreement that if she posted on social media as she had promised to do everything would run as normal. If not we would have to in reality ask her to step down, which we didn't want to do. Poppy point blank refused to carry on and was only willing to promote herself in the Golden Rivet calendar.

Poppy made the decision to separate herself, and from that moment my life became a living hell. She set the ball in motion by her own admittance posting she would have her 'revenge' over social media. Revenge for what I have no idea. She left Galaxy, it was us that tried to continue to work with her.

One of the first vicious attacks on social media was from Jacqueline stating a young nineteen-year-old girl's show title had been revoked, this was also sent by private messenger to my friends who later sent it on to me and that it was 'disgusting' and alluding to the fact I was a 'horrendous bully'. This from a woman that I thought a friend and someone trusted to work alongside me. I had done nothing apart from pay for her hotels, raise her profile by putting her and her daughter in newspapers, magazines and even on the TV. She even came away on all-expenses-paid Galaxy weekends that were so much fun and resurrected her sparkle. We had given Jacqueline her own special heaven. In return she gave me hell.

As well as the public posts, she messaged some my closest friends trying to get them to 'turn' on me, suggesting I had stripped her daughter of her titles and that I had been abusive and threatening. She even sent a written message to my photographer and my Supreme Champion plus several other girls that had also forwarded me the messages. If she was writing to my friends I was sure as shit she was copying and posting this same message to many others trying to club together a pool of supporters. Fortunately my friends are loyal and informed me what was going on and sent me her messages, all of which I have to this day. After a few days of goading and abuse, I copied in a lawyer friend on an email to her stating that whatever her issue was with me, then to let it go, leave me alone and get on with her own life and we should go our separate ways. At this point she wouldn't answer the telephone to me for a 'grown up' conversation so we could simply talk like adults and sort out any differences. She blanked me.

It seemed from her initial posts and messages she gathered a lynch mob to take me down that she herself in a previous written message to me had called a 'hit squad'. These people, for whom Jacqueline had previously showed contempt, were the nastiest people in the fitness industry with reputations for being outspoken over social media. There were approximately ten ugly trolls in the 'hit squad' and all bouncing off each others every word led by Jacqueline and Poppy as they both tried to keep under the radar 'directing' their very own plague of trolls.

Her next move was to ask her Facebook posse what the best time was to post, followed by another two posts stating '9pm is it then!!' and 'Tick Tock!'

At the advised time she made an ***Important*** announcement stating 'To make things absolutely clear. I competed in Miss Galaxy Universe twice and then I assisted in the organization. Please note I am not connected to Miss Galaxy Universe in any way whatsoever', to much vaunting from her hit squad who upped their daily attacks on me over social media and who were waiting for this very post as the green light to start the abuse.

I, like many, had built up a habit of looking at my phone first thing on waking up, and my inbox, Facebook page and message list was full of abuse.

It is not a good way to start a day. Many of those causing problems were repeat posters, vilifying me, despite me only ever meeting a couple of them. I received so many abusive personal messages and threats that to go to my phone was an exercise in fear – yet just the simple action of picking up my phone was becoming the most difficult part of my day. And the worst part was that I ignored people who were trying to give me support as I feared the next 'ping' would be someone calling me a liar, an abuser of women and children, a bully, a cunt, a narcissist, a dictator.

The saying 'words will never hurt me' is total bollocks. I have always prided myself on being the total opposite of those accusations pointed and even though I'd like to think I'm pretty resilient to the harsh realities of life, to be labelled as such cut deep to the core. These weren't one-off posts. There was a barrage of these posts all day every day being commented on and shared between the ten of them as they encourage even more people to join in. It spread like a disease. They were an unstoppable disgusting plague.

A liar? Get fucked. I am known for my truthfulness for a couple of reasons. Firstly it's my character; my blunt honesty has got me far. It's also got me into trouble but rather a truthful lion than a tactful mouse and I love the look on people's faces when you are so truthful it's painful. Secondly, and more for practicality, after my racing crash I have no short term memory, something quite embarrassing when suggesting a movie we've seen only two days before. However, having no short-term memory means I can't lie as I have no frame of reference to lie around.

A bully? For someone who vehemently opposes all forms of bullying this really hurt. To be labelled the very thing you are victim of didn't even occur until we set about fighting back, just to be accused of it destroyed me.

However, when I was called a dictator my team did the best to cheer me up. I am a director of a show. I direct and I *am* direct. I like discipline, good timekeeping and accuracy. I'm well-known for being strict and this is understood by everyone who knows me, so jokes included a gallery of dictators with my photograph added. This was the only one that made me giggle through the tears, because it was so ridiculous.

It's easy to self reflect and ask 'what did I do wrong?' Being a victim of cyberbullying is little different from being physically abused, we blame ourselves, we feel lonely, insecure, anxious and spend time trying to figure out what to do or where to go to avoid being harassed, yet the cyberworld is all-consuming and difficult to escape when all those around cannot survive without the internet. We surmise that it is our fault but the longer I reflected the more I was stunned and confused at how the events had unfolded.

Those who publicly supported me were also feeling the hit squad's backlash. Even model-turned-journalist Jodie Marsh who I had recently connected with was also condemned over Twitter because she was anti-bullying, yet I was an apparent bully. This is the only industry I have ever known that the more you help someone the more chance you have of getting totally fucked over by them. If you look at Jodie's posts on Facebook or you speak with her you will see we both suffer the same fate, which we do note to each other. Jodie is super nice and one of the most generous souls I have ever known; she's a shrewd character and her work ethic is second to none, yet her benevolence is repeatedly thrown back in her face.

I get it, the fitness industry is based on looks and media attention so attracts egotists yet once they taste limelight they change. As a show organiser I have seen it time and time again. They become superior as soon as they get in a magazine, they don't realise that the magazine didn't find them, I've actually 'talked' a good story to get people a column inch. They believe their own hype and their own bullshit, yet this was taking things to a whole new level.

Once this hate campaign against me escalated it was evident that it was carefully orchestrated. The Hooton's throughout made sure they didn't mention my name, yet not naming someone in defamation law is not a defence because if everyone knows who you are referring to then it's the same thing. Everyone knew, because the people who had joined in the messages, many had either said my name, my show's name or insinuated who I was. Even more stupidly many of the hit squad often prefixed threats with 'without prejudice' clearly not knowing what it means in legal terms.

The main person in the hit squad who was unimaginably nasty throughout the ordeal was Jacqueline's close friend Paul Corkery, a fitness photographer. I had never met him but there was something about him that tingled my spidey senses. I had no hesitation turning him down as our show photographer and openly advised girls against shooting with him. Subsequently we'd never seen eye to eye so it was of no surprise that he jumped on the bandwagon. What shocked me was that Jacqueline had sought friendship from Corkery, as when working on Galaxy, she had also stated she didn't trust him yet here they were suddenly stroking each other's ego all over social media. She even sent her daughter Poppy to do a sexy photo-shoot with him where she shockingly had her panties round her knees. Jacqueline was shooting with other photographers but never with Corkery even though he had openly said over social media 'I can't wait to shoot you and Poppy!' But Jacqueline knew he was a vile human being yet happy enough to feed her daughter to him. This really freaked me out.

Another one of the squad was Kerrie Bishop, better known as 'The Girl With The Golden Gun' as she had worked as the spray tanner on our show. I knew she had illegally taken money from the show so again it was of no surprise she was trying to discredit me while I was breathing down her neck.

Another vocal member of the squad was a bodybuilder who worked in her spare time as a prostitute. I was sent her profile from an escort website. One of her profile pictures was from a bodybuilding show wearing a bikini borrowed from the Miss Galaxy Universe Supreme Champion who was horrified and vowed never to wear it again, I can only imagine it being a target for many men's baby batter in some sort of bodybuilding sex kink. I had never met or even spoken to this woman yet she was happy to contribute abuse.

Another member who I also had never met or spoken to was the daughter of Billy Murray from the hit TV series *The Bill* and sister of Hollywood actress Jaime Murray. I'd never even heard of this girl, but she blatantly used my full name when calling me a 'fucking bully' on public posts to open a sluice gate of defamatory comments across social media. It was seriously horrendous. What made this worse was that social media shows she runs an anti-bullying and self-defence class for children in London's East End. These people are disgusting members of the human race.

One of the most vitriolic abusers was married to a police officer in the Met Police and building a female sisterhood empowerment business whilst she was ripping me down over social media. I had helped her in the past getting her a paid feature in the *Star* newspaper but she repaid me with hate and abuse. She promotes this 'Sisterhood' at a Scottish fitness expo but her social media abuse was fierce, I still have her every post. She was Hooton's right-hand woman and Paul Corkery's best friend. It's a sickness these people have.

Each of these bullies in turn shared their hate and each others to their own followers, and it didn't take long for the abuse to reach thousands of people. Where the fuck did these evil reptiles come from and what the fuck had I ever done to deserve this? All these people worked as a trolling team, it was clearly visible from every post across social media.

The gang mentality of cyber-abuse was quite topical at the time as the Justine Sacco case was in full flow. It was a case of a woman who tweeted a rather ill-advised statement which drew the censure of millions of people. While her poor attempt at humour had been taken out of context, it showed how quickly the internet can turn against someone.

In my situation, I hadn't said anything. There was no proof of me ever being rude or bullying to anyone, her hit squad were all egging each other on, and while the abuse spread to thousands of viewers I never caught up international infamy; yet the amount of online abusers is an irrelevance in many ways. Millions of people can attack and shame a stranger but similar damage can be done by a few select people who work in a very small circle within a niche industry who continued to shame me to friends and colleagues both in and outside of social media.

Justine Sacco must have felt like the world hated her. I didn't, because for me it was closer to home. I felt my business falling apart; all the respect I had earned throughout my life was gone with future colleagues in the fitness industry veering away, scared of my reputation as a bully rather than my true character of assisting the many in need. My status had simply disappeared. I was sure that everyone who knew me, other than my close circle of friends, now looked at me as an abuser, a cunt and a bully. You presume opinions change and it's personal.

There's no escape from social media especially when running a business through it. I'd wake up from a deep sleep and realise that I didn't actually want to be awake because I couldn't take another day of torment. I didn't want to get dressed, I didn't want to talk to anyone, I lost interest in everyone and everything and turned from an extrovert to a soulless introvert with life as an encumbrance. I would just lie in bed crying silently because I didn't want Lee to hear me, even though he knew. It was breaking him apart too as he couldn't make my sadness go away. I avoided seeing Mum and Dad even though we lived next door. When Mum did catch me she asked me why my eyes were red, I thought up some excuse and lied. On the odd occasion I did brave the outdoors I always wore sunglasses so no one could see my blood-shot eyes sore from crying. I smiled through pain and pretended everything was OK. OK – that state of happiness I usually saw only in those who had never really lived life and was a place I would have given my right arm for. Sleep was welcome relief but would only come from incessant crying. Hiding within the womb of my duvet doesn't help when the world outside taunts you so the darkness of solaced sleep was swiftly becoming my only respite. It is a dangerous place to be.

Flushing the trolls out of my life for good

Enough was enough. After three months of incessant abuse I called Greater Manchester police after I'd received suggestions of threats made against me. The police told me I needed a lawyer because it was a civil not criminal act and as I hadn't actually been physically attacked, they could do nothing. However PC McCann phoned Jacqueline Hooton to ask her to stop. It was an empathic if not toothless gesture. Jacqueline agreed, and PC McCann called me back to tell me the good news. I put the phone down with a sense of relief. It was short-lived. Within a couple of hours the abuse reached new levels of depravity.

I was pilloried for contacting the police by her hit squad, wasting police time and labelled selfish. Even worse, Jacqueline, who was abundantly aware of the pain she was causing boasted how she felt empowered and that if I 'succeeded in silencing her today' (because I had called the police) she was still contactable via email. How someone can feel empowered by ruining someone is beyond me but was an overt insight into her psyche. It was clear the abuse was to continue unabated unless I sought professional help. What amazed me was that all these retarded reptiles put everything down in writing allowing myself and friends to screen shot the lot.

Ironically, given Poppy Hooton's intended career, I went to see a psychologist and Lee told me to call the National Bullying Hotline. I spoke to an extremely helpful husband and wife team who really helped me understand what was going on. They gave me so much of their time it really made a difference. It was also time to get a legal team involved.

Although painful, friends such as my photographer Lowell and my former Supreme Champion sent me correspondence with an apology, as they understood the pain it would cause. They had received messages from Jacqueline being defamatory and trying to turn them against me. She believed my friends would side with her, but they all stuck their neck out for me. The picture was coming together nicely, the dots were joining up and it was abundantly clear that the hate campaign had been calculated beyond anything I had ever experienced. As soon as someone didn't side with her she blocked them on social media. It wasn't long before she had blocked around 400 Galaxy girls including the Supreme Champ when she told Jacqueline in no uncertain terms what she was doing was wrong.

I researched many different defamation lawyers and found GMS Law. I liked their reviews and staff profiles. When I first asked for advice, sobbing muffled my words. To have a good defamation case then you have to show damage and to show damage you need to have a 'reputation' and fit all of the criteria. As soon as I mentioned that I ran a successful all-female pageant, that I had been in hundreds of magazines and hosted TV shows, recited my life as a stunt double, powerboat champion and world fitness champion she stopped me and said that she needed me to speak directly with the boss of the law firm.

Richard Clegg, the owner of GMS Law, called me back. It was clear he had done some due diligence on me. It must have been a difficult conversation, not from a legal sense but from a communicative viewpoint, as I must have clogged up the microphone with snot while blubbering down the phone. Without seeing any proof he simply said, "Sarah, please don't worry. We'll take this on a no win no fee account and try and sort things out for you."

I felt immediate trust in him and sent him what evidence we had accumulated. I asked Lee to create a chronology of events. By just printing off every abusive message we managed to cover the entire lounge floor, which was heaven for our cats who played in the paper like kids in new snow until we locked them from the room, much to their annoyance.

Not all social media posts display times and dates, they simply say, '10 minutes ago' or 'yesterday'. It was so confusing but eventually Lee pieced it together. I was pretty useless, and all I contributed was to wet the paper and smudge the ink from tears. We taped all the printouts together like it was a children's school project and rolled them up before sending them to his office.

Richard and his staff were more than a legal team. I've known a lot of legal eagles in my life but these guys were different. Regardless of it being a sensitive case they were just amazing in the way they handled everything. Richard spoke to me whenever I needed him, he always returned my calls and nothing was too much trouble. It's easy to say 'well it's money in his pocket.' But in this case it wasn't, this was a no win no fee case. Nothing in life is guaranteed and this sort of case isn't easy because there are so many things to prove. Jacqueline Hooton had lit the touch paper and controlled abusers to do her dirty work, so for us we had to prove she was fully in control and that whatever she had actually said, it was alluding to it being about me. Unless she had a loaded gun then proving her guilt in legal terms would never be easy.

Richard told me that before he set the wheels in motion he had a duty of care to outline the realities of the case. A case of this nature could take two years and there was a high probability the abuse could get worse before it got better. I had to make the decision about whether to proceed. As soon as I said I wanted to, it was all systems go. I had Trump and his cronies giving me the shits from across the Atlantic, but that case was quite fun to handle; this case was close to home, literally and figuratively, and aged me as it took over my life.

The abuse continued. My phone would ping and I knew what was coming. Lee would tell me not to look but I had to. We had to catalogue everything. I sometimes didn't get dressed for days. I forgot how to smile, I felt sad 24 hours a day. I drank a bottle of wine every night, I stopped going to the gym, I had no energy, no lust for life. I was the living dead.

I didn't understand how this could happen to me. I was happily racing powerboats and having fun and doing fitness competitions when I started Galaxy to help others achieve goals and I concentrated on everyone else's happiness and progression. I gave everything to people like the Hooton's. I lost money on the first show and the shows barely broke even on the rest because I wasn't money hungry and we were non-profit making – I always put the money back into the show and the girls. I started to wonder why the fuck I had ever started Miss Galaxy Universe. I gave everything and all I got back was abuse, or that's what it felt like at the time.

By February 2014 I told my team I was closing the show down and everyone could fuck off; I didn't want anything to do with this pathetic egotistical industry. I was a simple female with zero complications or hang-ups. I just wanted to go back to racing or indeed anything else. Anything had to be better than this shit. My team wouldn't let me close the show, neither would Richard Clegg because then Jacqueline would have won.

Jacqueline encouraged all her followers to rise up against me declaring that my legal team 'couldn't sue all of them'. I again remained silent and let her ego hang her.

Friends picked up the slack. On top I remained calm when I needed to because I felt I had to lead by example. But underneath I was like a duck weighed down by an anvil, paddling like crazy to stay afloat. So even after being ripped apart I had to find the energy to carry on. I never replied to any abusive post and had to rise above it; hard to do when trying to attract competitors for the forthcoming show and remain positive for the competitors on social media.

I was broken but Lee, Averil, Lowell, Andy and his wife Rachel had my back and my legal team were always there for me emotionally.

When posts written by Jacqueline pointed to me being a bully, an abuser and narcissistic, she always denied it was about me, and said it was about someone else. So when asked via the lawyer on exactly who she meant, Jacqueline remained silent. If she could have answered just one of the questions it would have cleared much of it up yet she tangled herself in so many lies my lawyer found much of her paperwork contradictory. She never did answer the question. She couldn't. She avoided it because she was lying.

I eventually told Mum and Dad about a year after the abuse started. I was too embarrassed to tell my own parents and that hurt as much as the abuse itself. I have three brothers yet out of all of us I'm regarded as the strongest. How on earth could I be embarrassed about cyber abuse? I couldn't ever be bullied, not me, I'm a tough cookie. But I had been, I had been through the mill, I had been cyber-battered, I had been smashed in, beaten up and spat out and I would have given anything for it to have been a physical beating as I would have healed quicker.

Mum was devastated I hadn't told her before, but she knew something had been wrong. My parents are in their 70s, and still call a radio a wireless; social media is something they never use. When I told mum I just broke down. She did too; upset that she couldn't be there for me at the worst time of my life. She'd already been through the life-support machine with me, this would have been a walk in the park for her.

I had been forced to tell Mum and Dad as I was going to court to settle a dispute with spray tanner Kerrie Bishop, 'The Girl With the Golden Gun', serial abuser and in my eyes a thief. I had made it clear to Kerrie that I wouldn't let her get away with taking the Galaxy money and it ended up in the small claims court. While yet another legal case, this one was well within my comfort zone. Theft is theft and thieves need sorting.

I sued her in October 2014 for removal of money from the show in 2013. The case reached the national press with the hilarious headline 'Pageant Boss Browned Off'.

Bishop rocked up at court without any papers prepared, something the courts find discourteous to the legal process. Normal procedures ensued but when Kerrie called my husband a liar she was never going to win. Courts are a place to state your case not to start throwing shit – it's not a monkey house.

The judge turned to Lee and asked, "Mr Barrett, how would you reply to Miss Bishops statement that you are a liar?"

He didn't even think about the answer, "I'd reply to that by saying that I am very disappointed in her reaction, having been a Royal Marine for almost 20 years holding the long service and good conduct medal. Having never been in any form of trouble inside or outside of the military and holding the values that I do, I naturally am disappointed, Sir."

I sat there wondering where he'd hidden the autocue; it just tumbled off his lips with such eloquence that I couldn't even believe it was him. He didn't miss a beat nor show emotion. Kerrie Bishop sat seething and couldn't resist another outburst.

The judge called Ellie Jones, a witness I had brought, into the courtroom. Ellie had travelled quite a distance to give evidence for me but the judge felt he didn't need her statement after all so he asked her in and sat her down as he wanted thank her for travelling and staying overnight and assured her that just being here on the day was of great assistance in painting a picture.

The judge looked at the paperwork I had submitted. I had made sure it was clear, concise and colour-coded for ease of reference; judges have enough stuff to deal with so I think making the paperwork easy to follow is respectful to his position. He told me my calculations were wrong, which stumped me; I thought them as perfect, the last thing I wanted to do was make a mistake. He took his calculator out and told me that I had short changed myself and would be paid far more by Miss Bishop. I was sure that the quoted higher figure was incorrect but I wasn't going to say anything, he was the boss. He then added my travel and the hotel bills and the two days of work I had missed because of this.

The judge then paused before confirming that I had paid for Ellie's travel and accommodation. I told the judge I was happy to pick up Ellie's tab as it was my decision to ask her to appear. After all, I felt that was the right thing to do irrespective of Kerrie Bishop stealing from me; her bill had already swollen somewhat. He added it to the bill before asking Kerrie how she would like to pay. She explained it would have to be in small instalments. I informed the judge she was a homeowner so in fact could pay me in one go. The judge gave her two weeks to pay me.

The judge shook Lee's hand and thanked him on his service in the Royal Marines. He thanked Ellie and me before shaking our hands as well. Kerrie Bishop stormed off without thanking the court, which win or lose shows lack of deference to the court, a product of her misguided sense of entitlement and why she had ended up here in the first place.

While I was happy one hurdle had been overcome I still had the cyber-abuse case to contend with. Every time I talked about it the dark thoughts returned. It's fine to be on the receiving end but even though it had died down, just by talking about it rekindled all the pain. I was determined to take the case to the High Court, no matter how traumatic it may be, to highlight the suffering cyber-abuse can cause.

Jacqueline Hooton suddenly settled in May 2015. If you go to court you are either found guilty or not guilty. If you settle prior to court, not only do you save yourself a lot of money should the outcome not go your way, but you don't need to accept guilt. It's the old school saying, 'Never leave it to the judges'. She bottled it, she knew the truth would unravel once encountering the force of my prosecution barrister who would tie her up in lie after lie.

If I hadn't have been through hell for eighteen months, I would have refused her offer and continued to the High Court, but it wasn't about the money. It was about justice and allowing the courts to punish someone for their actions. Moreover, I was due to get married three weeks later. I'd already cancelled it once due to the pressure of the case, and I was damned if I was to cancel it a second time. Richard Clegg said to me, "Just enjoy your wedding. I don't want to hear off you for at least a month. It's over and leave us to do the rest. Don't think about anything else just have a great time."

Jacqueline Hooton to this day denies any wrongdoing. If she admitted to it, her business would be ruined. I'd question any innocent person why they would agree to pay £15,000 to settle a case before it went to court especially when they would have to pay the other party's legal fees, in my case £57,000, and her own costs which I imagine reflected mine. Cyberbullying likely cost Jacqueline Hooton over £110,000 and did nothing to enhance her reputation in trying to ruin mine. Her statement published in the *Mail Online* read:

"Regrettably I was sued for libel by Ms Donohue in April 2014 over comments I made on Facebook. On legal advice I settled those proceedings, which could otherwise have become very expensive by paying a sum of money to Ms Donohue. However, I made no admissions in respect of the claim advanced against me, gave no apology to Ms Donohue, nor was there any public statement made about the matter in court as part of the settlement. I am aware of a number of posts made by Ms Donohue on social media since this settlement, as well as emails and messages she has sent to several of my clients, professional contacts and my employer. All these publications have been passed to my lawyers and I do not intend to comment any further on the issue publicly. I would only caution those who seek to use social media platforms to express their views about the risks of doing so." The last line is the only thing I will ever agree with coming out of her mouth.

The settlement was national news and spread around the fitness industry like wildfire. By this time many fitness professionals had distanced themselves from the Hooton's and the hit squad had dissolved. I even had one of them apologise to me. She was upset with herself for being involved and no longer keeps in contact with any of them, she had no idea it would cause this much emotional damage and the sad thing was that she didn't even know me, only backing off when she saw how vitriolic the abuse had become. This took some guts and I'll never hold a grudge against those strong enough to apologise for doing wrong and totally respect her contrition. She was one of the best friends of the bully married to the police officer but they were no longer speaking. She even offered to speak to the *Mail Online* and admit to what had gone on and her part in it, she was that upset I had been so affected she would have put herself through similar. Myself and the journalist declined her offer after much thought, purely down to the damage she could be doing to herself. She remains a friend because forgiveness is everything.

It gave me no sense of satisfaction about not trusting the hit squad henchman Paul Corkery when, on 14 September 2016, he was sentenced to two years imprisonment for two offences of sexual assault by digital penetration and sexual touching of another female victim. He has been put on the sex offenders register and is subject to a Sexual Harm Prevention Order preventing him from working as a photographer unsupervised once released for ten years. It was said he was sexually manipulative and displayed potentially predatory behaviour. He breached his position of trust and unfortunately no one else saw what I saw in him a long time ago. I feel sorry for his wife and young child.

Social media allows everyone their freedom of speech regardless of the damage it can do. There was no confidentiality clause with the eventual settlement and I share my story to help other victims and it continues to help me come to terms with what happened. Mental recovery from this type of abuse doesn't happen overnight, ask any victim. She had been a cancer on my thoughts that I couldn't cut out for eighteen months. We all have our own way of dealing with it. I want people to see what I went through because anyone can be a bully and anyone can be bullied. I built a WordPress site of all the abuse which will last a lifetime and as a reminder to those whose names are visible that they should hang their head in shame. I still have every post they wrote, every message they sent and witnesses who came forward. What's in print will never disappear, it's there for everyone in the world to read. mycyberbullystory.wordpress.com

***

Throughout this whole ordeal the fitness market was changing. We had watched more shows spring up – in 2012 the industry only had two separate shows both of us putting on two shows a year but the total had risen to nine shows popping up all with several shows each a year in 2014. The total number of shows in the UK ballooned from four to over thirty. The industry was becoming diluted and to stay ahead of the game we had to start thinking about change or otherwise we would struggle to compete in an ever-growing market. Miss Galaxy Universe was all female and most shows are 70% male-dominated so we decided to widen my contest's scope to accommodate men therefore having to change the name. There was no way on God's earth I was going to alter it at the behest of any avaricious lawyer. I would rename it for my reasons at a time of my choosing that suited the business and its competitors.

We had to see the 2016 season out as girls had pre-entered and venues were booked and contracted, one of which was the O2 in London, but as we prepped for the final shows, we also were preparing for the new show and its launch with Andy Screen working to get the new website and promo ready.

The very last Galaxy was 5 November 2016 and would make way for the National Fitness Federation (NFF) launch in May 2017. It would again be the only fully functional fitness show in the UK catering for both men and women throughout the many different classes. It was refreshing to have a change and the NFF was looking forward to a great future as long as we didn't get similarly ridiculous hassles from the Namibian Farmers Federation or Notts Forest Fan club…

The first show was a huge success although disappointingly only three people opted to do the fitness tests so we had to cancel the functional side. This highlighted the fact that most people in the fitness industry who take part in these shows only want to look good and sadly performance doesn't interest them. The performance element is why I built the show in the first place. And it saddened me greatly. As we cleaned up after our inaugural show and prepped for the October show I received three emails in June. One from Chris Reindl Powerboats asking me to race their series across America in 2018. One from Diego Testa an Italian champion asking me to race in Italy. And one from my former teammate Martin Lai asking to me assist in launching the Asia Powerboat Series and to fly to Hong Kong with him in September for a display race. I printed the emails out and handed them to my husband. I barely paused to take a breath as I told him that racing meant more to me than the shows. The shows were all about other people and many of these people aren't particularly pleasant in an already unforgiving and egotistical industry. I spent my time giving and them taking. As time went on the mental reward of producing the most beautiful production in the industry had worn thin and with no one being interested in the performance side then what was the point in continuing when the side of the show I was passionate about was dead?

I had been bludgeoned by the bullying and now no one cared about the fitness tests. Fuck it, I emailed the theatre and cancelled the date, refunded competitors that had paid to do the show and made the calls to Chris Reindl and Martin Lai that I was fully available for the foreseeable future. Flights were booked and off I flew to Hong Kong. It was beautiful to be free. AWS Racewear kitted me out in a made-to-measure bright green race suit and I'm back in the driving seat and loving it.

After Trump's controversial comment about Mexican immigrants flooding over the US border in the summer of 2015, joint Miss Universe owners NBC cut their ties to him and stopped airing Miss Universe. Trump later bought out NBC's portion of Miss Universe and almost immediately sold the whole lot to IMG around September 2015. IMG also own the UFC which they bought for $4 million so pretty much have a wallet as deep as Trump's.

Legal paperwork from Trump's office had ceased around the time of his Mexican issue, naturally they were busy with bigger fish. I didn't think about it, notice it or even care why as I had never actually taken any of it seriously in the first place. It's only on looking back I can piece it together. After all, I shredded all Trump-related documents to make bedding for pets.

As someone who has always stood up for the small guy, it's rather empowering to know that Trump's powerful organisation couldn't win a battle against a farm girl from the north of England. This was just another fruitless attempt of life trying to bother me, and it had failed miserably, I'm not born to care for such trivialities and live for today, not for an unpredictable future.

There is no way after such a long in battle that you cannot retain an emotional attachment. Trump vs Donohue is a story that has been told umpteen times over endless dinners and drinks and no doubt will continue – the crux of the conversation being that I actually admired the fact that Trump and his henchmen clung onto me for a whole four years and it's rather validating that Donald J Trump cared enough to attempt shutting down little old me and my beautiful show. My paperwork had been signed off by Trump himself, yet I have no intention of selling his signatures on eBay. It gives me more pleasure to know that I played cat and mouse with the now President of the United States.

Chapter 15

My life, love and happiness

'Life just didn't get better than this.'

People often say I've had great life or that I've been lucky. Lucky? For racing boats or for almost leaving my mum and dad without a daughter? For running an all-female fitness show and helping women achieve their goals or for getting badly cyber-abused because of it? Newton's third law springs to mind.

I say we make our own luck by choosing a path and sticking to it regardless of what is thrown at us and with that great life people insist I've had, it has most certainly come with hurdles. Hurdles that some people couldn't have got over or coped with. If I died tomorrow I would die contented and accomplished, I seriously couldn't have had a more enjoyable life and wide range of extraordinary experiences.

I have had the highest highs, more than most people could experience in ten lifetimes and the lowest lows, so low that in the same situation people not as strong as myself or those without a support network have in fact committed suicide and it's a low that I would never wish on anyone. It's safe to say that my life has been an overload of emotions, but it's a curious life because after all, I'm just a simple village girl.

My parents aren't rich or famous, nor do they have friends in high places, scenarios which can so very often be found in those who have similar lifestyles to me where people deem us as 'lucky', many people are lucky above being talented and are born into a lifestyle, they have the easy way in and don't have to work for it. Mine just erupted. I had no aspirations of being the only female offshore racing driver in the world, in turn it making me a 'poster girl' for the most dangerous male-dominated sport in the world. I'm still now the most successful female offshore powerboat racer and the longest standing having raced over twenty-five years with well over 220 races under my belt.

My curious set of circumstances attracted three TV documentaries about my life from *Ripley's Believe it or Not*, BBC's *999* and even Channel 4. It also pasted me over magazine covers and saw me in hundreds of publications, with TV appearances, radio interviews, my own TV shows and being in movies.

I actually have a degree in Fashion and Textile Design, I presumed that one day I would be as good as my mum and grandma at making clothes. Instead I swapped my sewing machine for a powerboat, was even a pinup in *Soldier Magazine*, I hold several international sporting titles in two totally different sports and a speed record becoming 'Lady of The Lake'. Yes I sometimes sit back and think 'How the fuck did this happen?' But more than that I sit back and feel complete. My life has been wholesome and my husband is beyond awesome, a former Royal Marine of twenty years what more could a girl like me want out of life?

Life needs to be enjoyed to the full and as I made the decision to close the NFF show in June 2017. I knew that my life was going to become great once again.

So no, I haven't been 'lucky'; I have made the best out of every situation I have been in. My glass is always half full, never half empty. I have also always done the right thing, remained true to my word never backed down for anything or anyone or given in to those with wealth or power. I always try and look at things in a positive way. I also believe in karma.

So as I look back at my escapades over the years both good and bad, I take knowledge and some form of amusement away from each one.

Dad built me and taught me these valuable lessons in life as well as giving me the perfect upbringing, and Charles Burnett III is the man responsible for what I have in my life today. He gave me the opportunity to race offshore and it is through racing that my entire career was built. Not one person has built a career alone and without Charles Burnett III I would never have achieved such success and without my dad, I would never have coped with all life was going to throw at me.

Through powerboat racing and my fitness competitions my life had been amazing until the bullying stopped me in my tracks. It was a dark cloud that stayed for a while.

It was mid-2016 when I finally knew I was back to what I deemed normal. We were on our way to Charles Burnett's sixtieth birthday party in the Colorado mountains. Without doubt he throws the best parties, and only those he holds dear to him and he trusts are ever invited. I have yet to meet anyone with such flair for eccentricity, and his unrivalled talent for making everyone feel loved and his warm heart made him one of the most beautiful people that has every walked this planet. My love for Charles exceeds any love for a friend; he's a soul mate and someone to whom I owe so much. I'm sure he wouldn't see it like that but for me, this man is truly spectacular and I love having him in my life.

As soon as I received an email from the wonderful Ingrid, Charles' secretary who has been with him forever, I knew something was cooking. I opened it expecting something amusing to appear. I wasn't disappointed. A picture of Charles on a 'wanted' poster with a reward flashed before my eyes. It was an invite to his sixtieth birthday party with the theme of 'Heroes and villains of the 1800s' – so very Wild West. If Charles was throwing it we knew it was going to be the biggest one yet. Lee hadn't been to one of Charles's parties; however, he had done a track day when Charles had hired Brands Hatch so knew the occasion would be spectacular.

Within the hour I'd booked us two Virgin Atlantic Upper Class seats and hired a convertible yellow Mustang – my favourite car of all time. After all the shit we'd endured, we felt we deserved a little self-pampering.

We flew a few days early so we could make a holiday of the trip. We had done little research – I find too much travel planning inhibits my natural wanderlust and as the US has a whole host of amazing sights we just went in the general direction of the host hotel where we'd be staying a few days later. We got in the car, unfolded the courtesy map and pointed at Colorado Springs.

The scenery of snow-capped mountaintops in the distance and expanses of land which stretched as far as the eye could see underneath the blue skies and clean air washed over us like a cool breeze on a summers day.

We drove into Manitou springs, west of Colorado Springs, and immediately wanted to stay here forever. It has the look and feel of a small Wild West town with bars, boutiques and interesting buildings scattered throughout, all with a backdrop of snow-capped mountains accessible by the town's train that will slowly chug its way from 40 degree sunshine to bone-numbing cold. We spotted a motel in the town centre and just walked right in a grabbed a room for a few days of spa treatments, finest foods and decadent drinks all under the blissful sun that sparkled over glistening mountains that we intended to summit albeit courtesy of the Pike's Peak Cog railway.

The weather atop Pike's Peak itself could be classed as invigorating hence most people wear sensible footwear at the very least. I wore flip-flops. Being a Northern lass and an outdoors girl I don't get cold feet, in fact my feet melt snow as they are permanently hot, a strange but welcome phenomenon during the winter.

I thought a T-shirt more than adequate at 14,115 feet given everyone else wore huge jackets. I've often found it amusing how acclimatised to the conditions we become. My racing friends, Ian and Miranda Cutler and their son Thor, emigrated to Florida eighteen years ago. They wear jackets when I visit them in the colder months, yet I'm still red hot in a bra top and hot pants. The Peak was beautiful. We disembarked the cog railway into a snowdrift, there were men shovelling away whose job it seemed was to continuously clear snow from the track at the top so the railway could function. I felt like I was in another world. It was so bleak yet so beautiful. The air was refreshingly cold and the views amazing. It's said you can see the curvature of the earth from the very top and as we looked out as far as the eye could see with the sun starting to burn orange, there it was, a gentle curve. A beautiful sight never to be forgotten.

After a few days of heavenly Manitou Springs we drove over to the host hotel ready for the weekend's celebrations. With the roof down and the sun shining, we kicked up dust all across the desert roads and if it weren't for passing cars we could have been on the moon.

As we arrived Charles was standing right in the middle of the hotel car park deep in conversation with some hotel employees I hadn't seen him for almost two years so even before Lee had managed to stop the car I leapt out and jumped on Charles. It was so great to see him and his face lit up when he saw me. Manchester to Denver was the longest journey I had made for any celebration, but I wouldn't have missed this for the world.

Charles is the man who has everything so buying a present is never easy, but with Charles it's about amusement so we found a 'Burnett's' Vodka and wondered if a he actually owned the company. We also found a rodeo horse-shaped drinks holder in honour of his new venture of building a ranch.

We settled into the hotel and grabbed a drink and a snack. Charles was the magnet that brought people from all over the world together and it was great to see the same friendly faces who were at all his events. No one knew anything of what was in store for us that evening other than two coaches would pick us all up at 6.30 pm.

At 6.30 pm prompt, the first coach arrived and we clambered on board, it was so lovely to see people who I hadn't seen for many years. Sat across from me was 'Land Speed Louise' who I hadn't seen since I had been with Charles during speed week at the Bonneville Salt Flats when he was joining the 200 mph club. It wasn't long before we were snorting loudly recalling the events there, including Louise telling me to put sun factor all the way to my knicker line because the sun would reflect off the salt up my skirt and burn my thighs.

Louise is a world-renowned expert and writer for high-speed motorsport. She is a lady who can spin stories about all sorts of people from all over the world in some hilarious situations and it was amazing to see her again. The last time I had actual contact with her was when I was short listed for the female land-speed record hoping to reach 600 mph. The gig was offered to a female fighter pilot, which didn't surprise me. The record wasn't broken and fortunately the pilot survived, the car skidding onto its side at a speed so ridiculously fast it took three miles to come to a halt.

It was quite a profound moment looking back to the Salt Flats where I met Louise. Charles and I were flying to Las Vegas to drive a hire car through the desert up to the Utah–Nevada border signified by a simple white line on the road. At Vegas airport I was stopped for a security check. Nothing unusual there apart from the fact that I had just won a World Fitness title so was in extremely good shape and was wearing a tiny bikini top, a pair of mules and a skirt that most people would describe as a belt. I stood there bemused as the female security guard ran her hands over the tiny scraps of cloth I wore. As we collected our luggage, Charles thrust $100 in my hand and told me to keep myself amused on the slot machines until he had arranged the car. I told him I had my own money but he insisted that I would lose so rather I lose his than mine. I was amused that the airport was a gambling house so shrugged my shoulders, looked for the nearest machine, fed some money in and pressed some random buttons. I had no idea what the machines did other than flash lights and make strange noises. Charles returned twenty minutes later. I gave him my $250 winnings and with a grin told him he owed me lunch.

Not giving a hoot about his status is one reason I think I was the only UK powerboat racer who ever got invited to his functions. Charles may have given me glorious opportunities but I never bought into materialistic wealth; I never asked him for anything and even issued him the odd bollocking if I thought someone was using him. It used to drive me mad the way some UK leeches would gather around him clucking away just because he was wealthy and the queue of tossers lining up to take advantage of his generosity. As time would tell, friendship matters more than money and will outlast it, whatever the social status and here I was, sat in a luxury coach with wonderful happy and trusting people who were all well brought up, respectable, fun-loving and from all walks of lives from little old me to people that have been on the cover of *Forbes*.

Louise and I were still gossiping away as we turned off the main road and along a dirt track into the mountains, we kicked up dust for at least 30 minutes during which time Ingrid offered commentary over the microphone with snippets of information such as The Hooters, a famous American band, would be playing and we'd enjoy a Wild West shoot out and BBQ. Other than that she gave nothing away – a tour guide without guidance!

As the sun was about to slip behind the mountain tops we cornered a bend to see a line of military vehicles parked in front of a small wild west town straight out of a John Wayne movie.

Helped off the coaches, we were invited to look around this incredible spectacle. Charles had a staged town built just for us to watch a Wild West show. There was a saloon, and a jail-house, sheriff's office and of course an undertakers with a six foot coffin leaning up against the outside wall. The saloon had an upper deck and balcony and 'ladies' in their bustles and corsets were chatting to the cowboys below, and the sheriff was keeping an eye over everything going on. In front of the town there were two long benches for those that wanted to sit and grab a drink from one of the many waiters.

Many of the guests, wise to Charles' eccentricity chatted on how Charles was going to top the last party at his stately home where had he hired the Red Arrows to do a magnificent display over his house to raise funds for a military charity. He had even hired actors and soldiers to re-enact a battle complete with his collection of military vehicles and tanks. He had a pyrotechnics team to coordinate explosions in the grounds as WW2 planes flew low overhead. Soldiers advanced, tanks fired and bombs exploded. It was a remarkable spectacle made even more special as I had watched it all from the beautiful circular observatory at the top of the house that gave amazing vistas over the entire New Forest.

As we looked down across the mountains to the party area, flames flickered from huge fire pits dug into the floor. A huge open marquee, all set for dinner supported two manned bars that would help wash down the variety of animals laid out on the huge outdoor BBQ area without a wilted lettuce leaf or cheap burnt sausage in sight. A huge stage had been erected with professional rigging, lights and dance floor and to chill out several tepees had been erected full of cushions for those wanting to smoke weed away from those that didn't care to partake. Colorado was the first state to make smoking cannabis legal so it was great to see that Charles had thought of everything to make everyone welcome whatever their choice of substance.

Carousing cowboys took my attention back to the Wild West town; their flirting with corseted ladies setting the scene. Two cowboys flew through the swing door of the saloon entrance and fell brawling within an inch of a guest. The sheriff ran through a crowd of screaming women, and shot a pistol into the air trying in vain to break up the brawlers who continued down the street as more cowboys joined in scrapping their way past the undertaker, who amusingly took their measurements. Three of the cowboys dived behind a horse and cart and started a gun battle against gunslingers at the opposite side of the benches where we sat drinking cold wine and hollering in excitement. As one by one the cowboys died a bloody, yet comical death, the sheriff stood up and shooting his pistol into the air shouted, "Welcome to Charles Burnett III's Sixtieth Birthday Party!"

While it was a simple statement it had a profound effect on me. Friends and family had stuck by me and here was my reward – being invited across the world to a most fantastic party by one of life's beautiful people. It validated me as a good person, not just a survivor, but a thriver. This was reinforced with the offers flooding in to race across the world. Life was good.

Whatever challenges life throws, positives can be found in there somewhere, I promise there will always be one and whatever opportunities come our way, seize them. We make our own luck in life and positivity is the key to everything.

The day following Charles's birthday party Lee and I sat in an outdoor Jacuzzi overlooking the crystal-topped mountains behind Colorado Springs, steam pouring off our bodies. Life just didn't get better than this. I had overcome what will always be the worst time of my life and I was ready to take on whatever life threw at me. After all, **the world is never enough.**

About the author

Born in Yorkshire 47 years ago, Sarah Donohue is a successful sportswoman holding international titles in two entirely different sports.

Thriving in the male dominated arena of offshore powerboat racing for over 25 years, Sarah is the highest achieving female in a male dominated sport.

With a lust for life like no other, her energy has no boundaries getting the best out of all opportunities for herself and those around her. A believer that we are who we choose to be. One of life's motivators.

This fitness and powerboat champion, stuntwoman, TV Presenter, motivational speaker and former showgirl takes anything life throws at her.

She has a degree in Fashion & Textiles, is a qualified PT, Insanity instructor and swim teacher. Sarah has written for several fitness publications including Men's Health, UltraFIT Magazine, Front Magazine and Loaded Magazine. She has also been a former fitness advisor on the Trisha Goddard Show.

Sarah was also named as a 'Woman of Achievement' having been invited to the prestigious 'Woman of the Year' awards in London for her work in helping women achieve their goals through motivation.

Lightning Source UK Ltd.
Milton Keynes UK
UKHW02f0637290518
323380UK00009B/532/P